GED® TEST REASONING THROUGH LANGUAGE ARTS (RLA) REVIEW

Other titles of interest from LearningExpress

GED® TEST REASONING THROUGH LANGUAGE ARTS (RLA) REVIEW

NEW YORK

CONTENTS

CHAPTER 1 **Introduction to the GED® RLA Test** 1

About the GED® RLA Test 2

Question Types 2

How to Use This Book 7

Test Taking Tips 7

Eliminating Answer Choices 9

Keeping Track of Time 10

Preparing for the Test 11

The Big Day 12

Good Luck! 12

CHAPTER 2 **Diagnostic Test** 13

Part I 17

Part II 29

Answers and Explanations 30

CHAPTER 3 **Reading Comprehension: Big Picture Tools** 37

Reading the Passages 38

Tips for Fiction Passages 40

Tips for Nonfiction Passages 41

Author's Purpose 42

Point of View 45

Theme 47

Synthesis 51

Reading More Closely 55

Interpreting What You Read   57

Quiz   59

Answers and Explanations   62

Review   65

CHAPTER 4   **Reading Comprehension: Close-Reading Skills**   67

Make Connections   67

Main Idea and Supporting Details   68

Reading Comprehension Review   73

Summarizing   77

Fact and Opinion   79

Organizational Structure   81

Inferences   87

Making Comparisons between Passages   89

Quiz   90

Answers and Explanations   97

Review   101

CHAPTER 5   **Language and Grammar: Reading Skills**   103

Word Parts   103

Parts of Speech   106

Context Clues   118

Multiple Meaning Words   119

Frequently Confused Words and Homonyms   120

Literary Devices   121

Language and Grammar Review   123

Answers and Explanations   125

Review   128

CHAPTER 6   **Language and Grammar: Grammar Skills**   129

GED® Test Strategies   129

Sentence Construction   130

Capitalization   136

Using Apostrophes to Create Possessive Nouns and Contractions   140

Sentence Punctuation   142

Sentence Structure   145

Usage   145

Mechanics   146

Organization   146

Quiz   148

Answers and Explanations   149

Review   151

CONTENTS

CHAPTER 7 **The Extended Response Essay: Tips and Scoring** 153

About the GED® Test Extended Response Question 153
Before You Write Your Essay 154
What's in an Essay 155
How Your Essay Will Be Scored 160
Extended Response Practice 163
Extended Response Practice Sample Essays 169

CHAPTER 8 **The Extended Response Essay: Planning and Revising** 173

How to Write a Powerful Essay 173
Thinking Styles 174
Organization of Your Essay 179
Example of an Extended Response Essay 181
Revising an Essay 189
Sample Extended Response Question 189
Practice Essay 191
The Final Steps 195
Quiz 195
Answers and Explanations 198
A Final Word 206
Review 208

CHAPTER 9 **GED® RLA Practice Test 1** 209

Part I 210
Part II 226
Answers and Explanations 232

CHAPTER 10 **GED® RLA Practice Test 2** 249

Part I 250
Part II 267
Answers and Explanations 275

ADDITIONAL ONLINE PRACTICE 291

GED® TEST REASONING THROUGH LANGUAGE ARTS (RLA) REVIEW

1 ▶ INTRODUCTION TO THE GED® RLA TEST

This book is designed to help people master the basic reading skills and concepts required to do well on the GED® Reasoning through Language Arts (RLA) test. Many people who are preparing for this particular GED® test have not been in a school setting for some time. This means reading skills have gotten rusty or have been forgotten altogether. Others may have been in a school setting, but have not mastered various essential reading skills. By focusing on basic reading skills, this book will give its readers a better grasp of key reading concepts.

This book is not designed to prepare people to take the GED® test immediately afterward. Instead, its goal is to provide the necessary foundation of reading skills required for the GED® Reasoning through Language Arts test. Without these fundamental skills, it would be difficult for a person to prepare for the test effectively, much less earn a passable score. However, once these basic reading skills are understood, a person is then on the right path toward learning the concepts needed to succeed on this particular GED® test.

About the GED® RLA Test

In previous versions of the GED® test, the Language Arts section was divided into two separate tests: Reading and Writing. The new GED® test combines these into a single test. Questions in this section will ask you to do things like identify the main idea or theme in a reading passage or determine the meanings of words within a passage. The RLA section also tests your knowledge of grammar, sentence structure, and the mechanics of language. Sharpening your reading and writing skills is important for the GED® test, and not only for the Reasoning through Language Arts section: The GED® Social Studies test and the GED® Science test also measure your ability to understand and communicate ideas through writing.

The Reasoning through Language Arts test will contain a number of reading passages, each 400 to 900 words in length. Approximately 75% of these passages will be nonfiction, and the other 25% will be fiction.

Because the new GED® test is all given on the computer, you will see a number of different question types that are more interactive than the usual multiple-choice questions.

How Is the Test Delivered?

You will take your GED® test on a computer. Although you absolutely do not need to be a computer expert to take the GED® test, you should be comfortable using a mouse and typing on a keyboard.

How Long Is the Test?

You can choose to take all four GED® tests at once, or you can take each test separately. The entire exam will take about seven hours to complete. The timing for each subject area alone is as follows:

- Mathematical Reasoning—115 minutes
- Reasoning through Language Arts—150 minutes (including a 10-minute break)
- Science—90 minutes
- Social Studies—90 minutes

Question Types

The traditional **multiple-choice** questions will still be the main type you will see on the RLA test, and each item will have four possible answer choices to select from. This is a change from previous GED® tests, which had five choices for each multiple-choice item. There is still only one correct answer choice for each item. This eliminates the possibility of answer choices such as "All of the above" or "Both A and B," and allows you to focus on selecting the one correct answer.

On the RLA test, all multiple-choice items will refer to a reading passage; each passage will be followed by six to eight items. The layout for multiple-choice items related to a passage will be split-screen—the passage will appear on the left, and the multiple-choice items will appear on the right.

Drag and Drop

For these questions, you will need to click on the correct object, hold down the mouse, and drag the object to the appropriate place in the problem, diagram, chart, or graph that you're given.

Of course, within this book you can't drag and drop items. For the purposes of *GED® Test Reasoning through Language Arts (RLA) Review*, you will choose from a list of items, as you would on a typical drag-and-drop question, and write the correct answer(s) in the appropriate spot.

Drop Down

In drop-down questions, you will need to select the answer or phrase to complete a sentence or problem from a menu that drops down with the click of a button.

Drop-down questions are very similar to multiple-choice questions, so you will not see them in the two tests within this book.

Fill-in-the-Blank

These questions ask you to manually type in answer(s) to a problem rather than choose from several choices.

Fill-in-the-Blank

A fill-in-the-blank question asks you to type information into one or more blank space(s). There are no answer choices given to you—you must come up with what you think is the correct answer and type it in the blank.

To answer the question, type in what you think is the correct word or phrase for each blank.

Try this practice question.

 Henry has $5 more than Oliver, and the same amount of money as Murray. Together, they have $85. How much money does Oliver have?

_____ dollars.

The fill-in-the-blank questions in this book look almost exactly like the ones you'll encounter in the online test, but here you will of course have to write in your answer instead of typing it.

Hot Spot

For hot-spot questions, you will be asked to click on an area of the screen to indicate where the correct answer is located. For instance, you may be asked to plot a point by clicking on the corresponding online graph or to click on a certain area of a map.

Hot Spot

Hot spot questions ask you to choose a certain place on an image.

To answer the question, click on the correct spot of the image provided. You can change your answer by simply clicking on another area.

Now, you try.

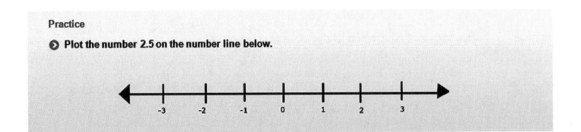

Practice

Plot the number 2.5 on the number line below.

In this book, you will be asked to draw a dot on a specific point or to circle a certain part of a diagram.

Short Answer

Short-answer questions are similar to fill-in-the-blank questions—you must type your response on the provided lines. However, these questions require you to write a paragraph instead of a word or two, usually in response to a passage or an image. Each should take about 10 minutes to answer.

Short Answer and Extended Response

These question types ask you to respond to a question by typing your answer into a box. With short answer and extended response questions, your answer will range from a few sentences to an essay. Like with fill-in-the-blank, there are no answer choices given to you.

You should feel comfortable typing on a keyboard in order to answer these questions, since there is a time limit for each test.

- Short answer questions can be answered with just a few words or sentences—they will probably take about 10 minutes to complete.

- Your extended response question is an essay, and is much longer—it will take 45 minutes to complete.

To answer these question types, enter your response into the text box provided. Here is an example of a response box:

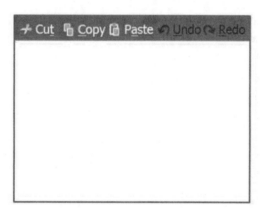

Notice that at the top of the box you will find tools to help you edit your answer if necessary.

Like fill-in-the-blank questions, short-answer questions in this book look as they will online—you will just write in your answer instead of typing it.

Extended Response

For extended response questions on the RLA exam you will be given 45 minutes to read one or two informational articles (a total of 550 to 650 words) and type a response on a computer using a simple word-processing program. This question requires you to read the prompt (the passage provided), create an argument based on it, and write a strong essay with evidence and examples.

When using this book, you can choose to either hand-write your essay or type it on a computer.

When and Where Can I Take the Test?

There are three testing opportunities per year in each subject area. To find a GED® test center, visit the link below, choose your location, and enter your zip code: www.gedtestingservice.com/testers/locate-a-testing-center.

You can sign up for any or all of the GED® tests online at this link, depending on the availability of spots in your area.

How Much Will the Test Cost?

Each of the four GED® tests costs $30, for a total of $120 for all four tests. You can pay for any or all parts of the test you are ready to take. There may be additional fees, depending on the state in which you take the test. Check the official GED® test website for complete test information.

How Are the Tests Scored?

A minimum score of 145 is required to pass each test. Each question on the GED® test is assigned a different point value depending on its difficulty. You will find out your score or scores on the same day you take the exam.

Reasoning through Language Arts

There are 48 questions and one Extended Response question on the RLA test. You will have 150 minutes to complete the entire exam, with one 10-minute scheduled break.

For most of the questions on the RLA test, you will be given a reading passage, followed by 6 to 8 questions that test your ability to understand and analyze what you have read.

Drop-down items are mostly used on the GED® RLA exam to test grammar and English-language mechanics. Drop-down questions are inserted in the middle of paragraphs. You will be asked to "drop down" a menu with several sentence choices, and choose the one that fits best grammatically in the sentence.

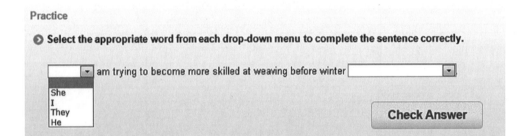

Passage Types for Reading Questions

Twenty-five percent of the reading passages on the RLA test will be literature. This includes historical and modern fiction, as well as nonfiction like biographies or essays. You might generally think of literature as fiction (invented stories), but literary texts can also be nonfiction (true stories).

Seventy-five percent of the reading passages will be from informational texts, including workplace documents (like memos or letters). These passages will often cover topics in social studies and science. The RLA test also will feature historical passages that are considered part of the "Great American Conversation." These include documents, essays, and speeches that have helped shaped American history.

There are no poetry or drama passages on the RLA test.

Extended Response Question

As you learned earlier in the chapter, the extended response item requires you to find and use information from the reading passage (or passages) to answer the question in a well-thought-out essay. You will be asked to analyze an issue and likely also asked to provide an opinion on what you have read. You will have 45 minutes of your total RLA time to complete this essay—that includes brainstorming, writing a draft, writing a final version, and proofreading your work.

How to Use This Book

In addition to this introduction, *GED® Test Reasoning through Language Arts (RLA) Review* also contains the following:

- **The LearningExpress Test Preparation System.** Being a good test taker can boost anyone's GED® test score. Many of the skills and strategies covered in this book will be familiar to anyone who has taken many multiple-choice tests, but there is a large difference between being "familiar with the strategy" and being "excellent at using the strategy." Our goal is to get you into that second category, and this chapter offers you the means to do so.
- **A Diagnostic Exam.** It's always helpful to see where your reading skills stand. Therefore, we recommend taking the diagnostic test before starting on the content chapters. By taking the diagnostic test, you should be able to determine the content areas in which you are strongest and the areas in which you might need more help. For example, if you miss most of your questions on the nonfiction passages, then you know that you should pay extra attention when the book discusses the best ways to approach nonfiction passages.

  The diagnostic test does not count for any score, so don't get caught up on how many you got right or wrong. Instead, use the results of the diagnostic test to help guide your study of the content chapters.
- **Content Chapters.** These chapters form the heart of the book. Here we cover the basic reading concepts discussed earlier. To help you understand all these ideas, every chapter has sample questions, helpful tips, and summaries, as well as explanations of the concepts being discussed. We recommend reading these chapters in order and not skipping around, as many of the concepts in the earlier chapters are built on in the later chapters.

- **Two Practice Tests.** Once you have a better grasp of the basic reading skills, the best thing to do is to practice those skills. Both our practice tests are designed to be similar to the real GED® Reasoning through Language Arts test in terms of question types and passage content.

  Taking these tests under timed conditions will help you gain familiarity with taking a timed reading test, which can help you in your GED® test preparations. However, if you would prefer to work on the questions untimed in order to focus on mastering the basic concepts of the content chapters, that's not a bad idea, either. Either way is helpful preparation.

Test Taking Tips

Selecting the Best Answer

You know all the reasons why test takers should read the passages and questions carefully. Now comes the part that makes all the difference: selecting the best answer. When all is said and done, this is the part of the test that matters most. To do well on the GED® test, it is essential that you select the best possible answer to each question.

Try to Answer the Question before Reading the Choices

As soon as you finish reading the question, think about what the best answer would be. Then, see if your answer is among the choices listed. If so, there's a good chance that it is correct, but don't mark the answer right away. Read all the choices first to be sure your answer is really the most complete option.

Read Every Choice

As you read the answer choices, you may determine that the first choice looks really great. But don't stop there! Read every single choice, no matter how wonderful any one of them appears to be. You may find that one of the first answers looks good but that the last one is even better.

Read Each Choice Carefully

Remember how important it is to be sure you read every single word in a question? The same holds true for reading each answer choice. Read each choice slowly and carefully, paying attention to every word. Take the time to read each answer choice twice before making your selection. Slight differences in wording can make one answer choice better than the others.

Use the Information in the Passage

Make sure that you choose an answer based solely on the information in the passage. You may already know a lot about the topic, which is great; however, the correct answers are in the passage. This test is not asking about what you knew before you read the material; it only wants to find out whether you are able to identify the correct information in this text.

Avoid Careless Mistakes

There will probably be answers you know right off the bat. Don't rush on these. Even if a question appears to be easy, read the question and answer choices carefully before making your selection. Careless mistakes can lower your score.

Watch Out for Absolutes

If certain words are found in answer choices, they should catch your attention. Look for words such as these:

- always
- never
- forever
- every

It is unlikely that the correct answer choice includes these inflexible words. Very few things are *always* true or *never* occur. Be suspicious if an answer choice suggests otherwise.

Pay Attention to Except and Not

Be sure you read every word in a question and pay close attention to the words *except* and *not*. It is easy to overlook these words by reading too quickly, and they completely change the question.

One trick for correctly answering these questions is to cover *except* or *not*, read the question, then look for the answer choice that does *not* belong.

Read Each Question for What It Is

Have you ever read a test question and wondered, *"What is this* really *asking?"* It can be easy to read too much into a question. Try not to do that on this test. The good news is, there are no trick questions on the GED® test. Just pay attention to what is being asked and select the best answer.

Choose the Best Answer

As you look through all the answer choices, you may find that more than one could be correct. Make sure that the answer you choose *most completely* answers the question. Just because a statement is true or looks like an acceptable choice does not mean it is the *best* answer. Carefully evaluate each choice before making a selection. Also, make sure your choice is the best answer *based on the passage*, not based on your own assumptions or beliefs.

TIP

Tempting answer choices are often listed before the best answer choice. Read all the answers carefully and make sure you completely understand each option before selecting the best response.

Read the Question Again

After you have selected your answer, read the question one more time. Make sure that your choice actually answers the question that was asked. Read the question, the appropriate section of the passage, and any visual aids, then read your answer choice. Does your answer make sense? If so, great! If not, now is your chance to try again.

Trust Your Instincts

Did you know that your first answer is usually correct? If you know that you have carefully read the passage and each answer choice, you have probably selected your best choice.

You may have time at the end of the test to look back over some of your answers. Unless you find an obvious mistake that you are certain about, don't change your answers. Research has shown that your first answer is usually right.

Answer Every Question

Make sure you do not leave any answers blank. Any question that is not answered is considered wrong, so take your best guess. There is no guessing penalty, so it is better to guess than to not answer a question.

BOOST

If you have been diagnosed as having a learning disability or physical handicap, you may be entitled to special accommodations for taking the GED® test. Be sure to check with the testing center you will be attending ahead of time to find out what, if any, documentation you might need to provide.

Eliminating Answer Choices

There may be times when you have no idea which answer choice is correct, and your only option is to take your best guess. In this situation, it is important to eliminate as many incorrect answer choices as possible, then select among those that remain.

Think of it this way: If you randomly choose one of the four answer choices, you have a 1 in 4 chance of getting it right. That's a 25% chance. Not bad, but definitely not in your best interest.

Suppose you are able to eliminate one of the answer choices. Now, you have a 1 in 3 chance of guessing correctly. Your odds just increased to 33%. Eliminate two choices and you have a 1 in 2 chance of answering correctly. This 50% chance of getting the answer right is much better than what you started with. Now, your random guess is much more likely to be the correct answer.

A few hints follow on how to make your best guess. These are only hints and will not work every single time. It is always better to use what you know and select the best answer based on the passage. Use these hints if your only option is making a random guess.

Look for Similar Answers

If you find that two of the answer choices are almost exactly the same, with the exception of a few words, eliminate the other answers and select between these two.

Also Look for Opposite Answers

You may notice that two of the answer choices are opposites.

Which is true about the duck-billed platypus?
a. It lays eggs.
b. It is a bird.
c. It does not lay eggs.
d. It is a vegetarian.

Notice that choices **a** and **c** are opposites, and obviously, both cannot be correct. So, you can automatically eliminate at least one of these answers. In this case, choice **a** happens to be correct. However, keep in mind that in another question, it is possible that both of the opposite answers could be wrong.

Get Rid of Extremes

Sometimes one answer may seem very different from the rest. In this case, eliminate the extreme answer.

Where did the story take place?

a. Alabama

b. Florida

c. Georgia

d. Paraguay

The answer choices here include three southern states and a foreign country. Paraguay seems a little extreme among the other choices in the list. If you are going to try to eliminate an answer so that you can make your best guess, Paraguay might be the most logical choice to eliminate.

Look for Grammatical Hints

Some questions may require you to choose the answer choice that correctly completes a sentence. Look for any choices that do not fit grammatically and eliminate these. For example, if the beginning of the sentence is written in past tense and an answer choice is in present tense, there's a good chance that the answer is incorrect.

If you are asked to choose a missing word or to identify a word with the same meaning, eliminate any choices that are a different part of speech.

The attorney was late for the meeting and asked us to brief her quickly on what had taken place so far.

What best tells the meaning of *brief* in the sentence?

a. concise without detail

b. to summarize in writing

c. a synopsis of a document

d. to give necessary information

In the sentence, *brief* is a verb, so the correct answer will also be a verb. Choice **a** is an adjective, and choice **c** is a noun. These can be eliminated, leaving only answers **b** and **d**, which are both verbs. In this case, **d** is the best choice.

Keeping Track of Time

Remember that this is a timed test. Being aware of how much time has passed and how much time remains can make a tremendous difference in your overall performance.

Wear a Watch

Be sure to wear a watch on the day of the test. Check the time as the test begins and figure out the time at which the test will end. The test administrator will probably update you on how much time remains throughout the test. However, it's a good idea to be able to check for yourself.

Don't Rush

Remember the old saying "Slow and steady wins the race"? Yes, there is a time limit. Yes, you need to pace yourself. However, if you rush, you'll be more likely to make mistakes. Work quickly, but most important, work carefully.

> *It's better to answer some of the questions and get them right than to answer most of the questions and get them wrong.*

Keep an eye on your watch, but keep your focus on doing your best.

TIP

Most people who have not passed the GED® test actually had the knowledge needed to pass. So what was the problem? They ran out of time. Don't let this happen to you! Pace yourself, monitor the time, and keep moving.

Use Your Time Wisely

Don't spend too much time trying to select a single answer. If a question has you stumped, take your best guess and move on. You can always come back later if you have extra time at the end. Wasting time on one tricky question can prevent you from having time to answer another that you might think is a breeze.

TIP

Sometimes, if you skip a tough question and come back to it later, you will find it easier to answer the second time around. Information and clues in other questions may help you figure out the best answer.

Wrap Things Up at the End

You already know the importance of keeping an eye on the time. If you find that there are only a couple of minutes left and you have not yet finished the test, start guessing. Any answer that is left blank will automatically be marked wrong. Go ahead and take a stab at any remaining questions; quickly get an answer marked for every test item. At this point, what have you got to lose? You may or may not get them right, but at least you tried, and as previously noted, there is no guessing penalty.

Preparing for the Test

Like so many things, the key to doing well on the GED® test is preparation. You're already on the right track by reading these chapters. A few other tips to help you prepare are discussed in this section.

Practice, Practice, Practice

Taking a practice test, such as the ones in this book, is a terrific way to be sure you are ready. These practice tests help you in several ways:

- You will know what types of questions to expect.
- You will become comfortable with the format of the test.

- You will learn about your own strengths and weaknesses.
- You will be aware of what you need to study.

As you take the practice tests, pay attention to the types of questions you get right and those that are more challenging. For example, you may find that the questions about main ideas are really easy. That's great! You might also find that you miss a lot of the questions that deal with themes. No problem. Now you know what skills to study.

Create Opportunities for Even More Practice

You probably read different types of passages all the time, either in magazines or newspapers, in novels, or on the Internet. As you read, think about the types of questions you will find on the GED® test. Then, ask yourself questions about your reading material. For example, you might ask yourself:

- What is the main idea of the passage I just read?
- What details support the main idea?
- What were the conflict and resolution in this story?
- What context clues helped me determine the meanings of unfamiliar words?
- What is the theme (or tone or mood) of the passage?

Another idea is to work with a friend and write questions for each other based on passages you select. You could also summarize passages, underline key words, circle the main idea of each paragraph, and highlight supporting details.

Know Yourself

Figure out what works best for you. For example, not everyone benefits from reading the questions before reading the passage. Some people may find it helpful to scan a passage for the main idea before reading; others may not. Try different strategies as you work through the practice questions and pay attention to which strategies you find most comfortable and most beneficial.

Be Ready the Day Before the Test

Being ready mentally and physically can help you do your best on the test. Here are some suggestions:

- Start studying and preparing in advance; don't plan on cramming for the test in the few days before you are scheduled to take it.
- The day before the test, take a break and relax. Go for a walk, call a friend, or see a movie. Don't stay up late to study.
- Have anything you want to take with you ready ahead of time. Set out your pencils, sweater, watch, or anything else that you need to take to the test location in the morning.
- Make sure you get plenty of sleep the night before the test. If you're concerned that you won't be able to fall asleep, get up extra early the morning before the test. That way, you'll be ready for bed early that evening.

The Big Day

You've studied, you're well rested, and now you're ready to take the GED® Reasoning through Language Arts exam! Now that test day is here, make the most of it.

Get Off to a Good Start

First, set your alarm early enough so that you won't have to rush. Not only will you feel more relaxed and have time to get settled before the test starts, but you also might not be allowed to enter the testing center if you are late. Make sure that being on time is one thing you won't have to worry about.

Then, be sure to eat a well-balanced breakfast. You need to keep your energy up, and you certainly don't want to be distracted by the sound of your stomach growling. If today is going to be a long day of testing, bring a bottle of water, a piece of fruit, or some trail mix to snack on between sessions.

Also, dress in comfortable, layered clothes and bring a sweater. Feeling like your shoes are too tight or being too hot or too cold can be distractions. Do everything you can to be sure you feel great and are on top of your game today!

Keep Your Cool

You've studied, you've practiced, and now you're ready. Don't let your nerves get the best of you. Getting worked up will not help you get your highest possible score. In the overall scheme of things, the GED® test is just a test. If things don't go as well as you'd hoped today, consider this a practice run. You have three chances in a calendar year to pass the test. Try to stay calm and focus on doing your best.

Carefully Read the Directions

If you are unsure about the directions or what exactly you are supposed to do, be sure to ask the test administrator before you begin the test. He or she cannot help you with specific test questions or vocabulary, but you may be able to get the information you need to clarify the test's instructions.

Good Luck!

Now that you are familiar with the GED® test, you can begin your powerful practice. The exams in this book are designed to be as close as possible to the actual tests you will see on test day. Each question in the exams that come with this book is accompanied by a very detailed answer explanation—you will be able to see not only why the correct answer is right but also why each of the other choices is incorrect. You will also see sample essays at all levels for the Extended Response items.

Best of luck on your GED® test study journey and on your test-taking experience!

2 ▶ DIAGNOSTIC TEST

CHAPTER SUMMARY

This is the first of the three practice tests in this book based on the GED® Reasoning through Language Arts test. Use this test to see how you would do if you were to take the exam today.

This diagnostic practice exam is of the same type as the real GED® Reasoning through Language Arts test. It consists of 50 multiple-choice questions and one essay question. These questions test your skills in comprehension (extracting meaning), application (using information), analysis (breaking down information), and synthesis (putting elements together).

The answer sheet you should use for the multiple-choice questions is on the following page. Then comes the exam itself, and after that, the answer key. Each answer on the test is explained in the answer key to help you find out why the correct answers are right and why the incorrect answers are wrong.

Diagnostic Test

1.	ⓐ	ⓑ	ⓒ	ⓓ
2.	ⓐ	ⓑ	ⓒ	ⓓ
3.	ⓐ	ⓑ	ⓒ	ⓓ
4.	ⓐ	ⓑ	ⓒ	ⓓ
5.	ⓐ	ⓑ	ⓒ	ⓓ
6.	ⓐ	ⓑ	ⓒ	ⓓ
7.	ⓐ	ⓑ	ⓒ	ⓓ
8.	ⓐ	ⓑ	ⓒ	ⓓ
9.	ⓐ	ⓑ	ⓒ	ⓓ
10.	ⓐ	ⓑ	ⓒ	ⓓ
11.	ⓐ	ⓑ	ⓒ	ⓓ
12.	ⓐ	ⓑ	ⓒ	ⓓ
13.	ⓐ	ⓑ	ⓒ	ⓓ
14.	ⓐ	ⓑ	ⓒ	ⓓ
15.	ⓐ	ⓑ	ⓒ	ⓓ
16.	ⓐ	ⓑ	ⓒ	ⓓ
17.	ⓐ	ⓑ	ⓒ	ⓓ

18.	ⓐ	ⓑ	ⓒ	ⓓ
19.	ⓐ	ⓑ	ⓒ	ⓓ
20.	ⓐ	ⓑ	ⓒ	ⓓ
21.	ⓐ	ⓑ	ⓒ	ⓓ
22.	ⓐ	ⓑ	ⓒ	ⓓ
23.	ⓐ	ⓑ	ⓒ	ⓓ
24.	ⓐ	ⓑ	ⓒ	ⓓ
25.	ⓐ	ⓑ	ⓒ	ⓓ
26.	ⓐ	ⓑ	ⓒ	ⓓ
27.	ⓐ	ⓑ	ⓒ	ⓓ
28.	ⓐ	ⓑ	ⓒ	ⓓ
29.	ⓐ	ⓑ	ⓒ	ⓓ
30.	ⓐ	ⓑ	ⓒ	ⓓ
31.	ⓐ	ⓑ	ⓒ	ⓓ
32.	ⓐ	ⓑ	ⓒ	ⓓ
33.	ⓐ	ⓑ	ⓒ	ⓓ
34.	ⓐ	ⓑ	ⓒ	ⓓ

35.	ⓐ	ⓑ	ⓒ	ⓓ
36.	ⓐ	ⓑ	ⓒ	ⓓ
37.	ⓐ	ⓑ	ⓒ	ⓓ
38.	ⓐ	ⓑ	ⓒ	ⓓ
39.	ⓐ	ⓑ	ⓒ	ⓓ
40.	ⓐ	ⓑ	ⓒ	ⓓ
41.	ⓐ	ⓑ	ⓒ	ⓓ
42.	ⓐ	ⓑ	ⓒ	ⓓ
43.	ⓐ	ⓑ	ⓒ	ⓓ
44.	ⓐ	ⓑ	ⓒ	ⓓ
45.	ⓐ	ⓑ	ⓒ	ⓓ
46.	ⓐ	ⓑ	ⓒ	ⓓ
47.	ⓐ	ⓑ	ⓒ	ⓓ
48.	ⓐ	ⓑ	ⓒ	ⓓ
49.	ⓐ	ⓑ	ⓒ	ⓓ
50.	ⓐ	ⓑ	ⓒ	ⓓ

Part I

Directions: Choose the *one best answer* to each question.

Questions 1 through 7 refer to the following excerpt from a novel.

Will Anne Miss Green Gables?

It was a happy and beautiful bride who came down the old carpeted stairs that September noon. She was the first bride of Green Gables, slender and shining-eyed, with her

(5) arms full of roses. Gilbert, waiting for her in the hall below, looked up at her with adoring eyes. She was his at last, this long-sought Anne, whom he won after years of patient waiting. It was to him she was coming. Was

(10) he worthy of her? Could he make her as happy as he hoped? If he failed her—if he could not measure up to her standards. . . .

But then, their eyes met and all doubt was swept away in a certainty that everything

(15) would be wonderful. They belonged to each other; no matter what life might hold for them, it could never alter that. Their happiness was in each other's keeping and both were unafraid.

(20) They were married in the sunshine of the old orchard, circled by the loving and kindly faces of long-familiar friends. Mr. Allan married them and the Reverend Jo made what Mrs. Rachel Lynde afterwards

(25) pronounced to be the "most beautiful wedding prayer" she had ever heard. Birds do not often sing in September, but one sang sweetly from some hidden tree while Gilbert and Anne repeated their vows. Anne heard it

(30) and thrilled to it. Gilbert heard it and wondered only that all the birds in the world had not burst into jubilant song. The bird sang until the ceremony was ended. Then it wound up with one more little, glad trill.

(35) Never had the old gray-green house among its enfolding orchards known a merrier afternoon. Laughter and joy had their way; and when Anne and Gilbert left to catch their train, Marilla stood at the gate

(40) and watched them drive out of sight down the long lane with its banks of goldenrod. Anne turned at its end to wave her last goodbye. She looked once more at her home and felt a tinge of sadness. Then she was

(45) gone—Green Gables was her home no more. It would never be again. Marilla's face looked very gray and old as she turned to the house which Anne had filled for years with light and life.

Adapted from L.M. Montgomery,
Anne's House of Dreams

1. Which of the following words best describes what Gilbert feels toward Anne?
   a. love
   b. respect
   c. gratitude
   d. nervousness

2. What happened when Gilbert's and Anne's eyes met?
   a. He wondered whether he was worthy of her.
   b. He wondered what their life would be like.
   c. He realized they were meant for each other.
   d. He thought Anne would miss Green Gables very much.

3. Based on the excerpt, what was probably the hardest change for Anne?
   a. becoming a wife
   b. saying goodbye to Marilla
   c. not being free to do what she wanted
   d. Green Gables not being her home any longer

4. Based on the excerpt, which description best characterizes the relationship between Marilla and Anne?
  a. Marilla felt tired from having taken care of Anne.
  b. Marilla raised Anne from childhood and cared about her.
  c. Marilla was sad that Anne left because she would have to leave, too.
  d. Marilla and Anne disagreed about Gilbert being a good husband.

5. Which of the following best describes what the author means when she says "this long-sought Anne" (lines 7 and 8)?
  a. Anne was no longer a young woman.
  b. Anne did not fall in love with Gilbert right away.
  c. Anne was patient with Gilbert.
  d. Anne had nearly married someone else.

6. Of the characters in this excerpt, whose inner thoughts are hidden from the reader?
  a. Anne
  b. Gilbert
  c. Marilla
  d. Mr. Allan

7. How does the bird's singing relate to Gilbert's and Anne's marriage?
  a. The bird's singing was distracting to those watching the service.
  b. The bird's singing mirrored the joy of the wedding service.
  c. The bird's singing seemed to suggest sad events in the future.
  d. The bird's singing was worrisome to the bridal couple.

Directions: Choose the *one best answer* to each question.

Questions 8 through 14 are based on the following passage.

Raymond Dean
Green Valley Farm
3421 Rte 32
Stone Ridge, NY 12430

Dear Mr. Dean:

(A)
(1) I am presently a student at ulster county community college and my field of study is agriculture. (2) I am studying all types of farming techniques, and only prefers organic methods for growing vegetables. (3) I have learned much about the latest techniques for growing food organically and I know that since you are one of the largest organic growers in the area, I will learn a great deal more from you and your employees.

(B)
(4) This is why I would like to apply for a summer position with your farm. (5) I hope to get a permanent job with you after I graduate. (6) I believe the experience of working with the Green Valley Farm professionals would, enhance my education greatly. (7) I want to let you know that I would consider an unpaid internship at your farm. (8) That is how anxious I am to work with you. (9) Maybe I could borrow some money from my parents or get a second job to support myself. (10) I am enclosing my resume as well as my references from teachers and a former employer.

(C)

(11) I first learned about your farm from a teacher. (12) He has high regard for your work. (13) He was suggesting that I write you and make this request. (14) I hope I will hear from you. (15) In the near future.

Sincerely yours,

Mark Tanzania

8. Sentence (1): I am presently a student at <u>ulster county community college</u> and my field of study is agriculture.

   Which is the best way to write the underlined portion of the sentence?
   a. ulster county Community College
   b. Ulster county community college
   c. Ulster County Community college
   d. Ulster County Community College

9. Sentence (2): I am studying all types of farming <u>techniques, and only prefers</u> organic methods for growing vegetables.

   Which is the best way to write the underlined portion of this sentence?
   a. techniques, so I prefer
   b. techniques which are
   c. techniques, but prefer
   d. techniques that don't prefer

10. Sentences (4) and (5): This is why I would like to apply for a summer position with your farm. I hope to get a permanent job with you after I graduate.

   Which is the most effective combination of sentences (4) and (5)?
   a. I am applying for a summer job, but I hope to get a permanent position.
   b. Applying for a job now in the hopes that you will hire me after I graduate.
   c. I would like to apply for a position with your farm, today, and then later after I graduate.
   d. I would like to apply for a summer position with your farm in the hopes of having a permanent job with you after I graduate.

11. Which revision would improve the effectiveness of paragraph (B)?
   a. move sentence (5) after sentence (10)
   b. move sentence (9) to the end of the paragraph
   c. remove sentence (6)
   d. remove sentence (9)

12. Sentence (6): I believe the experience of working with the Green Valley Farm professionals would, enhance my education greatly.

   Which correction should be made to sentence (6)?
   a. insert a comma after <u>professionals</u>
   b. replace <u>working</u> with <u>to work</u>
   c. change <u>believe</u> to <u>believed</u>
   d. remove the comma after <u>would</u>

13. Sentences (11) and (12): I first learned about your farm from a teacher. He has high regard for your work.

Which is the most effective combination of sentences (11) and (12)?

a. First I learned about your farm from a teacher he has high regard for your work.

b. I learned about your farm from a teacher who has high regard for your work.

c. My teacher has high regard for your work, I learned about your farm.

d. A teacher who has high regard for your work and I first learned about your farm.

14. Sentence (13): He was suggesting that I write you and make this request.

Which correction should be made to sentence (13)?

a. change <u>make</u> to <u>made</u>

b. change <u>you</u> and <u>make</u> to <u>you. Make</u>

c. change <u>was suggesting</u> to <u>suggested</u>

d. change <u>was suggesting</u> to <u>have suggested</u>

Questions 15 through 18 refer to the following excerpt from a short story.

Will He Appear on National Television?

"I think half the world has shown up for this audition." Gene was talking on his cell phone to his girlfriend. "I can't wait to perform. I know I'm in fine voice, and they are going to
(5) love the song I chose."

"Well, good luck. I will be thinking of you."

Although he sounded upbeat with his girlfriend, in truth Gene was anything but
(10) confident. He had staked so much on the audition, and he had no idea what the judges would really think of him. He realized for the first time that he was scared. Even so, he wanted to succeed so much he could almost
(15) taste it. Just imagine competing on national television. He took a long breath in. It was hard to believe he was actually going to perform for the judges.

He had arrived exactly at nine and had
(20) been in line for over three hours. He could hear his heart beating loudly. Right then, Gene heard his name being called. He went into the building and was ushered into the audition room.
(25) "Yes, I'm here," he answered.

Gene looked at the judges sitting at the table. They seemed bored and unimpressed.

"Well, what are you going to sing for us today?" one of the judges asked him. "Time
(30) After Time," Gene told him, his voice quavering a bit.

"Okay, let's see what you've got," said another judge who was tapping the table with a pencil.
(35) Gene felt a knot in his throat and didn't know if he could go on. He remembered what his voice coach told him: "Just take a moment before you start. Close your eyes. Take a deep breath, and then let go." Gene

(40)   closed his eyes and took a breath and then a
sweet voice began emanating from his
mouth. The judges seemed to disappear. He
could have been anywhere. He was in his
own world.

(45)   Suddenly it was over, and he stood in
front of the judges feeling very alone and
vulnerable. He could feel the sweat on his
brow.

          "Well, that was a surprise," said the first
(50)   judge. "I never would have predicted that."

          "What do you think? Does he go
through?" All four of the judges gave him a
thumbs up. "You're in, kid," the first judge
said. "Don't make us regret our decision."

(55)   "Oh, no, sir. You won't regret it," Gene
said as he nearly skipped out of the room.

15. Based on the excerpt, what does Gene most
likely think about the audition?
  a. It will give him a chance to make a good
living.
  b. It is something he had wanted to avoid.
  c. It is a chance for him to be discovered.
  d. It will make him famous in a short time.

16. When does the scene in this excerpt take place?
  a. early morning
  b. late afternoon
  c. early afternoon
  d. early evening

17. Which is the best description of Gene's
performance?
  a. a good try but not good enough
  b. a fine voice but without true conviction
  c. a bit slow to start but ultimately wonderful
  d. a showy voice but not much rhythm

18. What is the main effect of the author's use of
phrases such as "could almost taste it," "took a
long breath in," and "beating loudly"?
  a. to show how long Gene had been waiting
  b. to show that Gene was talented
  c. to show that Gene had been exercising
  d. to show how important the audition was to
Gene

*Questions 19 through 25 are based on the following
passage.*

Gorée Island

(A)

(1) Europeans played a large part in bringing slaves to America from west africa.
(2) European countries sent out explorers
who sailed down the west coast of Africa.
(3) They came in contact with the people
there. (4) They traded with them, but they
also captures many of the people. (5) These
people were sent to the New World where
they became slaves. (6) Most of them ended
up working on farms and plantations.

(B)

(7) Some Africans were sent from Gorée, a
small island off the coast of what is now Senegal. (8) There are about nine and a half million people in Senegal today. (9) They stayed
in dungeons until the ships from the New
World came to take them to America and the
Caribbean. (10) Some Africans also profited
from the slave trade. (11) A group of free
African women, called *signares*, sold food to
the European traders for the enslaved people
and also owned many slaves herself.

(C)

(12) Today the dungeons where they stayed are a museum. (13) Hundreds of people visit this museum each year to see where the slaves were held. (14) They view the dungeons and the House of the Slaves, which is where the masters lived. (15) Their is a memorial statue right outside the house showing African slaves in chains. (16) A visit there would be very educational. (17) You will learn a great deal from the guides about what happened there.

19. Sentence (1): Europeans played a large part in bringing slaves to America from west africa.

Which correction should be made to sentence 1?

a. replace <u>played</u> with <u>were playing</u>
b. insert a comma after <u>America</u>
c. insert a period after <u>large part</u>
d. change <u>west africa</u> to <u>West Africa</u>

20. Sentences (2) and (3): European countries sent out explorers who sailed down the west coast of Africa. They came in contact with the people there.

The most effective combination of sentences (2) and (3) would include which group of words?

a. coast of Africa while they
b. coast of Africa where they
c. coast of Africa instead of
d. coast of Africa but they

21. Sentence (4): They traded with them, but they also <u>captures</u> many of the people.

Which is the best way to write the underlined portion of this sentence?

a. had been captured
b. was capturing
c. will capture
d. captured

22. Which revision would improve the effectiveness of paragraph (B)?

a. move sentence (7) to the end of the paragraph
b. remove sentence (8)
c. remove sentence (9)
d. move sentence (11) to the beginning of the paragraph

23. Sentence (11): A group of free African women, called *signares*, sold food to the European traders for the enslaved people and also owned many slaves herself.

Which correction should be made to sentence (11)?

a. change <u>owned</u> to <u>owns</u>
b. change <u>A group</u> to <u>A groups</u>
c. insert a comma after <u>people</u>
d. replace <u>herself</u> with <u>themselves</u>

24. Sentence (15): Their is a memorial statue right outside the house showing African slaves in chains.

Which correction should be made to sentence 15?

a. move <u>right</u> to the end of the sentence
b. replace <u>Their</u> with <u>There</u>
c. change <u>is</u> to <u>are</u>
d. change <u>slaves</u> to <u>Slaves</u>

25. Sentence (17): You will learn a great deal from the guides about what happened there.

The most effective revision of sentence (17) would begin with which group of words?

a. If you go, you
b. Even if you go, you
c. However, you
d. Learning a lot

Questions 26 through 31 refer to the following employee memo.

What Will the New Procedures Do?

Memo

To: Employees of IMPEL

From: Management

Re: New Security Procedures

(5)   Date: June 15

As a result of some incidents that have occurred with unauthorized persons in secure parts of Building A, as of June 30, new procedures will go into effect for security in

(10) that building. From now on, all employees reporting to work should enter through the employee entrance at the side of the building on Murray Street. No employee is to enter through the main entrance. In order to be

(15) admitted, each employee must have a valid photo ID. The ID needs to be swiped to unlock the door. Make sure not to allow another person to enter with you even if you know the person. Each employee needs to

(20) swipe his or her own ID in order to be registered as being on the job.

The main entrance will be for visitors only. The receptionist there will call the party that the visitor is coming to meet so that he

(25) or she can come to the main desk to escort the guest to his or her office. Visitors will be given temporary passes, but they cannot have full run of the office.

In addition, all employees will also be

(30) required to log in on their computer when they begin work and log out when they take a break. Make sure to log out and in when taking lunch breaks.

If an employee sees someone whom he

(35) or she believes is unauthorized to be in Building A, that employee should take immediate action and report the event to Mr. Shields, our head of security. Do not

approach the person, but simply call Mr.

(40) Shields's office. His extension is 890. If there is no answer, make a written report and e-mail it to cshields@impel.com.

If employees have any questions regarding these regulations, please contact

(45) the Human Resources department at extension 550. Ms. Hardy will be able to respond to your queries. Thank you for your cooperation in this matter. We feel that with these additional procedures, our workplace

(50) will be made more secure for everyone concerned. Ideally, this will result in improved work output, since any possibility of a security breach will be prevented.

26. Which of the following best restates the phrase "security breach" (line 53)?
   a. a compromise in the safety of the office
   b. a blow to the confidence of employees
   c. a distraction because of an employee's personal problems
   d. a defense against employees not doing their jobs

27. Based on the excerpt, which of the following can be inferred about management?
   a. They are concerned about the safety of employees.
   b. They believe that the office is completely secure.
   c. They want employees to fill out time sheets.
   d. They want to track employee work habits.

28. Which of the following could be prevented by the new security procedures?
   a. visitors entering through the main entrance
   b. employees swiping IDs to open doors
   c. employees entering through the side entrance
   d. unauthorized persons wandering around Building A

29. Imagine an employee sees a person in Building A without an ID badge. According to the memo, which of these actions should the employee take?
  a. call Mr. Shields's office to make a report
  b. tell the person to leave the building
  c. call the receptionist in the main entrance
  d. report the event to Ms. Hardy

30. Which of the following best describes the style in which this memo is written?
  a. complicated and unclear
  b. academic and dry
  c. straightforward and direct
  d. detailed and technical

31. Which of the following best describes the way in which the memo is organized?
  a. by listing information in the order of importance
  b. by sequence of events
  c. by presenting a problem and then a solution
  d. by comparing and contrasting issues

Questions 32 through 37 refer to the following excerpt from a novel.

Will His Mother Let Him Leave?

"Beatrice," he said suddenly, "I want to go away to school. Everybody in Minneapolis is going to go away to school."

Beatrice showed some alarm.

(5)   "But you're only fifteen."

"Yes, but everybody goes away to school at fifteen, and I *want* to, Beatrice."

On Beatrice's suggestion, the subject was dropped for the rest of the walk, but a
(10)   week later she delighted him by saying, "Amory, I have decided to let you have your way. If you still want to, you can go away to school."

"Yes?"

(15)   "To St. Regis's in Connecticut."

Amory said nothing, but he felt a bolt of excitement along his spine.

"It's being arranged," continued Beatrice. "It's better that you should go away.
(20)   I'd have preferred you to have gone to Eton and then to Christ Church, Oxford. But it seems impracticable now—and for the present, we'll let the university question take care of itself."

(25)   "What are you going to do, Beatrice?"

"Heaven knows. It seems my fate to spend my years in this country. Not for a second do I regret being American—indeed, I think that regret is very typical of ignorant
(30)   people. I feel sure we are the great coming nation, yet"—and she sighed, "I feel my life should have slipped away close to an older, mellower civilization, a land of greens and autumnal browns. . . ."

(35)   Amory did not answer, so his mother continued, "My regret is that you haven't been abroad. But still, as you are a man, it's better that you should grow up here under the snarling eagle—is that the right term?"

(40)   Amory agreed that it was.

"When do I go to school?"

"Next month. You'll have to start East a little early to take your examinations. After that you'll have a free week, so I want you to
(45)   go up the Hudson and pay a visit."

"To who?"

"To Monsignor Darcy, Amory. He wants to see you. He went to Harrow and then to Yale—became a Catholic. I want him
(50)   to talk to you. I feel he can be such a help." She stroked his auburn hair gently. "Dear Amory, dear Amory. . . ."

Adapted from F. Scott Fitzgerald, *This Side of Paradise*

32. Which of the following best expresses the main idea of the excerpt?
a. A boy's mother agrees to let her son go to a boarding school.
b. A boy's mother would like her son to visit schools in other countries.
c. A boy wants to make his mother happy.
d. A boy wants to get away from his hometown.

33. Based on the information in this excerpt, which of the following would Beatrice most likely prefer to do?
a. learn about American history
b. have a potluck dinner with friends
c. spend time in England
d. teach English to schoolchildren

34. Why does Beatrice most likely think it is better for Amory to grow up in America?
a. He would not like Europe.
b. He is good at sports.
c. Schools are easier in America.
d. He was born in America.

35. Based on Beatrice saying, "I feel my life should have slipped away close to an older, mellower civilization, a land of greens and autumnal browns" (lines 31 to 34), what does she suggest about America?
a. She thinks it is similar to England.
b. She believes it is a land of great energy.
c. She assumes it is a weak country with little future.
d. She decides then to adopt it as her home.

36. How does Amory calling his mother by her first name influence the excerpt?
a. It shows that Amory and his mother are not close.
b. It shows that Beatrice wants to appear to be Amory's sister.
c. It shows that Beatrice resents being a mother.
d. It shows that Amory and his mother's relationship is not typical.

37. Why does Beatrice want Amory to visit Monsignor Darcy?
a. She thinks that Monsignor Darcy can convince Amory to go to school closer to home.
b. Monsignor Darcy is Amory's uncle.
c. She wants Amory to become Catholic.
d. She feels that Monsignor Darcy can help Amory because he went to Harrow and Yale.

Questions 38 through 42 refer to the following excerpt from a review.

What Does the Reviewer Think of *Last Fight*?

Last Fight may be one of the biggest blockbusters of the summer, but it doesn't live up to the buzz around it. In this science fiction tale of epic proportions, viewers are
(5)　propelled forward to a future when Earth is populated by androids and humans. These survivors of an ancient civilization live in a sterile world covered by a plastic dome. The dome is for protection from aliens who
(10)　attack Earth on a regular basis. It also cuts down on such environmental problems as air pollution and global warming.

　　　The plot centers around a young man named Raal and his quest to forge a peace
(15)　between the humans and the aliens. His is a

(20) difficult task, considering the aliens have no desire to stop trying to overcome Earth and its inhabitants. While Raal (George Armstrong) is a likeable character, he lacks the ability to change expression to any extent. As a result, his acting range is quite limited. He is something of a dreamer, and perhaps the message here is that there is no place for dreamers in the future, but I will not detail

(25) the plot or the ending. I don't want to spoil it for those people who may actually want to view the film. Still, let it be said that events do not go well for young Raal.

(30) The high point of the movie for me was the performance by veteran actor Bruce Cameron as the sage Kel. He has shown over and over his ability to transform even the most mundane character into someone fascinating to watch. It may be worth seeing

(35) the film just for his performance.

Besides being far-fetched, the movie concentrates too much on special effects, including 3-D, but that of course may be a draw for many viewers. Its cost was also

(40) enormous. Not much that is green is in this film.

38. Which of the following is the main idea of the excerpt?
a. The author is giving the reasons movies should not use special effects.
b. The author is detailing the kind of acting that he prefers.
c. The author is providing his impressions of a science fiction movie.
d. The author is explaining why he enjoys science fiction movies.

39. Which of the following best expresses the reviewer's opinion of *Last Fight*?
a. It was too expensive to make and is too long.
b. It was enjoyable because there was some great acting in it.
c. The reviewer hopes that most people will turn out for the movie.
d. It has little depth and relies too much on special effects.

40. If it is known that the author of this review had written numerous science fiction scripts, none of which were ever made into a movie, how would this most likely affect the reading of this review?
a. The experiences of the author give his or her opinion greater value.
b. The author's knowledge of the genre may be questioned.
c. Much of the negativity might be construed as sour grapes.
d. The author's personal experiences have no influence on the review whatsoever.

41. Which of the following best describes the style in which this review is written?
a. technical
b. humorous
c. academic
d. ornate

42. According to the author, which word best describes *Last Fight*?
a. provocative
b. lighthearted
c. solemn
d. overblown

Questions 43 through 50 are based on the following passage.

How to Write a Cover Letter

(A)

(1) A cover letter that accompanies your résumé is of great importance, the cover letter gives the employer a general impression of you. (2) In fact, if the cover letter don't interest the potential employer, the employer may opt not to read through the résumé at all. (3) So make your cover letter effective by keeping it short and bring up points that will interest the reader.

(B)

(4) Before you start to write, make sure you have an updated résumé. (5) Then research the company so you can include information about itself that might relate to the position you are hoping to fill. (6) Research will also help you prepare for an interview. (7) When you are ready to write your letter make sure to include the name of the person the title, the correct company name, and address. (8) If you don't know the name of the person to who you are writing, use "Dear Sir/Madam."

(C)

(9) When you get to the body of the letter, use the first paragraph to say why you think you would be good for the position. (10) Also include, why you would want to work for the company. (11) Use the next paragraph to tell about your experience and matching it to the job. (12) Let the employer know that you are enthusiastic about the prospect of working for the company. (13) The last paragraph should be brief.

(14) Should include a strong statement that will make the employer want to interview you. (15) At the end of the letter, give your contact, information and conclude with either "sincerely yours" or "yours truly."

43. Sentence (1): A cover letter that accompanies your résumé is of great importance, the cover letter gives the employer a general impression of you.

Which correction should be made to sentence (1)?
a. insert a comma after <u>résumé</u>
b. remove the comma
c. replace <u>gives</u> with <u>give</u>
d. replace the comma with <u>because</u>

44. Sentence (2): In fact, if the cover <u>letter don't interest</u> the potential employer, the employer may opt not to read through the résumé at all.

Which is the best way to write the underlined portion of sentence (2)?
a. letter did not interest
b. letters don't interest
c. letter haven't interest
d. letter doesn't interest

45. Sentence (3): So make your cover letter effective by keeping it short and bring up points that will interest the reader.

Which correction should be made to sentence (3)?
a. change <u>keeping</u> to <u>will keep</u>
b. change <u>interest</u> to <u>interesting</u>
c. change <u>it</u> to <u>its</u>
d. change <u>bring</u> to <u>bringing</u>

46. Sentence (5): Then research the company so you can include information <u>about itself</u> that might relate to the position you are hoping to fill.

Which is the best way to write the underlined portion of sentence (5)?

a. about yourselves

b. about herself

c. about himself

d. about yourself

47. Sentence (7): When you are ready to write your letter make sure to include the name of the <u>person the title</u>, the correct company name, and address.

Which is the best way to write the underlined portion of sentence (7)?

a. person; the title

b. person, the title,

c. person. The title

d. person and the title

48. Sentence (8): If you don't know the name of the person <u>to who</u> you are writing, use "Dear Sir/Madam."

Which is the best way to write the underlined portion of sentence (8)?

a. to which

b. that

c. which

d. to whom

49. Sentence (11): Use the next paragraph to tell about your experience <u>and matching</u> it to the job.

Which is the best way to write the underlined portion of sentence (11)?

a. getting to have matched

b. and to have matched

c. and to match

d. yet to match

50. Sentence (14): Should include a strong statement that will make the employer want to interview you.

What correction should be made to sentence (14)?

a. insert <u>It</u> before <u>Should</u> and use lowercase <u>should</u>

b. change <u>will make</u> to <u>is making</u>

c. replaced <u>interview</u> with <u>interviewing</u>

d. change <u>employer want</u> to <u>employer. Want</u>

Part II

1 Question

Read the following passages. Then, read the prompt and write an essay taking a stance. Use information from the passages to support your essay.

President Franklin Roosevelt's Message to Congress on Establishing Minimum Wages and Maximum Hours, May 24, 1937

"Today, you and I are pledged to take further steps to reduce the lag in the purchasing power of industrial workers and to strengthen and stabilize the markets for the farmers' products. The two go hand in hand. Each depends for its effectiveness upon the other. Both working simultaneously will open new outlets for productive capital. Our Nation so richly endowed with natural resources and with a capable and industrious population should be able to devise ways and means of insuring to all our able-bodied working men and women a fair day's pay for a fair day's work. A self-supporting and self-respecting democracy can plead no justification for the existence of child labor, no economic reason for chiseling workers' wages or stretching workers' hours.

Enlightened business is learning that competition ought not to cause bad social consequences which inevitably react upon the profits of business itself. All but the hopelessly reactionary will agree that to conserve our primary resources of man power, government must have some control over maximum hours, minimum wages, the evil of child labor and the exploitation of unorganized labor."

Letter to the Editor Regarding Minimum Wage Increase, January 3, 2014

Dear Editor:
I have seen many people speak out in support of raising the minimum wage in recent weeks, but I have yet to see anyone offer an informed alternative view. The truth is, if we increase the minimum wage for all American workers, we will undoubtedly do irreparable harm to our economy. The more we keep government from intruding into the workplace, the better.

Raising the minimum wage means that employers have to come up with the extra money to pay their workers more. How will they do this? By firing workers to reduce costs, or by charging more for their goods and services. If they fire workers, then those workers will now be earning less than they did before . . . not exactly a great solution to raise the standard of living. If they raise the price of goods and services, then people will have to spend more on life essentials such as food and transportation. So the benefit of higher wages will be eaten up by the increased expenses faced by the average worker.

When I was growing up, I made twenty-five cents an hour washing cars. I used that money to put myself through college to get my engineering degree. I used that degree to get a job designing bridges for the state of Texas. I didn't sit there at the car wash complaining about how little I earned; I used that opportunity to better myself. I just wish more people these days were willing to do the same.

Sincerely,

Ralph Phillips

Prompt

These two passages present different arguments regarding the issue of minimum wage. In your response, analyze both positions to determine which one is best supported. Use relevant and specific evidence from the passages to support your response.

Answers and Explanations

Part I

1. a. Although Gilbert may feel *respect* and *gratitude*, the word that best describes his feelings is *love*. It is clearly indicated in his actions. *Nervousness* is not supported by the excerpt.

2. c. This choice is clearly supported by what the excerpt says happened when their eyes met—"and all doubt was swept away in a certainty that everything would be wonderful." The other choices may enter into the scene between them, but they do not occur when their eyes met.

3. d. It is clear from the ending of the excerpt that this was the biggest and hardest change for Anne. That is why she felt a "tinge of sadness." The other choices are not supported.

4. b. There are hints in the excerpt that support this answer, such as Marilla looking "gray" when Anne was leaving and how Anne had filled the house with "light and life." The other choices are not supported by the text.

5. b. Based on the information in the excerpt, this is the correct answer. The text says that Gilbert had won her "after years of patient waiting." This supports choice **b**, not the other choices.

6. d. The author gives the readers clues about what all the other characters are thinking, but the reader does not learn anything about Mr. Allan.

7. b. The text says that not many birds sang in September but that one sang sweetly while Gilbert and Anne repeated their vows. It even "wound up with one more little, glad trill" after the ceremony was over, seeming to mirror the joy of the wedding service.

8. d. Choice **d** is correct because it capitalizes all the words that make up the proper name of the college. Choices **a**, **b**, and **c** are incorrect because they capitalize some, but not all, of the words in the proper name.

9. c. The best revision of this sentence reads, "I am studying all types of farming techniques, but prefer organic methods for growing vegetables." Therefore, choice **c** is the best response. Choices **a**, **b**, and **d** change the meaning of the sentence.

10. d. Choice **d** is the best answer. This contains all the relevant information that is needed. Choice **a** is very general, and it is unclear what permanent position is wanted by the letter writer. Choice **b** is grammatically incorrect because it lacks a subject for the verb *applying*. Choice **c** is awkward and unclear.

11. d. Choice **d** is the best response, since this information is not central to the main point of the letter, which is asking for an internship. Choice **a** doesn't make sense when it is moved. Choice **b** doesn't work since the information is not material to the topic. Choice **c** would mean removing an important sentence from the paragraph.

12. d. Choice **d** is correct because it removes an unnecessary comma from the sentence. Choice **a** is not correct because it would insert an unnecessary comma. Choices **b** and **c** are not correct because these contain the wrong forms of the verbs.

13. b. Choice **b** is the best response. This sentence replaces the repetitive *he has* with the pronoun *who*. Choice **a** is a run-on sentence so it is incorrect. Choice **c** does not combine the sentences, but simply puts an inappropriate comma between them. Choice **d** improperly joins the sentences with *and*.

14. c. Choice **c** is correct because this action happened once in the past and is not ongoing. Choice **a** is not correct because the verb *made* is in the past tense, not the present tense, the way it should be. Choice **b** is the wrong answer because it creates a phrase and doesn't address the verb problem. Choice **d** uses an incorrect form of past tense.

15. c. This is the best answer. The audition will give him a chance to be discovered. The audition will not make him become famous or give him a chance to make a good living.

16. c. The excerpt says Gene got to the audition site at 9:00 A.M. and had been waiting more than three hours (line 20). That would make the time after noon.

17. c. This answer reflects what happens in the story. At first he was slow to start, but then he sang very well and passed the round of auditions.

18. d. This answer reflects the feelings that Gene was having about the audition. For instance, a person's heart often beats loudly—or seems to beat louder than usual—when a person is experiencing an important moment in life.

19. d. Choice **d** correctly capitalizes a proper noun. Choice **a** changes the verb into an incorrect tense. Choice **b** inserts a comma that is not needed, and choice **c** makes the second sentence a fragment.

20. b. Choice **b** is correct because it combines the ideas in both sentences with the relative pronoun *where*. Choice **a** uses a transition word that changes the meaning of the sentences. Choice **c** creates a confusing sentence, and choice **d** changes the meaning of the sentences.

21. d. Choice **d** is correct because the verb form fits the subject, and the tense is correct as well. Choice **a** is not correct because the tense and the verb in the first part of the sentence do not match the subject. Choices **b** and **c** are both incorrect because they pick incorrect tenses—one in the past continuous tense and the other in the future tense.

22. b. Choice **b** is correct. This sentence has nothing to do with the main topic of the paragraph, which concerns the slaves being held in Gorée Island. Choice **a** is not correct because this is a topic sentence and clearly the opening of the paragraph. Choice **c** has important information about the slaves in it. Choice **d** wouldn't make logical sense.

23. d. Choice **d** is correct since the subject (*women*) is plural, not singular. Choice **a** is incorrect because this is the wrong verb tense for the sentence. Choice **b** is grammatically incorrect since *a* is singular and *groups* is plural. No comma is needed after *people*, so choice **c** is incorrect.

24. b. Choice **b** is correct because it replaces the homonym *their*, a possessive pronoun, with *there*, meaning *that place*. Choice **a** does not make sense. Choice **c** would result in a verb that does not agree with the subject. Choice **d** is incorrect because there is no reason to capitalize *slaves*.

25. a. Choice **a** is correct because this phrase links a visit to Gorée Island with learning from the guides. Choice **b** is incorrect because it changes the meaning of the sentence. Choice **c** uses an inappropriate transition. Choice **d** is wrong because it turns the sentence into a dependent clause.

26. a. This phrase means that the security was somehow broken, so choice **a** is correct. This can be seen in the very first section of the memo: "As a result of some incidents that have occurred with unauthorized persons in secure parts. . . ." The other choices are not suggested by these words. They have nothing to do with security being compromised.

27. a. The point of the memo is that there were some security incidents that needed to be addressed. Based on the memo, choice **b** is clearly not correct, and the others are not suggested by the memo, either.

28. d. If you read the memo carefully, you will see that this is the one option that the new regulations will help prevent. It is mentioned in the first paragraph.

29. a. Again, a close reading of the text will reveal that this is what an employee is to do first if a stranger is seen in Building A. This can be found in the fourth paragraph.

30. c. The memo is direct and to the point. It is not technical. It's quite clear and not at all academic.

31. c. The memo states a problem at the beginning and then describes the new regulations that will solve it—a way to keep unauthorized people out of secure parts of Building A.

32. a. This choice is clearly correct. It contains the main idea of the excerpt. The dialogue is about a boy wanting to go away to school and his mother finally agreeing to it.

33. c. It seems clear from the dialogue in the excerpt that Beatrice would prefer to be in England rather than do any of the other activities. She seems not to mind America, but she does long for England.

34. d. This is the most logical choice, although it is never actually stated in the excerpt. There is no mention of the father, although he may or may not live in America. The other choices are not supported by the passage, either.

35. b. This is the only choice suggested by the lines spoken by Beatrice. She is comparing England's mellow nature to America's energetic spirit.

36. d. This is the best and most all-encompassing answer. This mother and son do not seem like most mothers and sons. The way they relate and talk suggests an atypical relationship.

37. d. This is the most obvious reason that Beatrice wants Amory to meet Monsignor Darcy. She says he went to Harrow and Yale, and she wants Amory to talk to him.

38. c. This is what the review is mostly about. The reviewer does address the other answer choices, but they do not represent the main intent of the review.

39. d. Based on what the reviewer says about the movie, this is the best answer. He says the main character's acting is bad. He does not mention the length of the film, either.

40. c. This is the most logical choice. People reading the review would take into consideration that the reviewer has never had any of his or her science fiction scripts made into a movie. This would definitely taint the review, as he or she might be overly critical.

41. b. The review is somewhat *humorous*, or at least that is its intention. Although the 3-D aspect of the film is mentioned, that's not really enough to call the review *technical*. A technical review would probably have discussed the 3-D aspect at more length. None of the other choices properly describes the writing style of the review.

42. d. This word best describes what the reviewer feels about the movie. Overall, the reviewer is not very impressed with the film, so a positive choice like **b** could be eliminated. None of the other choices accurately describes the author's opinion.

43. d. Choice **d** is correct because it adds an appropriate conjunction to join the two sentences. Choice **a** inserts an unnecessary comma, and by removing the existing comma you create a run-on sentence, so both choices **a** and **b** are incorrect. Choice **c** replaces the correct form of the verb with an incorrect form.

44. d. Choice **d** is correct because the singular verb *doesn't* agrees with the singular noun *letter*. Choice **a** is incorrect because this is the wrong verb tense for this sentence. Choice **b** is incorrect, not because of the verb, but because of the plural form of *letter*. The sentence is referring to one letter, not multiple ones. Choice **c** is incorrect because this is a plural form of the verb.

45. d. Choice **d** is correct because it uses a verb that is parallel to *keeping*. Choices **a** and **b** are incorrect because they use an incorrect form of the verb. Choice **c** is not correct because it changes the pronoun object into a possessive.

46. d. Choice **d** is correct because this pronoun refers back to the antecedent *you*. Choice **a** is incorrect because it refers to more than one *you*. Choices **b** and **c** are incorrect because they refer to either *she* or *he* as antecedents.

47. b. Choice **b** is correct because commas are used between lists of items. Choices **a** and **c** are incorrect because they create sentence fragments. Choice **d** is not correct because *title* is not the last item in the list of items.

48. d. Choice **d** is correct because the preposition *to* takes the objective form of the pronoun *who*. Choice **b** is incorrect because *that* refers to an animal or thing, but not a person. Also, *which* does not refer to a person, so choices **a** and **c** are incorrect.

49. c. Choice **c** is correct because it matches the preceding verb *to tell*. Choices **a** and **b** are incorrect because they do not match *to tell*. Choice **d** is incorrect because it creates a confusing sentence.

50. a. Choice **a** is correct because it adds a subject to properly complete the sentence. Choice **b** changes a correct verb form into an incorrect one, as does choice **c**. Choice **d** is incorrect because it turns the sentence into two fragments.

Part II
Sample 6 Scoring Essay

President Roosevelt and letter-writing citizen Ralph Phillips represent perspectives on the minimum wage from very different time periods. During Roosevelt's administration, the country was facing its worst Depression in history; in 2014, the country had rebounded from a dramatic Recession but was deeply divided on both who was responsible for the crisis, and how it should be addressed.

Among FDR's New Deal initiatives was a proposal to establish a minimum wage and maximum hours for American workers. In this message to Congress, he suggests that protecting and investing in the American workforce would improve conditions for industrial workers and for farmers who are dependent on market demand, drawing on Americans' sense of ability and resourcefulness, ideals of democracy, and national ego. He cites child labor and exploitation of unorganized labor as the primary justifications for these measures.

However, Ralph Phillips' letter focuses on the downsides of such an initiative—employers required to adhere to an increased minimum wage would be forced into "firing workers to reduce costs" or "charging more for their goods," which would increase the burden on the workers it was meant to help. He justifiably points out that workers will need to be fired in order for employers to pay the remaining workers more. While these logistical concerns might initially appear to be more persuasive than FDR's appeal to the enlightened American spirit of enterprise, Phillips concludes with a petulant "I made twenty-five cents an hour washing cars" anecdote that willfully ignores class and economic realities of the modern era. He even appears hypocritical—he thinks the government should stay out of the private employment arena, but took a job for a government office! Besides, nobody could put themselves through college making a quarter an hour today—Phillips thus proves himself to be one of the "hopelessly reactionary" individuals FDR despaired of reaching in his message. FDR's address is best supported because he addressed it to a legislative body that could make a difference and sought to inspire Congressional leadership to intervene on behalf of the American worker.

This essay introduces compelling evidence from each source, organizes its points logically by moving from beginning to end in each essay, then comparing the two, and concludes by making an argument about which essay is better supported, and why. It demonstrates fluency in Standard American English conventions, including spelling and grammar.

Sample 3 Scoring Essay

In his message to congress, President Franklin Roosevelt says that the government should assist people to prevent exploration and child labor, even if it damages the economy. America is rich enough to paying workers fairly for their work. Ralph Phillips wrote a letter to the editor saying about how it would be to hard to have a minimum wage because of it having increase costs for employers and actually basically reduce employment.

He worked hard to put himself through school and says everyone should—but what if you can't even find a car wash job? What if you have other obstacles? Roosevelt may have less of plans but he is at least talking to the right people instead of just giving up.

This essay uses less specific, more simplistic evidence from each source, and features no direct quotes or broader context. Its organization is basically logical but lacks a coherent beginning-middle-end structure or specific analysis of each argument. The grasp of Standard American English is weaker—the pronoun "He" in the second paragraph is clear and there are other syntax issues.

Sample 0 Scoring Essay

They both make differnt points about minimum wagers in America. Phillips says the min. wage would only do bad things to the economy and supports his argument with personal stories about working hard. So he is more persuasive. roosevelt says America is rich and so should pay its workers more no matter what.

This essay fails to introduce its sources, what types of documents they are, or when they were written. There are no specific quotes, the essay is much too brief, and its structure is disorganized—it draws a conclusion before analyzing FDR's argument. The grammar, spelling, and syntax are all substandard.

Extended Response

For this prompt, an extended response should include some discussion of how the two passages differ in viewpoint regarding the issue of minimum wage. Specifically, Roosevelt's message to Congress emphasizes the need for government to establish livable requirements for wages and working conditions, while the letter to the editor asserts that government should keep out of private enterprise as much as possible. A successful extended response should also analyze the arguments presented in each passage. For the Roosevelt passage, the arguments focus on an appeal to emotion and charitable cooperation among all Americans. For example, Roosevelt refers to the way a "self-respecting democracy" should run. The letter to the editor, on the other hand, relies largely on personal experience to support its argument. Mr. Phillips also offers a logical argument regarding the effects of a minimum wage increase that some could consider one-sided; following the logic of this argument, workers should be paid as little as possible to keep everyone employed and to keep the price of goods low. A keen reader might even note the potential conflict between Mr. Phillips's assertion that government should stay out of the affairs of business, and the fact that he got a job working for the government.

3 ▶ READING COMPREHENSION: BIG PICTURE TOOLS

CHAPTER SUMMARY

Many of the questions on the GED® RLA test are designed to uncover how well you understand and think about what you read. You'll need to read the passage carefully in order to answer the question correctly. In some cases, the answer will be obvious to you; in other cases, you'll have to do a little detective work to figure out the correct choice.

Answers and explanations for all practice questions are at the end of the chapter.

This chapter covers tips and strategies for answering questions about big picture concerns like Author's Purpose, Point of View, and Theme, as well as how to read effectively and efficiently, how to select and eliminate answers, and how to manage your time.

Reading the Passages

Pay Attention to the Purpose Question

As you may already know, each passage is preceded by a purpose question. This question is printed in bold and is there to give you a purpose and focus as you read. Use this question to your benefit. Read it carefully, and think about what you might read about in the passage.

Suppose the following is one of the purpose questions on your test:

Who Is Knocking?

How can this help you? Well, before you even begin reading, you know that in the passage, you will read about someone knocking. Because the purpose question doesn't tell you who that is, you know you need to look for that information as you read. For some reason, this is going to be important for you to know.

> The purpose question is just there to provide a focus for your reading; you will not have to answer this question.

Read the Questions First

Another way to help you focus on important information as you read a passage is to take a quick look at the questions *before* you begin reading. This will help you know what information to look for in the passage.

1. How does the author feel about the topic?

By reading the questions ahead of time, you know you need to look for words and details that offer clues about the author's attitude toward the subject matter. This could help focus your attention as you read and possibly save time in the long run.

First Scan, Then Read

You may find it helpful to quickly scan the passage to identify the main idea, then go back and read the passage carefully. Knowing the main idea first can help you identify supporting details as you read. This also lets you know what information you should be looking for when you read the passage slowly and critically the second time.

Use Context Clues

Don't get upset if you come across an unfamiliar word in a passage. Use what you have learned about context clues to figure out the meaning. Try doing the following:

- Notice how the word is used in the sentence.
- Read the surrounding sentences.
- Look for hints such as synonyms, antonyms, examples, and definitions.
- Think about what would make sense in the context of the passage.

To correctly answer the questions, it is imperative that you completely understand each passage.

Notice Important Details

As you read, pay attention to words, phrases, and details that seem to be important to the meaning of the passage. Be on the lookout for the information listed here:

- key words
- names of real people
- names of characters
- names of locations
- dates
- headings
- specific details
- clues about mood or tone
- hints about the theme
- point of view

Read Everything

As you read, you may come across information that is set off in brackets. These are explanatory notes that can provide valuable information.

Information in brackets [such as these] can be helpful in selecting the best answer.

It may be tempting to skip over the information in the brackets, especially if you're beginning to feel the time crunch. Don't skip anything. Be sure to read all the information you've been given. It may be there for a good reason.

Classify Information

As you read, be sure to recognize the difference between the main idea and supporting details. Also, be sure to recognize whether a statement is a fact or an opinion. Classifying statements correctly can help you completely understand the passage and mentally organize the ideas you have read.

Don't Forget the Visuals

Any time a passage includes visual displays, pay close attention to them! They are probably there for a reason and often include extremely valuable information that will deepen your understanding of the passage. Visual aids that you might find include the following:

- maps
- charts
- graphs
- diagrams
- illustrations
- photographs

Read the titles, labels, and captions as well as the information contained within the visuals themselves.

Read the Passage Completely

Some people find it helpful to read the questions before reading the passage. That's great; however, you need to read the passage completely before trying to actually *answer* the questions, even if the questions appear to be simple. Most of the questions will require you to understand the entire passage completely in order to correctly answer them. Remember, this is not the time to assume that you know what the passage is about. Read the entire text carefully, then answer the questions.

Carefully Read the Questions

This may seem obvious, but it is vital that you read each question carefully and make sure you completely understand exactly what is being asked. In fact, read each question twice. How can you select the correct answer if you misread or do not understand the question?

Which of the following is least likely to occur next?

Suppose you read this question too quickly. You might miss the word *least*. This one simple word completely changes the question. Overlooking one word in a question could cause you to select the wrong answer choice.

Also, it may be tempting to assume that you know what the question is asking, especially if several similar questions are grouped together and you're feeling rushed for time. But remember—just because it would be logical for a certain question to come next, there's no guarantee that it will.

Pay Attention to Line Numbers

Some questions may refer to line numbers in the passage. Be sure to refer back to the passage and read the information in that line again. It is important to understand the words and information in the correct context.

> *What is the meaning of the word* buffet *in line 17?*

You're probably familiar with the word *buffet* and could easily give a definition. But, this word does have several meanings. Without reading line 17, how will you know which meaning is correct?

> *(17) Heavy raindrops and hail continued to buffet the tiny cabin throughout the night.*

Now that you've read the word in the correct context, you will be able to select the appropriate meaning.

TIP

Any information that is offered within a question is important! It would not be there if you didn't need it.

Tips for Fiction Passages

Prose fiction passages involve imaginary people and events. While you may see prose fiction passages that contain arguments and evidence to support a viewpoint or conclusion, the author's main intent for prose fiction is generally to entertain. These passages are more likely to focus on tone, style, setting, point of view, and making inferences about the characters and the world.

Make Inferences

Often in prose fiction passages, the author intentionally leaves out some information. This requires readers to make inferences about the plot, characters, or set-

ting. Use the information that is implied to "fill in the blanks" and create your own complete mental picture. For example, you can infer what type of person a character is by paying attention to what other characters say or think about him. You can put together information about the sights, sounds, and smells described in a story to infer the setting.

> *As Maxwell stepped outside, he noticed the sounds of the cows mooing in the distance and could make out the silhouette of the barn on the opposite side of the field. This was nothing like the city he was used to.*

> What is the setting of the story?
> **a.** a barn
> **b.** a big city
> **c.** a farm
> **d.** a zoo

The writer mentions a city, but this is not the setting. Because we know that Maxwell hears cows and can see a barn on the other side of the field, we can infer that he is on a farm (choice **c**). If the barn were the setting, he would be in it or near it; it would not be in the distance.

Notice Names

Pay close attention to the names of people and places, as well as to dates and key words. These are often important to remember if you are going to accurately understand the story.

Pay Attention to Details

Details can help you determine many things about a story. This information is invaluable when answering questions about plot, conflicts, mood, point of view, and theme. If you get to a question about one of these and are unsure of the answer, look back in the passage and see what insight the details can offer.

Tips for Nonfiction Passages

The GED® RLA test focuses on three types of nonfiction reading passages. These have been chosen to ensure that you have an understanding of practical reading and writing situations that you might encounter in the professional world.

Informational Science Passages

These passages will focus on one of two areas within the scientific realm. The first is human health and other biology; this may include topics such as respiration and the interdependence of animal species. The second is energy-related systems; this may include topics such as photosynthesis, climate, and gas combustion.

The emphasis of these passages is not to test you on unfamiliar scientific principles; you will not be expected to provide additional scientific knowledge on the topics presented. These passages will likely focus on your ability to correctly understand the steps in a process, and your ability to explain how the steps relate to each other.

Informational Social Studies Passages

These passages will focus on the theme of the Great American Conversation, which includes discussion of elements of American government and how it relates to society. The passages featured here will likely include excerpts from well-known historical documents, such as the Preamble to the U.S. Constitution, as well as other writings of significant figures in American history. These passages may also include texts from modern-day political figures, and can appear in forms as various as speeches, letters, laws, or diaries.

Informational Workplace Passages

These passages are meant to resemble the kinds of documents you are likely to encounter in a modern workplace setting. These documents may include letters, e-mails, instruction manuals, memos, or lists of policies, among others.

The purpose of the nonfiction passages on the test may be to entertain, inform, or persuade readers. The testing standards of the GED® Reasoning through Language Arts test place a particular emphasis on the understanding and analysis of arguments and evidence, so expect passages that focus on presenting a viewpoint or position on an issue. Regardless of their purpose, these passages are based on actual people, topics, or events and will offer information, facts, and details about the topic.

Notice Details

Watch for details such as statistics, dates, names, events, section headings, and key words that are included in the passage. You may see these again when you get to the questions. However, do not select an answer choice simply because it matches something from the passage; many incorrect answer choices are also taken from the text. This is to ensure that you are understanding the passage and not just skimming for a correct answer.

Pay Attention to Descriptive Language

Descriptive language can offer clues about an author's views on a topic. For example, if an author describes a car as a "beast," that author probably feels that the vehicle is very big or powerful. After you find the main idea, begin looking for language, facts, and details that reveal or support the author's point of view.

Look for Evidence

Keep in mind that each paragraph of a nonfiction passage will have a main idea. The rest of the paragraph will include details to support the main idea. As you read, search for this evidence. Facts, examples, descriptions, and other information that helps explain the main idea are essential to understanding the text and will probably be the subject of at least some of the questions.

Draw Your Own Conclusions

Some types of nonfiction passages will include opinions on a particular topic. In some cases, you will be given two passages that offer different views on the same topic. Pay special attention to the evidence and reasons presented to support the view presented in each passage. Then, draw your own conclusions regarding the author's ability to present and support that opinion. For the extended response item on the test, reaching your own conclusions and expanding on the evidence and views presented in the passages is critical if you want to score well.

Author's Purpose

To fully understand what we read, we need to be able to figure out why the passage was written. An author always has a reason, or purpose, for writing. The **author's purpose** for writing a passage is usually one of the following:

- to entertain
- to inform
- to persuade

Understanding the author's reason for writing can help you better understand what you read. Different types of texts usually have different purposes. Many stories, plays, magazine articles, poems, novels, and comic strips are written to **entertain**. They may be fiction or nonfiction and may include facts, opinions, or both, but the purpose for writing them is to tell a story. These are intended to entertain readers and are meant for pleasure reading.

This summer while vacationing in Florida, I went parasailing with my mom. It was the most thrilling adventure I'd ever had! We floated from a giant parachute, hundreds of feet above the water, and soared over the beaches.

This passage was written to entertain. It was intended to tell a story about the author's adventure. It does not try to teach any information, nor does it try to convince you to share an opinion about the topic.

Textbooks, encyclopedias, and many newspaper articles are written to **inform**. Their purpose is to give the reader information or to teach about a subject. Such passages will usually contain mostly facts and may include charts, diagrams, or drawings to help explain the information.

Parasailing is a sport in which a rider is attached to a large parachute, or parasail. The parasail is attached to a vehicle, usually a boat, by a long tow rope. As the boat moves, the parasail and rider rise up into the air.

This paragraph teaches readers about the sport of parasailing. It contains facts and information about the topic. Readers may enjoy reading about the subject, but the author's reason for writing the passage was to inform.

Other material, such as commercials, advertisements, letters to the editor, and political speeches, are written to **persuade** readers to share a belief, agree with an opinion, or support an idea. Such writing may include some facts or statements from experts, but it will most likely include the author's opinions about the topic.

One of the most dangerous sports today is parasailing. Each year, many people are seriously injured, or even killed, while participating in this activity. Laws should be passed that prohibit such reckless entertainment. If people want to fly, they should get on an airplane.

The author of this paragraph wants to convince readers that parasailing is a dangerous sport. The text includes not only opinions, but also facts that support the author's stand on the subject. Notice that strong words and phrases, such as *seriously injured*, *should*, and *reckless*, are included to stir up emotions in the readers. The author's purpose for writing this passage was to persuade readers to agree with his or her beliefs about parasailing.

BOOST

Did you know that the GED® test was originally created for military personnel and veterans who did not finish high school? That was in 1942. Five years later, New York became the first state to make the test available to civilians. By 1974, the GED® test was available in all 50 U.S. states.

Let's practice what you've learned about recognizing the author's purpose. Read the paragraph and determine whether it was written to entertain, inform, or persuade.

It was a quiet summer evening. The moon was full, and the sky seemed to hold a million stars. Outside, only the sounds of the crickets could be heard.

What was the author's purpose for writing this passage?

_____

Did you recognize that the author's purpose was to entertain? The text did not try to teach anything or convince you to hold a certain opinion. It was simply written for the reader to enjoy.

Read the passage for key information and answer the following five questions.

Instructions for License Renewal

A driver's license must be renewed every four years. A renewal application is sent approximately five to seven weeks before the expiration date listed on the license. Individuals who fail to renew within three years of the license expiration date are not eligible for a renewal and must repeat the initial licensing process. To renew a license, you must visit a Motor Vehicles Agency. You must present a completed renewal application; your current driver's license; acceptable proof of age, identification, and address; and proof of social security in the form of a Social Security card, a state or federal income tax return, a current pay stub, or a W-2 form. You must also pay the required fee. If all the documents and payment are in order, your photo will be taken and a new license will be issued.

1. What documents does one need to renew a driver's license?

2. What documents represent proof of social security?

3. How often must one renew a driver's license?

4. How does one obtain the renewal form?

5. True or False: You can renew your driver's license by mail.

Read the following passage and determine the meaning of the italicized word from its context.

6. By the time our staff meeting ended at 8:00, I was *ravenous*. I had skipped lunch and hadn't eaten since breakfast.

Ravenous means
   a. like a raven, birdlike.
   b. extremely hungry, greedy for food.
   c. exhausted, ready for bed.
   d. angry, quite upset.

Read the passage and answer the six questions that follow.

Robert Johnson is the best blues guitarist of all time. Johnson had a tremendous impact on the world of rock and roll. Some consider Johnson the father of modern rock: His influence extends to artists from Muddy Waters to Led Zeppelin and the Rolling Stones. Eric Clapton has called Johnson the most important blues musician who ever lived. It is hard to believe that Johnson recorded only 29 songs before his death in 1938, yet he left an indelible mark on the music world. Again and again, contemporary rock artists return to Johnson, whose songs capture the very essence of the blues, transforming our pain and suffering with the healing magic of his guitar. Rock music wouldn't be what it is today without Robert Johnson.

7. According to the passage, from what musical tradition did Robert Johnson emerge?
   a. rock and roll
   b. jazz
   c. blues
   d. classical

8. Johnson died in
   a. 1927.
   b. 1938.
   c. 1929.
   d. 1940.

9. True or False: Johnson influenced many rock artists, including Led Zeppelin and the Rolling Stones.

10. Contemporary rock artists turn to Robert Johnson for
   a. musical influence.
   b. life lessons.
   c. recovery from painful injuries.
   d. advice.

11. The most appropriate title for this article would be
   a. "A Fleeting Life"
   b. "The World's Greatest Musician"
   c. "Blues Guitar Legend Robert Johnson"
   d. "Learning the Guitar"

12. Indicate whether the following sentences are *fact* or *opinion*:
   a. Robert Johnson is the best blues guitarist of all time.
   b. Eric Clapton has called Johnson the most important blues musician who ever lived.
   c. Rock music wouldn't be what it is today without Robert Johnson.
   d. Robert Johnson died in 1938.

Read the passage and answer the eight questions that follow.

There will be dire consequences for residents if a shopping mall is built on the east side of town. First, the shopping mall will interfere with the tranquil and quiet atmosphere that we now enjoy. Second, the mall will attract a huge number of shoppers from a variety of surrounding areas, which will result in major traffic congestion for those of us who live here. But most importantly, to build the shopping mall, many of us will be asked to sell our homes and relocate, and this kind of displacement should be avoided at all costs.

13. The main idea of this passage is that the shopping mall would
  a. be great for the community.
  b. not change things much.
  c. be bad for the community.
  d. be a good place to shop.

14. *Displacement* is a good word choice because
  a. it is compatible with general reading level and the formal writing style of the article.
  b. the writer likes to impress readers by using big words.
  c. it is the only word that is suitable or appropriate.
  d. it is easy to understand.

15. This passage is organized
  a. in chronological order.
  b. by cause and effect.
  c. by order of importance.
  d. both **b** and **c**

16. This passage uses which point of view?
  a. first person
  b. second person
  c. third person
  d. no point of view

17. This passage is written from whose perspective?
  a. that of the residents
  b. that of an outside consultant
  c. that of the shopping mall developer
  d. the reader's perspective

18. The choice of the word *dire* suggests that the consequences of the merger would be
  a. minimal.
  b. expected.
  c. disastrous.
  d. welcome.

19. Which words best describe the style of this passage?
  a. informal, conversational
  b. descriptive, storylike
  c. formal, businesslike
  d. scattered, confusing

20. The tone of this passage is
  a. sad.
  b. foreboding.
  c. threatening.
  d. joyous.

Point of View

It is important to think about who is telling the story. This narrator may be someone who is a part of the story, or it may be someone outside of the events. The **point of view** refers to who is telling the story, which makes a difference in how much information the reader is given.

Some stories use a **first-person** point of view. In this case, one of the characters is telling the story, and readers see the events through this person's eyes.

After the game, Henry and I grabbed a pizza with the rest of the team. We hung out for a couple of hours, then headed home. By then, I was totally exhausted.

Notice that when an author uses a first-person point of view, the narrator uses the pronouns *I, me, us,* and *we,* and it seems as if the character is speaking directly to the reader. The narrator knows only his or her own thoughts and feelings, not those of the other characters, and often shares his or her attitudes and opinions with the readers.

Other stories use a **third-person** point of view, in which the narrator is not a character in the story and does not participate in the events.

> *After the game, Deon said he would join Henry and the rest of the team for pizza. They stayed for a couple of hours before heading home, exhausted.*

When a story is told from the third-person point of view, the narrator will use pronouns such as *he, she,* and *they* when discussing the characters. Also, the narrator often knows the thoughts and feelings of every character.

Let's practice what you've just reviewed. Read the next three paragraphs, think about who is telling the story, and determine the point of view of the passage.

> *As soon as the bell rang, a tall, thin woman with dark hair rose from behind the desk. The class quieted as she began to speak.*
>
> *"Good morning, class," she stated. "I am Ms. Wolfe, and I will be your English teacher this semester. Go ahead and open your books to the table of contents, and let's get started."*
>
> *Ms. Wolfe picked up the text from her desk, and opened it to the first page.*

What is the point of view of this passage?

_____

This passage is written in the third-person point of view. The narrator is not a character in the story. Notice that the pronoun *I* is included in the passage. However, it is spoken by one of the characters, not the narrator.

Read the passage and answer the question that follows.

Ms. Crawford has been a model citizen since she moved to Springfield in 1985. She started out as a small business owner and quickly grew her business until it was one of the major employers in the region. In 1991, her company was profiled in *BusinessWeek* magazine. Her innovative business model includes a great deal of community work and fundraising, the rewards of which have brought deep and lasting benefits to Springfield and its citizens. Today, she is being honored with Springfield's Citizen of the Century Award to recognize all her cutting-edge efforts on behalf of our community.

21. This paragraph uses what point of view?
   a. first-person point of view
   b. second-person point of view
   c. third-person point of view
   d. It can't be determined from the information provided.

Read the passage and answer the question that follows.

There will be dire consequences for residents if a shopping mall is built on the east side of town. First, the shopping mall will interfere with the tranquil and quiet atmosphere that we now enjoy. Second, the mall will attract a huge number of shoppers from a variety of surrounding areas, which will result in major traffic congestion for those of us who live here. But most importantly, to build the shopping mall, many of us will be asked to sell our homes and relocate, and this kind of displacement should be avoided at all costs.

22. This passage uses which point of view?
  a. first person
  b. second person
  c. third person
  d. no point of view

Theme

As we read, we look for and try to understand the messages and information that the author wants to share. Sometimes, the author's message is very obvious. Other times, we have to look a little harder to find it. The **theme** of a story is its underlying message. In a fable, the moral of the story is the theme. In fiction, this overall message is usually implied, rather than being directly stated, and may involve the following:

- attitudes
- beliefs
- opinions
- perceptions

The theme often leaves you with ideas, a conclusion, or a lesson that the writer wants you to take away from the story. Often, this lesson relates to life, society, or human nature. As you read, think about what the author's message might be. Consider the characters' words and actions, the tone, the plot, and any repeated patterns to see what views of the writer these portray.

Think about the story of the three little pigs. One could say that the theme of this story is that it is best to do a job the right way the first time. The author does not directly state this message, but this is a lesson or opinion that readers might take away from the story.

As an example, say you're reading a novel about a poor woman's journey from Korea to the United States in the 1940s. It may describe the details of the character's childhood on a farm in Korea, the boat trip that she took as a young adult to San Francisco, the elderly man who swindled her out of her life savings because she didn't speak English, the difficulties she had finding a job, and the satisfaction she ultimately felt as she worked hard to make a living. These are the facts of the plot, but the theme of the novel is something very different. Here are some possible themes:

- The theme could be *a message or lesson*. For instance: *You can reach your goals more easily if you block out your problems and focus only on your goal.*
- The theme could be *a question*. For instance: *Do you lose part of yourself when you leave your culture? Is it better to stay where you are and face the difficulties there, or do you become more of your real self when you leave your culture and make your own way in the world?*
- The theme could be *a specific idea about life or people*. For instance: *Desperation brings out the very worst in people and the very best.*
- The theme could also be *a simpler, more general concept*. For instance, perhaps the novel is an exploration of the theme of youth and aging.

Note that more than one theme may be valid for a work of fiction, and other readers may come to a different conclusion than you do. This is part of the reward of reading fiction—seeing the ideas behind what you read and discussing those ideas with other people. (Often these are ideas about life, which will be interesting to you as you make your own way in the world.)

Although a work of fiction may have more than one possible theme, don't worry that this will cause confusion on the GED® RLA test. Every question about theme on the GED® RLA test will have only one, clearly correct answer. There are no "trick" questions on the exam.

Finding the Theme

As you read a work of fiction closely, pay attention to the following elements in order to find the theme:

- **Repetition:** Note whether the author repeats certain words, phrases, symbols, actions, or ideas, or whether certain characters reappear throughout a story. This is often a clue that those words, phrases, characters, and so on have a special importance in the story—and to the theme.
- **Connections:** In many stories, one specific thing may not be repeated, but if you look closely, you'll find that the writer uses repetition in a more complicated way. For example, let's say the first chapter of a book takes place in a house by a river, which is flooding after a bad storm. The climax of the book takes place on a train that's traveling through the dusty plains of Texas. The end of the book takes place on a street in New York City, where children have uncapped a fire hydrant and are playing in the water. While a river, a plain, and a fire hydrant are very different things, there is a pattern running through the book: water—either too much or too little. Ask yourself if this pattern helps to reveal the theme.
- **Timing:** Consider when events occur in a story and whether there is a pattern. For example, let's say in one short story, whenever the main character, a firefighter, puts on his firefighting uniform in the morning, a mouse—a common symbol for cowardice and weakness—peeks its head out of a hole in the wall. Is this pattern a reminder that we all have to battle our weaknesses? Or that even when someone acts bravely, he or she is still vulnerable? Patterns are usually connected to the theme and can help us understand it.
- **Omission:** Often it's what a writer *doesn't* write about that's most important. Is there a detail or event that's glaringly left out of the story? This may be directly tied to the theme.

Practice

Read the passage and answer the questions that follow.

Four Simple Tips to Help You Land a Great Job

Whether you're just graduating and entering the job market for the first time or you're changing careers, searching for a job is never easy. In today's high-tech society, many potential employers are turning to social media to learn more about you.

"Before you even walk through the door for your first interview, it is highly likely the person waiting on the other side has seen more than just your resume," says Lauren Berger, CEO of Intern-Queen.com. "The way you present yourself online speaks volumes to hiring managers about your tech savvy and comfort level with social media—both critical skills demanded by virtually every employer."

With technology playing an established role in our lives and social networks easily accessible to potential employers, establishing a strong digital footprint and personal brand is crucial to success. So how can you use technology to land that first job and make the best first impression?

Here are four top tech tools and social media tips for landing your dream job:

1. Get organized. While it may seem like a minor detail, one of the first things you should do is get a professional e-mail address. The college e-mail or cutesy address you created back in high school won't impress a job recruiter.

2. Leverage your networks and set informational interviews. Make a target list of employers you'd like to work for and do some research about them, identifying one person from each company whom you'd like to meet. Reach out to that person and explain that you're really interested in the company and what his or her department does. Then ask if he or she will take five minutes to sit down and tell you how he or she got started and give you some advice.

3. Put your best "digital foot" forward. You have one chance to make a first impression, so make sure it's a good one. This means not only dressing professionally but also using your style (both online and off) to demonstrate your personal interests. Building your personal brand and establishing relationships within the industry will help open doors to opportunities you may not have discovered otherwise. Make sure that your online presence is up to date and also reflects your best attributes. This includes maintaining a consistent resume and work experience information across your networks to build familiarity among possible recruiters.

4. Lead with your strengths. Ask your friends and previous employers what your strengths are, and use specific examples during your interview to highlight them. You can also use this opportunity to demonstrate your experience with technology. If you are consistently told how well organized you are, share a previous work experience that demonstrates how you used technology and what value this brings to the employer. If you have a laptop or a tablet computer, consider bringing it to the interview to show off your portfolio of work. This instantly demonstrates you're on the cutting edge of new technology—a value for any employer.

These seemingly simple tips can help you stand out from the crowd and boost your chances of finding that great job.

23. Of the following choices, which skills does the author emphasize as being important to potential employers?

   a. leadership and the ability to resolve conflict

   b. digital literacy and expertise with Internet communications

   c. loyalty and a strong work ethic

   d. creativity and knowledge of computer hardware

24. Based on the passage, which of the following statements would the author most likely make when advising someone who was recently laid off and is in the process of applying for jobs?

   a. Update your career wardrobe and hire a professional to revise your resume.

   b. Consider getting retrained in a field that is growing in career opportunities.

   c. Evaluate how your job qualifications can be demonstrated through the use of technology.

   d. Schedule as many informational interviews as you can at each company you are interested in, and attend a weekly job-support group.

Common themes you may have found in reading might include:

- Crime does not pay.
- It is important to be honest.
- Be happy with what you have.
- Money cannot buy happiness.
- Keep going when things get tough.
- Do not be afraid to try something new.

Give it a try. Look for the theme as you read the following passage.

Camilla usually looked forward to Friday nights, but this week was the definite exception. Instead of going to the movies with her friends, she would be stuck at home, helping Mom get ready for tomorrow's garage sale. As she walked into the house, Camilla could see that Mom was already prepared for the long night ahead of them.

"Hey, get that scowl off your face and throw on your overalls," Mom called out cheerfully. "It won't be that bad."

Camilla changed clothes and headed to the garage, dragging her feet the whole way. Mom was elbow deep in an old cardboard box. She pulled out a raggedy, old stuffed dog.

"Mr. Floppy!" Camilla cried, excited to see her old friend. "I haven't seen him in years!"

"Your very first soft friend," Mom reminisced. "I'm assuming you'll be keeping him? Or would you like a 25-cent price tag to stick on his ear?"

Camilla set the old dog aside. She would definitely keep him. She helped Mom empty the rest of the box, sticking price tags on other old toys and books. They continued through the boxes, stopping to look through old photo albums together, telling funny stories about some of the useless gifts they'd collected, laughing at the hand-me-down clothes that had arrived at their house over the years, and modeling the silliest of them.

After a few hours, Mom looked at her watch. "Wow! It's nearly 8:00 already. Should we order a pizza?"

Camilla couldn't believe how late it was. She looked at her mom—who was wearing dusty overalls, five strands of Aunt Edna's old beads, and Granny's wide-brimmed Sunday bonnet—and couldn't help but laugh out loud. This was the best Friday night she could remember.

What is the theme of the story?
a. Memories are a special part of life.
b. It is important to get rid of old items.
c. Families should spend weekends together.
d. Sometimes things turn out to be better than expected.

At the beginning of the story, Camilla did not want to spend the evening helping her mom. By the end, she was having a great time. Choice **d** is the theme of this story. Some of the other answer choices represent ideas that were presented in the story, but the underlying message that the author wanted to portray is that things can turn out to be more fun than we think they will be.

Synthesis

Suppose you were doing a research paper. You would select a topic, then to be sure you learned as much as possible, you would search a variety of texts to find information about that topic. After reading each of your sources, you would put together all the information you learned. This combination of information would provide a clear understanding of the subject.

As readers, there are times when we have to combine information to gain a complete understanding of the text. **Synthesis** means putting ideas from multiple sources together. Sometimes, readers synthesize information from different parts of a single text. Other times, they must put together information from more than one text.

Read the passage below.

Roger quietly walked to the shelf. He pulled his ball cap down on his head as he quickly looked at the items neatly lined up in front of him. Then, he grabbed a package of crackers, shoving it into his backpack as he hurried to the door, trying not to make any sound.

Think about what you know so far. Roger is being quiet; he grabs something off of a shelf and tries to quickly sneak out the door. What do you think is happening? Now, continue reading.

Roger's mom heard him opening the front door. She put the sleeping baby in her cradle, then hurried to see her son. "Honey, did you find something in the pantry to take for a snack?"

"Yeah, Mom," Roger replied. "I found the peanut butter crackers and grabbed a package. Those are my favorites. Thanks for getting them."

"Do you want me to drive you to baseball practice so you're not late?" Mom asked.

"No, I don't want you to wake Amy. I know she hasn't been sleeping much lately."

"You're a good big brother and a great son. Be careful."

Did this new information change your mind about what was happening? You may have thought Roger was being sneaky or doing something he should not have been doing. When you synthesize the new information, you gain a deeper understanding of the situation. Roger is being quiet so he doesn't wake up his sister, he's taking crackers that his mom bought for him off of a shelf in the pantry, and he's in a hurry to get to practice.

When you synthesize information, ask yourself:

- Why is this new information relevant?
- Why was the new information given?
- How does it relate to the first part of the passage?
- How does this help me gain a deeper understanding of what I've read?
- In what ways does the new information change my ideas about the passage?

Another common type of question found on the GED® Reasoning through Language Arts exam is an **extended synthesis** question. First, you will read a passage. Then, you will be given a question. An additional piece of information about the passage or the author will be given within the question itself. You will have to combine the new information with what you read in the text to gain a deeper understanding of the passage.

First, figure out how the new information relates to what you previously read. Then, try to determine how this information helps you understand the reading passage in a deeper or different way.

Let's try an example. Be sure to read the passage carefully so that you will be able to understand the question that follows.

The winter had been especially cold. A thick, snowy blanket had covered the landscape for what seemed like months. Each day, the stack of firewood beside the house grew visibly smaller and smaller. This concerned Ella terribly. She continued to hope that the snow would be gone before the firewood.

Ella turned away from the window and returned to her writing. Somehow, writing about summer made the house feel warmer. Feeling the sun's bright rays on her face, walking barefoot in the green grass, fishing with her family, swimming in the refreshing water—these were things Ella dreamed and wrote of during the long winter months.

Here's an extended synthesis question:

The author of the passage lived during the nineteenth century in the midwestern United States. Based on the information in the story, as well as knowing the information about the author, which of the following best explains Ella's concern over the firewood?
  a. Most nineteenth-century homes had large fireplaces.
  b. There was not much firewood available during the 1800s.
  c. Winters in the midwestern United States are extremely cold.
  d. Before electricity, people depended on firewood for heat and cooking.

Keep in mind that to correctly answer this question, you need to combine the information in the passage with the new information given in the question. Several answer choices could make sense. For example, it is true that many nineteenth-century homes had fireplaces and that winters in parts of the United States can be very cold. However, these facts do not consider the pieces of information that you need to synthesize.

From reading the passage, you know that Ella needs firewood. After learning the time period during which she lived, you are able to see how important firewood was for her survival. During the nineteenth century, homes did not have electricity. People had to have firewood to warm their homes and cook their meals. Choice **d** best synthesizes the information from both sources.

Let's try another example. Read the passage carefully, then read the question. Determine how the information in the question is related to the passage.

As the real estate agent walked up to the home, she admired her own photo on the "For Sale" sign in the front yard. She was anxious to get this home sold. Once inside with the homeowners, she explained the next step in selling their house.

"Your beautiful home has been on the market for several weeks now without any offers. We need to consider our options. The carpet is definitely a little bit worn in one bedroom, the bathroom wallpaper is a bit out of date, and the front yard could use some new flowers. These issues could be deterring potential buyers. I think it is time we lower the price of your home by at least 15%, if you want to get it sold."

The real estate agent will qualify for a large bonus if she sells one more house within the next month. Which of the following best describes the agent's motives in the passage?
  a. Her first concern is selling the house quickly so she can get the bonus.
  b. Her profit depends on the house selling for the highest possible price.
  c. She knows it is best for the owners to get the best price for their home.
  d. Her clients' home is currently overpriced for the neighborhood.

Based on the information in the passage, we do not know whether the home is overpriced, so choice **d** is incorrect. Choices **b** and **c** may be true. However, these do not take into consideration the additional information provided within the question. This information lets us know that if the house sells quickly, the agent will receive a large bonus. When added to the information in the passage that states that she wants to lower the price of the house, we can figure out that her moti-

vation for dropping the price is to sell the house quickly so that she can get the bonus. So, the correct answer is choice **a**.

TIP

Remember to carefully read the extended synthesis questions. Look for the additional information within the question and think about how this information relates to the passage. The information is there for a reason. You will be expected to use it as you consider your answer.

Compare and Contrast

We spend a good deal of our lives comparing and contrasting things. When we want to explain something, for example, we often **compare** it to something else (showing how two or more things are similar). We might say, for example, that mint chocolate chip ice cream tastes just like a peppermint-filled chocolate, or that our new boss looks a lot like Will Smith. When we want to show how things are different or not alike, we **contrast** them. We might say that our friend Sam looks nothing like his brother Pat, or that Italian is a much harder language to learn than Spanish.

Comparing and contrasting are common techniques in writing, too. They can be used for many reasons—for example, to describe a character more colorfully or to provide support for an argument that the writer is making.

Transitions Used to Compare and Contrast

As you read the next passage, about gardeners and parents, notice the transitional words and phrases that indicate when the writer is comparing (showing similarity) and when the writer is contrasting (showing difference). There are several transitional words and phrases writers use to show comparison and contrast.

Here are some words and phrases that can be used to show *similarity*:

- similarly
- likewise
- like
- just as
- in the same way
- and
- also

These words and phrases can be used to show *difference*:

- on the other hand
- on the contrary
- however
- nevertheless
- conversely
- yet
- but

Practice

Read the passage and answer the questions that follow.

Gardeners and Parents

Planting a garden is a lot like having a family. Both require a great deal of work, especially as they grow and as the seasons change. As summer days lengthen, your plants become dependent on you for sustenance, much like your children depend on you for food and drink. Like a thirsty child asking for a drink of water, your plants do the same. Their bent, wilted "body" language, translated, issues a demand much the way your child requests milk or juice. When their collective thirsts are quenched, you see the way they both thrive in your care. The fussy child becomes satisfied, and the plant reaches toward the sun in a showy display. You might also find that you have to clean the space around your plants much like you would pick up toys and clothes that have been left helter-skelter in your toddler's room. Similarly, plants shed spent petals, roses need to be pruned, and weeds need to be pulled. To keep children healthy, parents protect their children against disease with medicine, and gardeners do the same with insect repellent. To nourish them, parents give children vitamins, and gardeners use fertilizer, as both promote healthy growth. As children grow and become adults, they need less and less care. However, here's where the similarity ends. While plants die or become dormant during winter, children still maintain a vital role in the family unit.

25. In this passage, the writer compares being a parent to being a _____.

26. Which of the following pairs shows a **contrast**, not a comparison, between being a parent and being a gardener?
   a. Parents give vitamins to children to keep them healthy; gardeners give fertilizer to their plants to keep them healthy.
   b. Parents pick up toys and clothes in their children's room; gardeners pull up weeds around their plants.
   c. Children remain an important part of the family after they grow up; plants die or become dormant after the growing season ends.
   d. Children ask parents for milk or juice when they are thirsty; plants bend or wilt when they need water, showing gardeners that they are thirsty.

Reading More Closely

As you practice more and more with reading passages, you will begin to notice how specific sentences or paragraphs relate to each other and to the passage as a whole. When you are aware of how an author has structured his or her writing, it will help you understand the writer's meaning even better. Structure, word choice, description, and detail all give shape to a text and affect its meaning.

The following excerpt is from the speech that John F. Kennedy gave when he was sworn in as president in 1961.

> ### EXCERPT
>
> The world is very different now. For man holds in his mortal hands the power to abolish all forms of human poverty and all forms of human life. And yet the same revolutionary beliefs for which our forebears fought are still at issue around the globe—the belief that the rights of man come not from the generosity of the state, but from the hand of God.

As you read this passage closely, you should pay attention to certain words or phrases and how they build on each other.

The phrase *mortal hands* has a more powerful meaning than if the word *mortal* was not included. Words such as *revolutionary beliefs* and *forebears* reinforce Kennedy's appeal to the audience to make a connection with the birth of the nation.

The structure and word choice of the passage affect its tone and meaning and support Kennedy's purpose to inspire his audience. Later on in the speech are six paragraphs that all begin with the same pattern:

> *To those old allies whose cultural and spiritual origins we share. . . .*
> *To those new States whom we welcome to the ranks of the free. . . .*
> *To those peoples in the huts and villages across the globe struggling to break the bonds of mass misery. . . .*
> *To our sister republics south of our border. . . .*
> *To that world assembly of sovereign states. . . .*
> *Finally, to those nations who would make themselves our adversary. . . .*

This is a great example of the use of **repetition** and **parallel structure** to strengthen meaning and focus the listener's attention.

Practice

Read the passage and answer the questions that follow.

"The Magnolia Tree," from the Memoir *Cross Creek* (1942), by Marjorie Kinnan Rawlings

I do not know the irreducible minimum of happiness for any other spirit than my own. It is impossible to be certain even of mine. Yet I believe that I know my tangible desideratum. It is a tree-top against a patch of sky. If I should lie crippled or long ill, or should have the quite conceivable misfortune to be clapped in jail, I could survive, I think, given this one token of the physical world. I know that I lived on one such in my first days at the Creek.

The tree was a magnolia, taller than the tallest orange trees around it. There is no such thing in the world as an ugly tree, but the magnolia grandiflora has a unique perfection. No matter how crowded it may be, no matter how thickly holly and live oak and sweet gum may grow up around it, it develops with complete symmetry, so that one wonders whether character in all things, human as well as vegetable, may not be implicit. Neither is its development ruthless, achieved at the expense of its neighbors, for it is one of the few trees that may be allowed to stand in an orange grove, seeming to steal nothing from the expensively nourished citrus. The young of the tree is courteous, waiting for the parent to be done with life before presuming to take it over. There are never seedling magnolias under or near an old magnolia. When the tree at last dies, the young glossy sprouts appear from nowhere, exulting in the sun and air for which they may have waited a long hundred years.

The tree is beautiful the year around. It need not wait for a brief burst of blooming to justify itself, like the wild plum and the hawthorn. It is handsomer than most dressed only in its broad leaves, shining like dark polished jade, so that when I am desperate for decoration, I break a few sprays for the house and find them an ornament of which a Japanese artist would approve. The tree sheds some of its leaves just before it blooms, as though it shook off old garments to be cleansed and ready for the new. There is a dry pattering to earth of the hard leaves and for a brief time the tree is parched and drawn, the rosy-lichened trunk gray and anxious. Then pale green spires cover the boughs, unfolding into freshly lacquered leaves, and at their tips the blooms appear. When, in late April or early May, the pale buds unfold into great white waxy blossoms, sometimes eight or ten inches across, and the perfume is a delirious thing on the spring air, I would not trade one tree for a conservatory filled with orchids. The blooms, for all their size and thickness, are as delicate as orchids in that they reject the touch of human hands. They must be cut or broken carefully and placed in a jar of water without brushing the edges, or the creamy petals will turn in an hour to brown velvet. Properly handled, they open in the house as on the tree, the cupped buds bursting open suddenly, the full-blown flowers shedding the red-tipped stamens in a shower, so that in a quiet room you hear them sifting onto the table top. The red seed cones are as fine as candles. They mature slowly from the top of the tree down, as a Christmas tree is lighted.

27. To what does the author compare magnolia blooms?
  a. orchids
  b. candles
  c. Christmas trees
  d. jade

28. The passage describes the yearly cycle of a magnolia tree. Select the answer that puts the following statements in chronological order:
    1. The tree is covered in flower buds.
    2. The tree grows fresh green leaves.
    3. The air around the tree is perfumed.
    4. Leaves fall off the tree.
  a. 3, 2, 4, 1
  b. 2, 3, 4, 1
  c. 1, 2, 4, 3
  d. 4, 2, 1, 3

Interpreting What You Read

As we touched on, your job as a reader is not only to understand the literal meaning of a word, paragraph, article, or book, but to read between the lines in order to discover the full meaning of the text. Just as in spoken conversation, where you have many ways to communicate what you are thinking—through a joke, a story, even a facial expression—writers have many techniques to communicate with their readers.

Text with layers of meaning is often more colorful, more convincing, more emotional, or more meaningful than text that simply spells out what the author is trying to say in a clear, factual way.

It's important to try to pick up on a writer's clues, just as, for example, you would pick up on a look of disappointment when a friend says, "That's fine." You immediately recognize that your friend does not really think that whatever happened is fine. This section describes the techniques that writers use—many of which you probably have already picked up on—and how to identify them.

Interpreting Specific Words

On the GED® RLA test, you may be asked to figure out the definition of vocabulary words by looking at their **context**—the words and meanings that surround the vocabulary words.

For an example of how to do this, read the following paragraph about one of the nation's favorite pastimes.

Reality TV

Most reality TV shows center on two common motivators: fame and money. The shows transform waitresses, hairdressers, investment bankers, counselors, and teachers, to name a few, from obscure figures to household names. A lucky few successfully parlay their 15 minutes of fame into celebrity. Even if you are not interested in fame, you can probably understand the desire for lots of money. Watching people eat large insects, reveal their innermost thoughts to millions of people, and allow themselves to be filmed 24 hours a day for a huge financial reward seems to have mass appeal for viewers. Whatever their attraction, these shows are among the most popular on television, and every season, they proliferate like weeds in an untended garden. The networks are quickly replacing more traditional dramas and comedies with reality TV programs, which earn millions of dollars in advertising revenue. Whether you love it or hate it, one thing is for sure—reality TV is here to stay!

One of the more difficult words in the paragraph is *obscure*. With a little detective work, we can determine the definition of that word by looking at how it is used in the paragraph. Let's look at the context in which it appears:

> *The shows transform waitresses, hairdressers, investment bankers, counselors, and teachers, to name a few, from obscure figures to household names.*

Given the sentence, what can we tell about *obscure*? Well, since the shows transform waitresses, hairdressers, investment bankers, counselors, and teachers from one position—*obscure* figures—to another position—household names—that immediately tells us that an obscure figure and a household name are two different things.

Furthermore, we know from the sentence that the people in question are involved in typical, everyday jobs (waitresses, hairdressers, bankers, etc.) and that from this position, they are transformed into household names, which means they achieve some level of fame and notoriety. Now you can take a pretty good guess at the meaning of *obscure*.

Before they become household names, the waitresses, hairdressers, investment bankers, counselors, and teachers are

A. famous and notorious.
B. unknown and undistinguished.
C. unique and distinctive.

The correct answer, of course, is **B**. It certainly can't be **A**, because we know that these people are not yet famous. The reality shows will make them famous, but until that happens, they remain *obscure*. Answer **C** doesn't really make sense because we know from the passage that these people are waitresses, hairdressers, investment bankers, counselors, and teachers. Now, these are all very respectable jobs, but they are fairly common, so they wouldn't be described as unique or distinctive. Furthermore, we can tell that **B** is the correct answer because we can substitute the word *obscure* with the word *unknown* or *undistinguished* in the sentence and both would make sense.

How Much Context Do You Need?

In the previous example, you would still be able to understand the main message of the passage even if you didn't know—or couldn't figure out—the meaning of *obscure*. In some cases, however, your understanding of a passage depends on your understanding of a particular word or phrase. Can you understand the following sentence, for example, without knowing what *adversely* means?

> *Reality TV shows will adversely affect traditional dramas and comedies.*

What does *adversely* mean in this sentence? Is it something good or bad? As good a detective as you may be, there simply aren't enough clues in this sentence to tell you what this word means. But a passage with more information will give you what you need to determine meaning from context.

> *Reality TV shows will adversely affect traditional dramas and comedies. As reality TV increases in popularity, network executives will begin canceling more traditional dramas and comedies and replacing them with the latest in reality TV.*

In the passage, *adversely* most nearly means

A. mildly, slightly.
B. kindly, gently.
C. negatively, unfavorably.
D. immediately, swiftly.

The correct answer is **C**, negatively, unfavorably. The passage provides clues that allow you to determine the meaning of *adversely*.

Quiz

Now you've had a chance to review some of the skills needed to comprehend reading passages.

Directions: Read the following passages and choose the *one best answer* to each question.

Questions 29 through 33 refer to the following passage.

What Will Happen with the Painting?

After hours of rummaging through the various items that had been donated to the charity over the weekend, Natasha was ready to head home for the day. She had sorted the
(5) clothing, books, toys, housewares, and sporting goods into the appropriate bins and would tackle the task of pricing the items in the morning. With any luck, the items would find their place on the store shelves by
(10) tomorrow afternoon and be sold quickly.

As she turned to lock the door to the storeroom, Natasha noticed a framed canvas leaning against the wall. She wondered where it had come from and why she hadn't
(15) noticed it before now. She bent over to examine the artwork and was amazed at the bold colors and brushstrokes of the oil painting and the detail in the carved wooden frame. At the bottom corner of the
(20) piece, she noticed the signature of a world-famous artist. Amazed, she stared at the painting wondering whether it was authentic or a fake. Natasha carefully traced the frame with her finger, looking for any imperfections.
(25) She couldn't help but wonder why someone would part with such a beautiful, and possibly valuable, piece of art. She carefully covered the painting with a sheet and placed it in a closet where it would be safe.

(30) Natasha could not stop thinking about the painting. Her mind was filled with questions that kept her awake most of the night. Where had it come from? Was it really the work of a famous artist? Why would
(35) someone give away a piece of art that could potentially be worth thousands of dollars? Finally, she got out of bed and went to the computer. She found the name of an art history professor at the nearby university.
(40) Maybe some of Natasha's questions would finally be answered.

29. Which is most likely the author's purpose for writing this passage?
a. to tell readers a true story
b. to inform readers about art history
c. to entertain readers with a fiction tale
d. to teach readers about a famous artist

30. Which is the meaning of the word *authentic* in line 22?
a. old
b. genuine
c. famous
d. beautiful

31. Read the following sentence from the second paragraph:
Natasha carefully traced the frame with her finger, looking for any *imperfections*.

What is the meaning of *imperfection*?
a. perfect
b. improvement
c. type of disease
d. a flaw or defect

32. Which statement is an example of a text-to-world connection readers might make with the passage?

a. I remember when I found a high-fashion coat at a garage sale for only $5.

b. Art appreciation has been on the rise in major cities.

c. I need to clean out my attic and donate what I find to charity.

d. An art history book I read mentioned that people sometimes don't realize they own valuable pieces of art.

33. Natasha spent many years working in an art museum and has a keen eye for valuable oil paintings. The charity she now volunteers with donates money to the local children's hospital, which is known for its impressive research program. Which sentence most accurately describes Natasha?

a. She has a large art collection that she hopes to expand.

b. She plans to return to the university and teach about art.

c. She is generous and genuinely cares about helping others.

d. She hopes to work in the field of medicine or research someday.

Questions 34 through 38 refer to the following passage.

Will Others Change Their Minds?

Since I was a boy, it has been difficult to make friends. Many assumed that all aristocrats thought themselves better than others, but that was not the case. I never

(5) believed that being a member of the highest social class made me more important than anyone.

In the streets, people stepped far out of my way, as if trying to avoid me. I smiled and

(10) tried to make eye contact, but no one would meet my gaze. Groups of friends gathered on street corners and in cafes, laughing together. Loneliness filled my heart, and I longed to be a part of one of their groups. Yet somehow, I

(15) would be excluded by circumstances that many would call fortunate.

One day, I stopped at the farmers' market in town to buy a piece of fruit. As I paid the gentleman, a woman sneered and

(20) said, "Don't you have servants to do your shopping for you?" Several other customers giggled and turned their backs. Smiling politely, I thanked the man for the fruit and walked away, listening to the whispers

(25) behind me.

As I walked away, I noticed a young boy sitting alone beside the bakery. He was crying, and many people walked past him without stopping. I sat down beside him on

(30) the ground and asked why he was upset.

"I can't find my mother. I stopped to look in the window of the bakery. When I turned back around, she was gone," the boy explained.

(35) I put my arm around him, explaining that he was wise to stay in one place so that his mother could find him. "You must feel lonely," I said. "I feel lonely, too, sometimes.

(40) We'll stay here together until your mother returns."

Very soon, a frantic young woman came running down the street, calling out, "William! William, where are you?"

The boy jumped up, and his mother
(45) ran to us and scooped up her son in her arms, asking if he had been afraid.

"No, Mama," William explained. "This man kept me company."

The woman looked at me and seemed
(50) surprised, then smiled warmly and thanked me. William gave me a hug, then walked away, hand in hand with his mother. As they walked away, I realized a crowd had gathered to watch the commotion. One person in the
(55) crowd smiled at me, then another, then another. For the first time, I no longer felt like a lonely outsider.

34. Which sentence from the passage reveals its point of view?
   a. I smiled and tried to make eye contact, but no one would meet my gaze.
   b. Groups of friends gathered on street corners and in cafes, laughing together.
   c. "Don't you have servants to do your shopping for you?"
   d. He was crying, and many people walked past him without stopping.

35. Considering the point of view from which the story is told, which of the following is true?
   a. The narrator is not one of the characters in the story.
   b. The narrator knows the motivations of all the characters in the story.
   c. Readers will know the thoughts and feelings of only one character.
   d. Readers will know the thoughts and feelings of all the characters.

36. Reread the first paragraph. Which would best describe someone who is an *aristocrat*?
   a. friendly
   b. gloomy
   c. helpful
   d. wealthy

37. Which statement is an example of a text-to-self connection that readers might make with the passage?
   a. It was hard for me to make friends after I moved to a new town, and for a while, I felt like an outsider.
   b. Farmers' markets are growing in popularity.
   c. There was a missing child on the news last night, but he was found this morning, safe and sound.
   d. Our social studies book talks about class conflict throughout history.

38. What is the theme of the story?
   a. Friendship is a necessary part of life.
   b. It is difficult to find happiness without having great wealth.
   c. Even young children are able to make a difference in the world.
   d. It is important not to judge people before getting to know them.

Answers and Explanations

1. Completed renewal application; current driver's license; acceptable proof of age, identification, and address; proof of social security; money to pay required fee
2. Social Security card, state or federal income tax return, current pay stub, W-2 form
3. Every four years.
4. It is sent five to seven weeks before the current license expires.
5. False: You can renew only by visiting a Motor Vehicles Agency.
6. **b.** Because the writer hadn't eaten since breakfast, she is *extremely hungry, greedy for food.*
7. **c.** According to the passage, Robert Johnson emerged from the *blues.*
8. **b.** According to the passage, Robert Johnson died in 1938.
9. **True.** Johnson did influence many rock artists, including Led Zeppelin and the Rolling Stones.
10. **a.** The author mentions that contemporary rock bands such as Led Zeppelin and the Rolling Stones were influenced by Johnson's music. Johnson's legendary musical influence is communicated when the author writes, "Again and again, contemporary rock artists return to Johnson." Based on the text, the logical conclusion is that the contemporary artists are turning to Johnson for musical inspiration.
11. **c.** Although "A Fleeting Life" might be an appropriate description for Johnson's brief life span, it describes only one aspect of his life. On the other hand, specifying that Robert Johnson is a blues guitar legend is more specific and descriptive.
12. **a.** Is an **opinion**. It is debatable whether Johnson is the best blues guitarist of all time. Choice **b** is **fact**. This is verifiable information. Choice **c** is **opinion** because this is a debatable proposition. Choice **d** is **fact**. According to the passage, Robert Johnson died in 1938.

13. **c.** The first sentence is the topic sentence, which establishes that the shopping mall will be bad for residents of the town. The remaining sentences support that idea.
14. **a.** The style of the article is businesslike and formal, and is targeted to a sophisticated reader who would be capable of understanding a word such as *displacement.* Therefore, *displacement* is compatible with the style of the article.
15. **d.** The writer warns the readers of the effects that a shopping mall will have on residents of the town and arranges those effects in order of importance, saving the most important effect for last.
16. **a.** The first-person point of view is reflected in the use of the pronouns *us* and *we.*
17. **a.** The writer says that the shopping mall will have "dire consequences" for the residents and then uses the pronouns *us* and *we,* which identify the writer with the residents.
18. **c.** The effects the writer includes here are all very serious, especially the third effect—displacement. The writer has chosen the word *dire* to emphasize that seriousness.
19. **c.** The passage avoids any unnecessary description or details and uses formal rather than casual language.
20. **b.** Each sentence explains a negative effect that the shopping mall will have on the residents, and the negativity of this passage is heightened by the word *dire* and the phrase "avoided at all costs."
21. Answer: Choice **c** is correct. This paragraph uses the objective third-person point of view. There is no *I* or *we* (first person) or *you* (second person), and the only pronouns the paragraph uses are the third-person pronouns *she* and *her.*
22. Answer: Choice **a** is correct. The first-person point of view is reflected in the use of the pronouns *us* and *we.*

23. b. The main idea of the article is that employers are increasingly using social media, so using social media and other tech tools can improve your chances of finding a job. In the third paragraph, the author states, *With technology playing an established role in our lives and social networks easily accessible to potential employers, establishing a strong digital footprint and personal brand is crucial to success.* The writer then goes on to suggest tips for improving the way readers use e-mail and other Internet communications.

24. c. The underlying premise of the article is that having strong computer-literacy skills is important during job searches. More specifically, the author advises readers, *Make sure that your online presence is up to date and also reflects your best attributes.*

25. In this passage, the writer compares being a parent to being a **gardener**. Throughout the passage, the writer lists the many ways that he or she thinks being a parent is similar to being a gardener.

26. c. The last sentence of the passage points out one difference between being a parent and being a gardener: after parents raise their children, the children still maintain an important role in the family, but after gardeners raise plants, the plants die or go dormant in the garden.

27. a. The author states, *The blooms, for all their size and thickness, are as delicate as orchids in that they reject the touch of human hands.*

28. d. According to the author, on magnolia trees, *there is a dry pattering to earth of the hard leaves and for a brief time the tree is parched and drawn, the rosy-lichened trunk gray and anxious. Then pale green spires cover the boughs, unfolding into freshly lacquered leaves, and at their tips the blooms appear. When, in late April or early May, the pale buds unfold into great white waxy blossoms, . . . the perfume is a delirious thing on the spring air.*

29. c. This passage was written to entertain. It is not a true story, and although art history and a famous artist are mentioned, the author did not intend to teach readers about these topics.

30. b. The passage tells us that Natasha wondered whether the painting was "authentic or a fake." *Fake* is given as an antonym of *authentic.* So, *authentic* means *real,* or *genuine.*

31. d. The root of *imperfection* is *perfect.* The prefix *im-* means "not," so *imperfections* cause something to be not perfect. An *imperfection* is a flaw or defect that makes something not perfect. If you thought the answer was *perfect,* you selected the root of the word. If you chose "type of disease," you may have confused the word with *infection.*

32. b. Choices **a** and **c** are examples of text-to-self connections because they relate ideas from the passage to something personal. Choice **d** makes connections between the passage and other texts that have been read previously, so it is an example of a text-to-text connections. Choice **b**, making a connection between the passage and something happening in the world, is a text-to-world connection.

33. c. This is an example of an expanded synthesis question. To answer it correctly, you must combine the information given in the question with what you read in the passage. Because Natasha used to work in a museum and recognizes valuable oil paintings, she probably had a pretty good idea that the artwork was worth a lot of money. The charity that now has the painting donates its money to the children's hospital, which uses some of the money for research. Natasha was obviously excited about the painting being given to the charity, which is probably because the money it raises will be given to the hospital. If she is so excited, she must really care about the people who will benefit from the donation.

34. a. This passage was written from the first-person point of view. The narrator is one of the characters in the story, and he uses pronouns such as *I* and *me*. Notice that it sounds as if the narrator is talking directly to the reader.

35. c. Because the story tells a first-person account of the events, only the narrator's thoughts and feelings will be revealed to the readers. The narrator is a character in the story, and he knows only his own ideas and motivations, unless the other characters reveal their thoughts and feelings to him.

36. d. Context clues in the first paragraph explain that an *aristocrat* is "a member of the highest social class." Generally, people in this class have a lot of money. In this story, the aristocrat was also friendly, helpful, and possibly even gloomy. However, by definition, aristocrats are usually wealthy. As you read, remember to look for context clues in the sentences surrounding the word they help to define. In this case, the word *aristocrats* is used in one sentence, and the definition or explanation is in the sentence that follows.

37. a. Choices **b** and **c** are examples of text-to-world connections because they relate ideas from the passage to real-world events. Choice **d** makes connections between the passage and other texts that have been read previously, so they are examples of text-to-text connections. Choice **a**, making a connection between the passage and something personal, is a text-to-self connection.

38. d. In this passage, people made assumptions about the narrator without getting to know him. As it turned out, these assumptions were incorrect. After others saw his helpfulness and the way he cared for the little boy, they became aware of his true personality. The narrator longed for friendships and showed that he felt helping the little boy was important, but these ideas were not the overall message the author wanted to portray. Choice **b** is the opposite of what the narrator believed, as he did have great wealth but was not happy.

REVIEW

In this chapter, you have learned several strategies to help you better comprehend reading materials:

1. Point of view refers to who is telling the story. First-person point of view is when one of the characters tells the story and readers see the events through his or her eyes. Third-person point of view is when the story is told by a narrator who is outside of the story and does not participate in the events. However, he or she is often aware of the thoughts and feelings of all the characters.

2. Authors usually write for one of the following purposes: to entertain, to inform, or to persuade.

3. The theme of a story is the author's underlying message. Usually, these beliefs, attitudes, or perceptions are not directly stated; instead, the theme is a lesson that readers take away from the story. The words and actions of the characters, the tone, the plot, and repeated patterns in the story help to reveal the theme.

4. Synthesizing information means putting together information from multiple sources or from more than one location within a source. Combining information can help readers gain a deeper understanding of the text.

5. Making connections between the text and what they already know helps readers better understand the material. The types of connections readers make include text-to-self, text-to-text, and text-to-world.

6. Before you begin reading a passage, be sure to pay attention to the purpose question that precedes the passage as well as the comprehension questions that follow it.

7. Scan the passage first, then read it carefully, noticing important details and mentally organizing the information. Remember to read the information in brackets, the visual aids, and the captions as well.

8. After you read the passage completely, thoroughly read each question, paying close attention to any information stated within the question itself.

9. Try to answer each question before you actually read the answer choices. Then, read each choice carefully, paying close attention to every word, before selecting the best answer based on the passage.

10. When reading fiction passages, be sure to pay attention to details, such as the names of characters or places, and use the ideas that are included in the passage to infer information that the author has not included.

11. As you read nonfiction passages, look for evidence that supports the main idea of the passage. Be sure to pay close attention to details, names, dates, statistics, and descriptive language that can enhance your comprehension of the material and help you draw your own conclusions about the topic.

4 ▶ READING COMPREHENSION: CLOSE-READING SKILLS

CHAPTER SUMMARY
This chapter teaches you to identify main ideas and supporting details, summarize passages, distinguish fact from opinion, recognize organizational structure, and make inferences—key close-reading skills you'll need to succeed on the GED® Reasoning through Language Arts test.

While the previous chapter focused on higher-order concerns like the Author's Purpose and Point of View, this chapter provides more nuts-and-bolts tools that you'll use to answer questions about fiction and nonfiction texts. Now that you've mastered the bigger picture, it's time to zoom in and learn to break excerpts down and identify their component parts. When close-reading, or examining excerpts for elements that help you gain insight into the meaning of the text as a whole, you'll need to be able to focus on individual elements and understand what they contribute to the larger work.

Make Connections

To better comprehend text, it is important for readers to **make connections** between what they are reading and what they already know. Not only does this help readers gain insight, but it also helps to make the material more personal and relevant. This gives readers a deeper understanding of what they read.

There are three main types of connections that great readers make:

1. text-to-self
2. text-to-text
3. text-to-world

The connections readers make are neither correct nor incorrect. The same text may remind different readers of very different things. Connections with texts are personal, and they will mean different things to different readers. The important thing is that readers connect with the text in a way that makes it meaningful and understandable to them.

Text-to-Self

Connections that readers make between the reading material and their own personal experiences are **text-to-self** connections. These make the reading more personal. Statements that could help you make such connections include the following:

- This reminds me of when I . . .
- If I were this character, I would . . .
- If this ever happened to me, I might . . .

Think about the story we read about Camilla on page 50 and the garage sale. Perhaps it reminded you of a garage sale you had, of a time you came across sentimental items, or of a situation in which time flew by with your family. These would be text-to-self connections.

Text-to-Text

Text-to-text connections occur when readers are able to make connections between the reading material and a text that they have previously read. To make such connections, think about whether the text reminds you of any of the following:

- a different book by the same author
- a book with similar characters, settings, or plots
- a book that includes similar situations or events

- a book about a similar topic
- information you read in a textbook, newspaper, or magazine

Did Camilla's story remind you of another character who reconnected with his or her mom? Have you ever read an article about having a garage sale? Can you think of a book about discovering your family history? If so, these would be examples of text-to-text connections.

Text-to-World

Connections that readers make between the reading material and something that happens in the real world are **text-to-world** connections. To make this type of connection, think about whether the text reminds you of:

- information you read on the Internet
- something you saw on TV or heard on the radio
- events that are happening in the real world

If you connected Camilla's story to a television documentary on relationships between parents and teenagers or if it reminded you that there is a garage sale happening in your neighborhood this weekend, you made a text-to-world connection.

Main Idea and Supporting Details

Every passage you read, regardless of the type of material, has a main idea. The **main idea**, sometimes called the *big idea*, is the central message of the text. To determine the main idea, first identify the topic of the text. Then, think about the major point that the writer is trying to tell readers about the topic. For example, if the topic of a passage is loggerhead sea turtles, the main idea could be as follows:

Loggerhead sea turtles return to the beach where they were born to lay eggs.

This would be the most important idea that the writer wants you to take away from the passage. The rest of the passage would contain information to help explain the main idea. Examples, information, facts, and details that help to explain and describe the main idea are the **supporting details**. These help to strengthen readers' understanding of the main idea.

In the passage about sea turtles, supporting details could include the following sentences:

The turtles crawl onto the beach at night.

They dig a hole in the sand and lay their eggs in the hole.

After covering the nest with sand, the turtles return to the ocean.

Each of these supporting details gives information about the main idea.

There are four basic types of supporting details that writers include to give readers a deeper understanding of the central message of the text. Here are the types of supporting details:

- examples
- reasons
- facts
- descriptions

Being able to identify the main idea and supporting details is helpful in organizing the information in a passage. Readers are able to recognize the central message of the text and identify examples, reasons, facts, and descriptions to clarify and explain the message.

TIP

While the topic of a passage may be as short as a single word, the main idea of a passage is always a complete sentence.

Read the following paragraph. Look for the main idea and supporting details as you read.

Before becoming the sixteenth president of the United States, Abraham Lincoln showed a pattern of behavior that caused him to earn the nickname "Honest Abe." Early in his career, he worked in the grocery business. When his partner passed away, leaving behind a mountain of debt, Lincoln not only paid off his own part of the money, but also his late partner's share because this was the honest thing to do. Later, he worked as a lawyer. During that time in history, members of the legal profession were often recognized as being dishonest. However, Lincoln earned the reputation among his colleagues as being a man who never told a lie. He even gave a lecture during which he encouraged the audience to make honesty a priority in their occupations.

What is the main idea of the passage?

_____

_____

You probably recognized that the first sentence tells the main idea of the passage. You may have stated that the main idea is:

Abraham Lincoln earned the nickname "Honest Abe."

Abraham Lincoln showed a pattern of honesty throughout his life.

People called Lincoln "Honest Abe" because of the priority he placed on honesty.

Any of these would be correct. The main idea is the most important piece of information, about which the rest of the paragraph is written. Each of these choices captures that information.

> Which of the following is a supporting detail from the passage?
> a. Abraham Lincoln was the sixteenth president of the United States.
> b. Lincoln's behavior caused him to be known as "Honest Abe."
> c. Early in his career, Lincoln worked in the grocery business.
> d. Lincoln's colleagues recognized him as a man who never told a lie.

Did you recognize that answer choice **d** supports the main idea of the passage? This statement is an example of the honesty that caused people to call Lincoln "Honest Abe." Choice **b** restates the main idea. Choices **a** and **c** both contain relevant or interesting information, but they do not directly support the main idea, so they are considered minor details rather than supporting details.

What other supporting details are contained in the passage?

_____

_____

Supporting details from the passage include *Lincoln paid off his late partner's debt as well as his own* and *he gave a lecture encouraging the audience to be honest.* These statements support the main idea by giving some reasons why he became known for his honesty.

Some reading passages include more than a single paragraph. Every paragraph will have its own main idea. The main idea is stated in the topic sentence. The **topic sentence** basically sums up what the entire paragraph tries to explain.

Look back at the paragraph about Lincoln. Can you identify the topic sentence? It is the sentence that tells the basic message of the paragraph.

> *Before becoming the sixteenth president of the United States, Abraham Lincoln showed a pattern of behavior that caused him to earn the nickname "Honest Abe."*

This is the first sentence of the paragraph, and it is the topic sentence. Notice that it also contains the main idea. The topic sentence can be anywhere in the paragraph; however, it is generally either the first or last sentence. Being able to locate the topic sentence can be helpful in determining the main idea.

Excerpted from Marjorie Kinnan Rawlings's *Cross Creek*, a Memoir about Life on a Florida Orange Grove (1942)

I see no reason for denying so fundamental an urge, ruin or no. It is more important to live the life one wishes to live, and to go down with it if necessary, quite contentedly, than to live more profitably but less happily. Yet to achieve content under sometimes adverse circumstances requires first an adjustment within oneself, and this I had already made, and after that, a recognition that one is not unique in being obliged to toil and struggle and suffer. This is the simplest of all facts and the most difficult for the individual ego to accept.

A close reading of this passage requires that you first pay attention to the year in which it was published—1942. What significant events happened in the United States around this time? The nation was recovering from the Great Depression and had just entered World War II. Rawlings is writing about the years before this, but it is important to know that these events were happening because they may shape the viewpoint of the author.

In this excerpt, Rawlings talks about living the life one wants to live, even if it means suffering difficulties, instead of having more money but being less happy. She acknowledges that the struggle she faced was not really unique—everyone experiences difficulties. Rawlings implies that complaining about one's lot in life is a waste of time. This summarizes her point of view, which may have been shaped not only by her personal experiences but by what was happening in society at this time.

What might be Rawlings's purpose for writing *Cross Creek*? Based on her style and viewpoint, the reader can conclude that she wanted to provide readers with a glimpse of life in a Southern community, including its challenges and imperfections. In reading this memoir, a person might connect on some level with the struggles that Rawlings faced.

Practice

Read the passage and answer the questions that follow.

Excerpted from the Memoir *Cross Creek* (1942), by Marjorie Kinnan Rawlings

It is always bewildering to change one's complete way of life. I was fitted by temperament and by inheritance for farm and country living, yet to take it up after some thirty years of urban life was not too easy. I had known my maternal grandfather's Michigan farm, but there I was both guest and child, and the only duties were to gather the eggs from the sweet-smelling hayloft. I had known my father's Maryland farm, but that farm was his love, his escape from Washington governmental routine, and we lived there only in the too few summers. I had no duties there at all. There was only delight; the flowering locust grove; the gentle cows in pasture; Rock Creek, which ran, ten miles away from its Washington park, at the foot of the hill of the locusts, where my brother and I learned to swim and to fish for tiny and almost untakable fishes; long walks with my father through the woods where he hoped someday to build a home; jaunts with him behind Old Dan in the carriage, to the county seat of Rockville, or to buy mules at Frederick. These things got in the blood but were no preparation for running a farm oneself.

When I bought the Florida orange grove with my inheritance that represented my share of the Maryland farm, my father's sister Madeline wrote me in lament. "You have in you," she said, "that fatal drop of Pearce blood, clamoring for change and adventure, and above all, for a farm. I never knew a Pearce who didn't secretly long for a farm. Mother had one, Uncle Pierman was ruined by one, there was your father's tragic experience. I had one, once." I see no reason for denying so fundamental an urge, ruin or no. It is more important to live the life one wishes to live, and to go down with it if necessary, quite contentedly, than to live more profitably but less happily. Yet to achieve content under sometimes adverse circumstances requires first an adjustment within oneself, and this I had already made, and after that, a recognition that one is not unique in being obliged to toil and struggle and suffer. This is the simplest of all facts and the most difficult for the individual ego to accept. As I look back on those first difficult times at the Creek, when it seemed as though the actual labor was more than I could bear, and the making of a living on the grove impossible, it was Martha who drew aside a curtain and led me in to the company of all those who had loved the Creek and been tormented by it.

1. Madeline's attitude toward the writer's decision to purchase the farm could best be described as
  a. nostalgic for days gone by.
  b. enthusiastic but concerned.
  c. understanding but foreboding.
  d. indifferent.

2. The passage suggests which of the following about the writer's decision to purchase the farm in Cross Creek?
  a. She deeply regretted her decision because of the amount of work required to run the farm.
  b. She was ready to separate from her domineering family and live on her own on the farm.
  c. She was enthusiastic about owning the farm and appreciated the experiences that prepared her for this endeavor.
  d. She had a deep desire for rural life and knew she must fulfill this longing to be truly happy.

3. In the last sentence, *the Creek* refers to
  a. a farm in Michigan.
  b. an orange grove in Florida.
  c. Rock Creek, ten miles from Washington, DC.
  d. a farm in Maryland.

4. The phrase *it was Martha who drew aside a curtain* is a metaphor that could be best interpreted as
  a. Martha opened the curtains of the author's house, filling it with sunlight.
  b. Martha gave the author clarity by offering an inside perspective.
  c. Martha alleviated some of the author's burden at the Creek by opening the curtains and doing other household tasks.
  d. none of the above.

Reading Comprehension Review

Use the following passage to answer questions 5 and 6.

FDA Widens Look at Arsenic in Apple Juice

Some consumers are understandably surprised to learn that arsenic is present in water, air, and soil, and as a result, it can be found in certain foods and beverages, including apple juice and juice concentrates. Arsenic is present in the environment as a naturally occurring substance and also as a result of contamination from human activity, such as past use of fertilizers and arsenic-based pesticides, which may still be in the soil, explains Donald Zink, PhD, senior science adviser at the U.S. Food and Drug Administration's (FDA's) Center for Food Safety and Applied Nutrition. "While environmental contaminants like arsenic are unavoidable in food," says Zink, "the goal is to keep the levels of arsenic that people consume over the course of their lives as low as possible."

That's where the FDA and the U.S. Environmental Protection Agency (EPA) come in. Their job is to monitor food and the environment and take action when needed to protect the American public. The FDA has been testing and monitoring fruit juices, including apple juice, for arsenic content for more than 20 years, says Michael R. Taylor, the FDA's deputy commissioner for foods. "We are confident in the overall safety of apple juice consumed in this country because we continue to find that apple juice, on average, contains low amounts of arsenic."

In fact, the FDA's most recent tests done in 2010 and 2011 show on average about three parts of arsenic in every one billion parts of apple juice. That is lower than the 10 parts per billion (ppb) set by the EPA as the maximum level allowed in public drinking water.

"Our test results over many years support the overall safety of apple juice," says Taylor, "but we see a small percentage of individual samples tested that contain higher levels of arsenic. We want to minimize the public's exposure to arsenic in foods as much as we can." For that reason, the FDA plans to consider all the relevant evidence, and based on this work, it may set a guidance or other maximum level to further reduce arsenic in apple juice and juice products.

To further protect the public's health, the FDA is also taking the following actions:

- Enhancing its surveillance of arsenic in apple juice and juice concentrate. The agency will shortly have results for an additional 90 samples of apple juice and juice concentrate and soon after will sample additional types of juice and juice concentrates.
- Continuing to test samples of apple juice imported into the United States from China. The most recent results included more than 70 samples from China, and 95% of these contained less than the 10 ppb level used for drinking water.
- Working with the EPA to coordinate the review of the risk assessment being prepared and discussing other steps the two agencies can take to reduce the overall levels of arsenic in the environment and in foods.

The bottom line is that the FDA is working hard to ensure the safety of the foods people consume and to do so based on the best science. And the best thing families can do is to consume a variety of foods and beverages and follow a well-balanced diet consistent with the Dietary Guidelines for Americans.

5. What is *arsenic*?
   a. It is a preservative added to apple juice and other fruit juices to increase their shelf life.
   b. It is a naturally occurring element that can be hazardous to your health if you consume too much of it.
   c. It is a vitamin found in apple juice and other fruit juices that can be hazardous to your health if you consume too much of it.
   d. It is an artificial sweetener used in beverages to reduce calorie levels.

6. In the following sentence, what does *10 ppb* mean? *The most recent results included more than 70 samples from China, and 95% of these contained less than the 10 ppb level used for drinking water.*
   a. 10 percent per beverage
   b. 10 parts of pesticides in beverages
   c. 10 parts per billion
   d. none of the above

Use the following passage to answer questions 7 and 8.

Excerpted from *Army Letters from an Officer's Wife, 1871–1888,* by Frances M.A. Roe

Fort Lyon, Colorado Territory, October 1871.

After months of anticipation and days of weary travel we have at last got to our army home! As you know, Fort Lyon is fifty miles from Kit Carson, and we came all that distance in a funny looking stage coach called a "jerky," and a good name for it, too, for at times it seesawed back and forth and then sideways, in an awful breakneck way. The day was glorious, and the atmosphere so clear, we could see miles and miles in every direction. But there was not one object to be seen on the vast rolling plains—not a tree or a house, except the wretched ranch and stockade where we got fresh horses and a perfectly uneatable dinner.

It was dark when we reached the post, so of course we could see nothing that night. General and Mrs. Phillips gave us a most cordial welcome—just as though they had known us always. Dinner was served soon after we arrived, and the cheerful dining room, and the table with its dainty china and bright silver, was such a surprise—so much nicer than anything we had expected to find here, and all so different from the terrible places we had seen since reaching the plains. General Phillips is not a real general—only so by brevet, for gallant service during the war. I was so disappointed when I was told this, but Faye says that he is very much afraid that I will have cause, sooner or later, to think that the grade of captain is quite high enough. He thinks this way because, having graduated at West Point this year, he is only a second lieutenant just now, and General Phillips is his captain and company commander.

It seems that in the Army, lieutenants are called "Mister" always, but all other officers must be addressed by their rank. At least that is what they tell me. But in Faye's company, the captain is called general, and the first lieutenant is called major, and as this is most confusing, I get things mixed sometimes. Most girls would. A soldier in uniform waited upon us at dinner, and that seemed so funny. I wanted to watch him all the time, which distracted me, I suppose, for once I called General Phillips "Mister"! It so happened, too, that just that instant there was not a sound in the room, so everyone heard the blunder. General Phillips straightened back in his chair, and his little son gave a smothered giggle—for which he should have been sent to bed at once. But that was not all! That soldier, who had been so dignified and stiff, put his hand over his mouth and fairly rushed from the room so he could laugh outright. And how I longed to run some place, too—but not to laugh, oh, no!

These soldiers are not nearly as nice as one would suppose them to be, when one sees them dressed up in their blue uniforms with bright brass buttons. And they can make mistakes, too, for yesterday, when I asked that same man a question, he answered, "Yes, Sorr!" Then I smiled, of course, but he did not seem to have enough sense to see why. When I told Faye about it, he looked vexed and said I must never laugh at an enlisted man—that it was not dignified in the wife of an officer to do so. And then I told him that an officer should teach an enlisted man not to snicker at his wife, and not to call her "Sorr," which was disrespectful. I wanted to say more, but Faye suddenly left the room.

(continues)

Yesterday morning, directly after guard-mounting, Faye put on his full-dress uniform—epaulets, beautiful scarlet sash, and sword—and went over to the office of the commanding officer to report officially. The officer in command of the post is lieutenant colonel of the regiment, but he, also, is a general by brevet, and one can see by his very walk that he expects this to be remembered always. So it is apparent to me that the safest thing to do is to call everyone general—there seem to be so many here. If I make a mistake, it will be on the right side, at least.

7. Who is Faye?
   a. the person to whom Frances Roe is writing
   b. the general's wife
   c. Frances Roe's husband
   d. a soldier whom Frances Roe gets to know at Fort Lyon

8. In general, what seems to be Frances's attitude toward army protocol?
   a. disinterested and bored
   b. interested but furious
   c. devoted and serious
   d. curious but questioning

Use the following passage to answer questions 9 and 10.

Excerpted from the Short Story "To Build a Fire" (1908), by Jack London

Day had broken cold and grey, exceedingly cold and grey, when the man turned aside from the main Yukon trail and climbed the high earth bank, where a dim and little traveled trail led eastward through the fat spruce timberland. It was a steep bank, and he paused for breath at the top, excusing the act to himself by looking at his watch. It was nine o'clock. There was no sun nor hint of sun, though there was not a cloud in the sky. It was a clear day, and yet there seemed an intangible pall over the face of things, a subtle gloom that made the day dark, and that was due to the absence of sun. This fact did not worry the man. He was used to the lack of sun. It had been days since he had seen the sun, and he knew that a few more days must pass before that cheerful orb, due south, would just peep above the sky line and dip immediately from view.

The man flung a look back along the way he had come. The Yukon lay a mile wide and hidden under three feet of ice. On top of this ice were as many feet of snow. It was all pure white, rolling in gentle undulations where the ice jams of the freeze-up had formed. North and south, as far as his eye could see, it was unbroken white, save for a dark hair-line that curved and twisted from around the spruce-covered island to the south, and that curved and twisted away into the north, where it disappeared behind another spruce-covered island. This dark hair-line was the trail—the main trail—that led south five hundred miles to the Chilcoot Pass, Dyea, and salt water; and that led north seventy miles to Dawson, and still on to the north a thousand miles to Nulato, and finally to St. Michael on Bering Sea, a thousand miles and half a thousand more.

(continues)

But all this—the mysterious, far-reaching hair-line trail, the absence of sun from the sky, the tremendous cold, and the strangeness and weirdness of it all—made no impression on the man. It was not because he was long used to it. He was a newcomer in the land, a *chechaquo*, and this was his first winter.

The trouble with him was that he was without imagination. He was quick and alert in the things of life, but only in the things, and not in the significances. Fifty degrees below zero meant eighty-odd degrees of frost. Such fact impressed him as being cold and uncomfortable, and that was all. It did not lead him to meditate upon his frailty as a creature of temperature, and upon man's frailty in general, able only to live within certain narrow limits of heat and cold; and from there on it did not lead him to the conjectural field of immortality and man's place in the universe. Fifty degrees below zero stood for a bite of frost that hurt and that must be guarded against by the use of mittens, ear flaps, warm moccasins, and thick socks. Fifty degrees below zero was to him just precisely fifty degrees below zero. That there should be anything more to it than that was a thought that never entered his head.

9. Which of the following best expresses the theme of the passage?
   a. A person must have rigorous training to face the harsh elements of nature.
   b. It is extremely foolish to travel alone in unknown terrain.
   c. A person must learn to see beyond the facts to understand the meaning of life.
   d. With hard work and perseverance, a person can triumph over any adversity.

10. Which words describe the man as he appears in the passage?
   a. innocent, heroic
   b. knowledgeable, matter-of-fact
   c. rebellious, observant
   d. religious, young

TIP

Sometimes, the main idea is suggested but not directly stated. Remember to ask yourself what the topic is and what the most important thought is about the topic. This will help you determine the main idea of the text.

Summarizing

Have you ever given a book report or written a research paper? In either case, you read information from a text, then restated the most important ideas in your own words. This is called **summarizing**.

Being able to summarize information is one way to show how well you understood what you read because it requires you to focus on the main points and explain them. Think back to a research paper you have written. Chances are, you read a number of articles or books about your topic; however, your paper was probably only a few pages long. That's because you only included key pieces of information in your summary. You chose the main idea and the most important supporting details and restated these in the report.

Think back about the paragraph we read about "Honest Abe." What information in the text was the most important? How could you restate that in your own words?

Abraham Lincoln was known as "Honest Abe" for many reasons. He showed honesty in his early work life, set an example of honesty as a lawyer working among many dishonest colleagues, and encouraged others to practice honesty as well.

This summary has two sentences in it. The original paragraph about Lincoln was considerably longer. Because a summary focuses on only the most important information, it is generally much shorter than the original text. In fact, you might summarize an entire book in only a few sentences or paragraphs.

Read the following paragraph.

In the midst of New York Harbor stands a 305-foot tall, 225-ton symbol of freedom and democracy: the Statue of Liberty. "Lady Liberty," as she is affectionately known, was a gift of friendship from France and was dedicated on October 28, 1886. Officially named "The Statue of Liberty Enlightening the World," this highly recognizable structure contains much symbolism. For example, the torch itself is a symbol of enlightenment. The tablet of law held in her left hand contains Roman numerals representing the date of our country's independence, July 4, 1776.

Finally, the crown on the head of the statue has seven rays, one for each of the seven continents.

The statue is covered in copper, about the thickness of two pennies. Natural weathering has caused the copper to turn a light green color. When the statue was restored for its 100th birthday, the torch was replaced, and the new torch was covered with a thin layer of 24 karat gold. During the day, the sun's reflection lights the torch; at night, it is lighted by 16 floodlights.

To summarize the passage,

- determine the most important idea.
- decide what information can be left out.
- restate the information using your own words.

Now, let's summarize the passage.

What is the main idea of the entire passage?

_____

What are two important supporting details?

_____

_____

Write a summary of the passage in your own words.

_____

_____

_____

You probably recognized that the main idea is one of the following:

The Statue of Liberty is an important symbol.

The Statue of Liberty is a huge monument that represents many things.

Remember, there is not a single correct way to state the main idea. The important thing is that you recognize which information is the most important.

Next, figure out which supporting details are key. The size of the Statue of Liberty is definitely interesting. It could even be the central idea of another passage. However, in this example, these facts are not some of the supporting details that must find their way into a summary. The same is true about the date the statue was dedicated and the fact that the copper has turned green over the past century and a half. These are ideas that could be left out when you summarize the passage.

The most important supporting details would be those that address the symbolism associated with the statue. Information about the significance of the torch, the tablet, and the crown should be included in a thorough summary.

TIP

Don't forget! A summary must use your own words, not the words of the author. Restate the ideas that you read and make sure you are not copying what is written in the text.

Just like the main idea, there is more than one correct way to summarize a passage. Yours may be similar to the following summary:

> *The Statue of Liberty was a gift from France that symbolizes a number of ideas that are important to our country. The torch represents enlightenment, the tablet recognizes the date of our country's freedom, and the crown acknowledges the seven continents in the world.*

Remember learning that each paragraph has its own main idea? See if you can find the main idea in the second paragraph about "Lady Liberty." If you recognized the main idea as the fact that the Statue of Liberty is coated with a thin layer of copper, you're exactly right! Supporting details include information about the thickness of the copper and the fact that it has changed colors due to weathering.

Remember that understanding the author's purpose is critical to understanding the text itself. If the author's purpose in the previous passage was to persuade readers that the Statue of Liberty was long overdue for restoration, then the supporting details the author chose would probably have focused on the statue's recent state in a negative way. The author might have presented evidence that the structure represented a safety hazard due to its age, or that its weathered copper covering was an eyesore for those who visited it. As written, however, the passage is clearly written to inform the reader.

Fact and Opinion

You probably learned the difference between fact and opinion when you were younger. A **fact** is a true statement that can be proven.

> *California is located on the west coast of the United States.*

This is a fact. Look at any atlas, encyclopedia, or geography book, and you can verify, or prove, that this statement is true.

An **opinion** is a statement that reflects someone's personal views. Not everyone will agree with an opinion.

> *California's beaches are the most beautiful in the whole country.*

Many people would probably agree with this statement. However, this is the writer's personal view. If you were to talk with people sitting on the beaches in Hawaii, North Carolina, or Florida, you'd most likely find at least a few who disagree.

> **TIP**
>
> Words such as *beautiful*, *best*, *worst*, *should*, *terrible*, and *wonderful* often indicate an opinion. Look for clues that help you determine that a statement shares the feelings or beliefs of the author.

Writers often use a combination of facts and opinions to share their ideas. Being able to distinguish between these statements can help you gain a complete understanding of the passage. Strong readers are able to interpret the information in a passage and form their own opinions.

Four inches of snow fell overnight.

Can this be proven? Absolutely. A ruler or a weather report can be used to check how much snow fell. Because this statement can be proven, it is a fact.

We have had too much snow this winter.

Can this be proven? We could prove that snow has fallen, but how much is too much? Not everyone would agree that there has been too much snow. In fact, some people might think there has not been enough. This statement tells how someone feels about the snow, so it is an opinion.

Facts and opinions are both useful. They not only help writers get their point across; they can be useful to readers as well.

Suppose you want to buy tickets to a play and are trying to decide which play to attend. You would need to know facts such as where each play is being per-formed, the times and dates of the shows, and the cost of the tickets. These facts are helpful in making up your mind. But, you'll probably want to find some opinions, too. You could read reviews or talk to friends to find out which theaters offer the best seats, which actors and actresses are the most entertaining, and whether a particular play is completely boring.

The author's purpose for writing a piece can impact whether the text includes mostly facts, mostly opinions, or a combination of both:

- If the author's purpose is *to inform*, the text is likely to contain mostly facts.
- If the author's purpose is *to entertain*, a combination of facts and opinions will be included.
- If the author's purpose is *to persuade*, you can definitely expect to find opinions. However, facts that support or promote the author's opinion may also be included.

> **TIP**
>
> As you read nonfiction passages, look for facts that give information about the topic. If opinions are included, be sure to recognize them for what they are—the personal feelings of the writer, not verifiable information.

As you read the following paragraph, determine which statements are facts and which are opinions. Ask yourself:

1. Can this statement be proven or verified?
2. Would everyone agree with this statement?

The drama club of Meadowbrook Middle School put on a stage presentation of The Elves and the Shoemaker *earlier this month. The students performed before a sold-out crowd for all three performances. The highlight of the evening was a dance by the elves during the second act. Even the principal was seen laughing until tears filled her eyes. It was the first live performance the students put on this year, although plans for a spring musical were announced at the end of the evening. It is sure to be a huge success!*

A woodwind ensemble from the school band provided music before the show as well as during the intermission. This impressive group of young musicians was enjoyed by all. The amazing talent present in the school was obvious in everyone involved, from the actors and actresses to the stagehands and technical crew. Ticket sales for the performances earned nearly $900 for the school's fine arts department.

Did you determine which statements from the review of the play were facts and which were opinions?

Facts from the passage:

- The drama club of Meadowbrook Middle School put on a stage presentation of *The Elves and the Shoemaker* earlier this month.
- The students performed before a sold-out crowd for all three performances.
- Even the principal was seen laughing until tears filled her eyes.
- It was the first live performance the students put on this year, although plans for a spring musical were announced at the end of the evening.
- A woodwind ensemble from the school band provided music before the show as well as during the intermission.
- Ticket sales for the performances earned nearly $900 for the school's fine arts department.

Each of these statements could be proven by checking the school calendar, looking at the program for the performances, or checking with the accountant for the fine arts department. Even the statement about the principal could be verified through a photograph or video. She might even admit it.

Opinions from the passage:

- The highlight of the evening was a dance by the elves during the second act.
- It is sure to be a huge success!
- This impressive group of young musicians was enjoyed by all.
- The amazing talent present in the school was obvious in everyone involved, from the actors and actresses to the stagehands and technical crew.

All these are opinions because there could be people who would not agree with the author. For example, some audience members might have thought the highlight of the evening was when the musicians played, not when the elves danced. Also, *amazing* and *impressive* are words that often indicate an opinion.

Organizational Structure

When you write, whether the text is a story, a letter, or a research paper, you probably spend time planning the order in which you will present your ideas. It would not make sense to randomly write down your thoughts without any pattern or logical order. Before writing, you probably organize similar ideas together or tell actions and events in the order in which they happened. Without using some sort of organization, not only would you have trouble getting your thoughts across accurately, but your readers would also become terribly confused.

Writers want their texts to make sense. The whole point of writing is to share information and ideas with an audience, and writers carefully consider how to best arrange this information so that readers are able to follow their thoughts and fully understand the passage. The **organizational structure** of a passage is the way a writer arranges his or her ideas.

Common types of organizational structures that writers may choose include *sequence, cause and effect, compare and contrast, problem and solution, classification,* and *description.*

Understanding how information is presented can help readers

- organize and understand the passage.
- anticipate what ideas might be presented next.
- think about what information to look for.
- make predictions.
- connect ideas from different parts of the text.

To recognize which organizational structure an author has used, think about what he or she wants readers to know. If an author wants to be sure readers understand the order in which events occurred, sequence is probably used. If he or she wants readers to know what led up to a particular event, a cause and effect structure is likely to be found. Recognizing and understanding each type of organizational structure can make a big difference in how well you comprehend the material.

Now, let's talk about each type of organizational structure in a little more detail.

Sequence

The **sequence** of events is the order in which the events are discussed in a passage. When readers are able to recognize that a text uses a sequential organizational structure, they know that details, ideas, and events will be presented in a specific order. Often, the sequence used is either time order or order of importance.

Time order means that ideas and events are presented chronologically, or in the order in which they actually happened. Often, words and phrases such as the following indicate time order:

- first
- second
- next
- then
- last
- before
- after that
- following
- by the time
- as soon as

Writers often use time order when the correct order is important. For example, history books are often written in time order by beginning with the earliest events and leading up to the most recent. Correct order would also be important when readers are expected to follow steps in a particular sequence, such as directions, how-to articles, and recipes.

Of all days for it to happen, my alarm clock didn't go off this morning. As soon as I opened my eyes and saw sunlight, I knew it would be a race to make it to the bus on time. The first thing I did was jump in the shower, wash my hair quickly, then jump right back out. Next was the dash to the closet. Shirt on, jeans zipped, shoes tied, and down the stairs. By the time I reached the kitchen, Mom had my peanut butter toast wrapped in a napkin and ready to go. I ran out the door, and before it even slammed behind me, the bus pulled up to the curb. Yes! I made it!

The transition words in the paragraph help readers know exactly when each action happened. On the lines below, list the events of the paragraph in the correct order.

_____

_____

_____

_____

You probably figured out that the events occurred in this order:

1. The alarm clock did not go off.
2. The speaker opened his or her eyes.
3. The speaker showered.
4. The speaker got dressed.
5. Mom wrapped up the toast in a napkin.
6. The speaker ran out the door.
7. The bus reached the curb.
8. The door slammed.

Another sequence writers may use to organize their writing is by **order of importance**. They might choose to tell the most important idea first, followed by ideas that decrease in importance. This is a good way to catch the readers' attention by beginning with the strongest point.

Did you know that newspaper articles are often organized in order of importance? The most important information is usually listed at the beginning of the article, followed by less important information. The reason for this is that some readers do not take the time to finish the entire article. This organizational structure ensures that those readers do not miss the most important ideas.

Conversely, writers may begin by telling the least important idea, then list ideas or events in increasing order of importance, telling the most important idea last. This leaves readers with the strongest point freshest in their minds.

The Tri-City Tigers won the district soccer championship on Friday night! The final score was 5–2 in what was a very exciting game. Jackson Greenwood scored three goals for the

Tigers. Coach Abbott placed each team member in the game at some point. It was truly a victory for all!

The fact that the Tigers won the championship is the most important idea in the paragraph, so it is stated at the beginning. The final score is the second most important piece of information, so it is stated next. Jackson scoring two goals is next in importance, followed by the fact that all the players were involved in the win.

If the writer had chosen to tell the events in order of least to most importance, the paragraph could have been organized as shown here:

All members of the Tigers soccer team got a chance to play in Friday night's game, thanks to Coach Abbott. Jackson Greenwood scored three goals for his team. The final score of the exciting game was 5–2, giving the Tri-City Tigers the title of district champs!

Cause and Effect

As you know, a *cause* is something that makes something else happen. An *effect* is what happens as a result of the cause. For example, if you go to bed late, you'll be tired in the morning. Going to bed late is the cause; being tired in the morning is the effect.

At times, there is a cause and effect relationship between events in a passage. Authors may choose to use a **cause and effect** organizational structure, which focuses on such relationships, in the text. Recognizing a cause and effect structure lets readers know that they should be on the lookout for things that are the result of a given event. It also helps readers understand how events in the passage are related to one another.

Darnell studied every night for a week, so he got an A on his science exam.

How are these events related? Did one thing happen as a result of the other? Yes. Studying every night *caused* Darnell to do well on the test. He got an A *because* he studied so much. So, studying every night is the cause; getting an A on the exam is the effect.

Often, writers will include clues—words that signal a cause and effect relationship. Examples of such words are listed here:

- because
- so
- since
- then
- due to
- when
- as a result
- therefore
- if

Ella fixed French toast for breakfast since it was her parents' anniversary.

In this sentence, the clue word *since* indicates a cause and effect relationship. In the sentence about Darnell, the clue word *so* signaled the relationship.

Notice that either the cause or the effect can come first. In Darnell's example, the cause is first; in Ella's example, the effect is first. To determine which event is the cause and which is the effect, ask yourself which event is the result of the other.

Now it's your turn. Read the following paragraph. As you read, look for cause and effect relationships.

During the past quarter, our company had a record number of sales. As a result, we also saw a significant increase in profits. So, over the next few weeks, we will be able to hire additional employees in several departments to take on some of the workload. Current employees will also receive a bonus in their next paycheck as recognition for their contribution to our company's continued success.

What signal words were included to offer clues about the cause and effect relationships?

_____

As a result and *so* were used to highlight two of the relationships. However, you probably noticed that more than two relationships existed. Signal words are not always included. Be sure to read carefully and think about how the events in a passage are related, whether signal words are included or not.

Did you recognize all the cause and effect relationships in this paragraph?

The *cause*:

- a record number of sales for the company

The *effects*:

- a significant increase in profits
- the hiring of additional employees
- a bonus for current employees

Notice that a single cause had more than one effect. The opposite may also be true; a single effect can be the result of several causes.

Compare and Contrast

When we *compare*, we tell how two or more things are alike. When we *contrast*, we tell how two or more things are different. Writers often use a **compare and contrast** organizational structure to explain ideas, events, people, or objects by describing the ways in which they are alike or different. When readers recognize a compare and contrast structure in a passage, they look for similarities and differences between the topics.

Signal words often alert readers that things are alike or different in some way.

Similarities	Differences
▪ also	▪ but
▪ like	▪ yet
▪ both	▪ only
▪ alike	▪ differ
▪ similar	▪ unlike
▪ likewise	▪ rather
▪ the same as	▪ although
▪ at the same time	▪ however
▪ in the same ways	▪ different
▪ in the same manner	▪ less than
	▪ better than
	▪ nevertheless
	▪ on the contrary

By comparing and contrasting, writers are able to help readers gain a clear understanding of their ideas.

Chinchillas are small animals that are slightly larger and rounder than squirrels. Both animals are generally gray or brown in color. The chinchilla often has a bushy tail similar to that of a squirrel, although its ears are more round, like those of a mouse.

The comparisons and contrasts in this paragraph help describe chinchillas in a way that gives readers a clear picture of these animals.

What signal words did you notice in the paragraph?

_____

You probably recognized that *slightly larger and rounder than, both, similar to, although,* and *like* pointed out similarities and differences between the various animals.

There are two types of compare and contrast organizational structures that writers often use. **Whole-to-whole comparisons** completely discuss the first idea, event, or item and then completely discuss the second. For example, if a writer were comparing and contrasting sports, he might completely explain baseball, then completely describe soccer.

Part-to-part comparisons discuss one particular aspect of each topic, then discuss another aspect, and so on. For example, a writer might discuss the number of players on baseball and soccer teams, then discuss how points are scored in each game, and then discuss the rules for each game.

Problem and Solution

If an author elects to use a **problem and solution** organizational structure, a problem is discussed and is then followed by one or more solutions to the problem. When readers recognize this structure, they know that as they read, they should look for possible ways to solve the problem.

Construction of the new auditorium at Forest Lakes Middle School is scheduled to begin in early April, which will interfere with the school's planned Spring Fling Carnival because construction equipment will occupy a large portion of the area normally used for the event. The carnival committee believes it may be possible to reschedule the carnival for the middle of March, prior to groundbreaking on the construction project. If that is not possible, the committee may consider moving some of the activities indoors, reducing the need for some of the outside space. It has also been suggested that an alternative location, such as the nearby Little League fields, be used for the event.

What problem is the topic of the paragraph?

_____

The problem is that there may not be enough space for the school carnival after construction has begun on the new auditorium.

What solutions are suggested?

_____

_____

_____

Three possible solutions are suggested: change the date of the carnival, move some of the activities indoors, and change the location of the event. In a longer passage, the problem might be introduced in one paragraph, with each solution being discussed in separate paragraphs.

Classification

Sometimes, writers divide information about a topic into smaller sections that each focus on a group of related ideas or objects. This organizational structure is called **classification**, and writers use it to arrange ideas and information into categories. Each category contains ideas that are similar in some way.

Readers can recognize that classification has been used if the passage talks about different kinds of things, such as different kinds of animals, different types of transportation, or different kinds of sports. This structure lets readers know that ideas in each section will be somehow related.

TIP

Sometimes, section headers will be a clue that the organizational structure is classification. For example, a passage about animals might include section headers such as *mammals*, *reptiles*, *birds*, *amphibians*, and *fish*.

Dear Friends,

We are pleased that you are planning a trip to our resort! We are sure that you will find the vacation package that best suits your needs. Vacation packages are grouped into three categories. You may make your selection at any time prior to your arrival.

Room-only packages include your hotel room and access to the resort's three swimming pools. You may also enjoy the exercise equipment in the gym at no additional charge.

Bed-and-breakfast packages include your hotel room as well as access to the pools and gym. Breakfast in any of the resort restaurants is also included, or you may choose to order your morning meal from our room service menu.

All-inclusive packages include not only the offerings of the previous packages, but also lunch and dinner from any of the resort restaurants or room service. Each guest may enjoy three meals and two snacks each day, all included in the price of the package.

We look forward to your stay and would be happy to answer any questions. Feel free to contact us at any time for further assistance.

Sincerely,

Resort Manager

This passage uses a classification organizational structure. What is the topic of the letter?

_____

What were the categories that the information was divided into?

_____

You probably recognized that the topic is the resort's vacation packages, and the categories the packages are divided into include *room-only*, *bed-and-breakfast*, and *all-inclusive* options.

Description

When an author chooses a **description** as the organizational pattern for a passage, he or she will introduce the topic, then discuss attributes and characteristics that describe it. When readers recognize this organizational pattern, they know to anticipate finding details, attributes, examples, and characteristics that will help explain the topic.

> *For more than 200 years, the White House has been home to the presidents of the United States and is undoubtedly the most recognizable residence in the country. A view of the front reveals a two-story structure with rows of rectangular windows, columns in the center of the building, and our nation's flag flying over the roof. Indoors, the home boasts six levels, including 132 rooms, 35 restrooms, and 28 fireplaces. For recreation, the First Family can enjoy a tennis court, jogging track, swimming pool, movie theater, and bowling alley, all without leaving the comfort of their very famous home.*

In this paragraph, the topic was introduced in the first sentence. The following sentences describe what the White House looks like from the outside, the structure of the inside, and the recreational features of the building. Each of these details helps give the reader a clear picture of the topic.

Inferences

Sometimes, writers come right out and directly state everything they want readers to know. Other times, a writer will make suggestions about a person, place, event, or object without directly stating the information. To gain a complete understanding of the passage, readers have to read between the lines and construct meaning about the information in the text. An educated guess based on clues in the passage is an **inference**.

To make an inference, consider

- clues and hints in the passage.
- your own prior knowledge.
- observations.
- details in the text.

Making inferences is similar to drawing conclusions.

When readers make inferences, they recognize ideas that are implied.

> *Elliot showed his little brother around the school, making sure he would be able to find his locker, classrooms, and most importantly, the cafeteria.*

What information is implied in this sentence? Based on what we read, what we already know, and what makes logical sense, we can infer several things:

> *Elliot's brother is unfamiliar with the school.*

> *Elliot's brother is a new student.*

> *Elliot already attends the school.*

These ideas were not directly stated. However, if we read between the lines, we can infer that they are most likely true.

TIP

Keep in mind that inferences are not random, wild guesses. They are based on information that you have been given as well as what you already know. Inferences are *logical* conclusions.

BOOST

Did you know that about 71% of people who take the GED® test have already reached at least grade 10? In fact, one in ten college freshmen earn their GED® test credential before arriving on campus!

At times, you will have to make inferences to determine different things about a passage, such as the main idea, purpose, tone, or point of view. You will have to pay attention to the details in the text to infer this information.

To gain a complete understanding of the text, readers may have to make **multiple inferences** by considering information from various parts of the text. This requires readers to think about their purpose for reading, evaluate the importance of ideas and details, then decide what information is key to understanding what the writer wants them to know about the passage.

For example, suppose you are reading a passage describing how to make a birdhouse. Based on the purpose of the text, you know that it is essential to find the steps necessary to complete the project. If you came across information describing why birds migrate in the winter, you could categorize these facts as being unimportant to the purpose of this particular passage. If you came across information telling you to first measure a piece of wood, you would know that this detail is essential in understanding the text.

Readers also might need to consider information from various parts of the text to make strong predictions. Think of each piece of information as a piece to a jigsaw puzzle. The more pieces you have, the better equipped you will be to predict what the finished puzzle will look like. Consider each piece of information as it relates to what you have already read. Then, use this combination of ideas to infer what is likely to happen next in the text.

Considering all the pieces of information in a passage can also be helpful in making inferences about the author. What authors say, as well as what they do not say, can help readers recognize their attitudes, beliefs, biases, prejudgments, and opinions about the topic.

Four bands performed at the school's Winter Wonderland Formal. The ultimate hip-hop band Sticks and Stones rocked the crowd first. Nearly every student was on the dance floor the entire time they played. The drumbeat of their signature hit "Keep Movin'" undoubtedly stuck in everyone's heads for days. After their set, the bands Golden Child, Harvey's Dudes, and Stumped also played.

Which inference could be made about the passage?
a. The author is the drummer in a hip-hop band.
b. Sticks and Stones was the audience's favorite musical group.
c. Nearly all the students attended the Winter Wonderland Formal.
d. The author believes Sticks and Stones was the best band at the dance.

The author's opinion about the bands is obvious. You could probably read between the lines and infer that the author really enjoyed the performance by Sticks and Stones. Think about all the words and details he or she included when talking about the band. Then, think about what he or she *didn't* say; the author only quickly mentioned the other bands, without giving any information about the bands or their performances. Choice **d** is the best answer.

Connotative Meaning

Authors use words in certain ways to help them describe characters or events and create a particular mood or tone.

The **connotative** meaning of a word is its suggested meaning, as opposed to the literal or exact definition. For instance, if you are angry with someone and refer to him or her as a "rat," you are suggesting that the person is mean or disgraceful, not an actual rodent.

Writers use **figurative** language to create images with words and express ideas in creative ways. Figurative devices include metaphors and similes.

Making Comparisons between Passages

A number of questions on the GED® Reasoning through Language Arts test will involve comparing two passages that contain related ideas. For example, the text of Lincoln's Emancipation Proclamation might be followed by an excerpt from a speech by Confederate President Jefferson Davis regarding slavery. In this case, the two passages provide opposing viewpoints of a single issue. In other cases, the passages might deal with the same idea or theme but offer differences in style, tone, or even purpose. In any case, the most important questions to ask when comparing two passages are:

In what ways are the two passages similar?
In what ways are the two passages different?

When two passages are paired together, you will often encounter a question about the main idea or theme that is common to both passages. If you can identify the ways in which the two passages are similar, this will help you determine whether they share a single idea or theme. When two passages are placed together on the GED® test, you can be sure that they are related in some way—it's up to you to figure out exactly how they are related.

When comparing passages, remember to look at both the content and the form of the passages. Two passages with dramatically different forms, such as an e-mail and a news article, might actually contain the same main idea but differ in structure, style, tone, or intended audience. By contrast, two passages that are both excerpted from persuasive essays might share the same form, style, and intended audience, but offer opposing arguments and evidence on a topic.

For the extended response item on the GED® Reasoning through Language Arts test, you may be required to write a short essay comparing two passages that contain related ideas. When writing, it is especially important to mention the specific details in each passage that support the main idea. You may even want to quote small amounts of text from each passage to support your analysis. Be careful to avoid drawing comparisons between elements that are not important to the main idea or theme. For example, two passages may both be written in an informal style, but unless that style is important to understanding the author's purpose, it should not be brought up as a key point in your response.

Quiz

Now that you've had a chance to review some of the skills needed to comprehend nonfiction, read each of the following passages, then choose the one best answer to each question.

Directions: Choose the *one best answer* to each question.

Questions 11 through 15 refer to the following passage.

What Is Included in a Healthy Diet?

Most people recognize the importance of a healthy lifestyle. Part of this includes enjoying a balanced diet. Each day, people need to eat foods from each food group to
(5) be sure they are getting the benefits offered by each type of food.

It is recommended that people enjoy between 6 and 11 servings of food from the grain food group. These foods include
(10) bread, rice, pasta, and cereal. Those made from whole grains offer the most health benefits. Enjoying whole grain toast for breakfast, a sandwich on a wheat pita for lunch, and whole wheat pasta for dinner are
(15) ways to ensure that plenty of servings of these foods have found their way onto our plates.

We all know the benefits of eating plenty of fruits and vegetables, but do we
(20) really get enough every day? It is recommended that people enjoy three to five servings of vegetables and three to four servings of fruit every day. That may sound like a lot, but whipping up a fruit smoothie
(25) at the beginning of the day, having veggies and dip as a snack, and adding fresh berries to a yogurt parfait for dessert are ways to think outside of the box—a box of fruit snacks, that is.

(30) Getting enough protein doesn't have to mean eating two to three burgers each day. Did you know that beans, eggs, and nuts are considered protein as well? Sure, a burger, fish, chicken, or steak would be great at
(35) lunch or dinner, but including eggs at breakfast or a handful of almonds in the afternoon can cut down on the amount of meat in your diet, while still guaranteeing the protein your body needs.

(40) We all know the importance of dairy for strong teeth and bones. But don't feel that you have to drown yourself in skim milk to get your two to three servings a day. Remember that fruit and yogurt parfait?
(45) That's a yummy way to get a full serving of dairy. And how about the grilled cheese sandwich on wheat for lunch? Cheese is another way to get some dairy into your diet.

Eating a balance of food from each
(50) group is essential to staying healthy and feeling your best. Remember to mix it up. Try new things and be sure to get the servings you need each day.

11. Which statement from the passage is an opinion?
   a. Most people recognize the importance of a healthy lifestyle.
   b. Those made from whole grains offer the most health benefits.
   c. That's a yummy way to get a full serving of dairy.
   d. Cheese is another way to get some dairy into your diet.

12. Which organizational structure is used in the passage?
   a. sequence
   b. classification
   c. cause and effect
   d. problem and solution

13. What is the main idea of the passage?
    a. We need to include plenty of dairy in our diets.
    b. Most foods can be grouped into five basic types.
    c. A balanced diet is an important part of a healthy lifestyle.
    d. There are creative ways to be sure we eat the right nutrients.

14. Which detail supports the main idea of the third paragraph?
    a. A fruit smoothie can help us get enough servings of fruit.
    b. A box of fruit snacks offers an entire serving of fresh fruit.
    c. We all know the benefits of eating plenty of fruits and vegetables.
    d. We need between six and nine servings of vegetables and fruits daily.

15. Which choice best summarizes the passage?
    a. A balanced diet includes plenty of grains, fruits and vegetables, dairy, and protein to help us stay healthy. These foods can be incorporated into our diets in creative ways throughout the day.
    b. Protein and dairy are important foods that come from many sources. Meats, nuts, and eggs offer our bodies the protein we need, while milk, yogurt, and cheese give us dairy for strong bones and teeth.
    c. Eating the right kinds of foods is important to staying healthy. Exercise, plenty of sleep, and eating a balanced diet ensure that we have enough energy every day as well as the nutrients we need to build muscles.
    d. Each day, we need 6 to 11 servings of grains, especially whole grains. We can get these nutrients from breads, cereals, rice, and pasta. Including these foods at every meal will ensure that we get enough of them.

Questions 16 through 20 refer to the following passage.

What Types of Jobs Are Available?

Currently, Fairhaven Fine Furnishings has a job opening available in the warehouse. Daily job requirements include unloading trucks of furniture and accessories delivered
(5) by the manufacturers, organizing these items in the warehouse, locating and preparing items to fill customer orders, and loading these items onto our company's trucks for delivery. This job requires
(10) employees to be able to lift at least 100 pounds, operate a forklift, and demonstrate exceptional record-keeping abilities, as maintaining accurate inventory is of utmost importance. This job offers many
(15) opportunities for future advancement within the company. Many of Fairhaven's current management team members began their careers working in the warehouse. This is a full-time position, paying $17.75 per hour.
(20) Health insurance, including vision and dental benefits, will be available after 90 days, assuming the employee receives an acceptable performance evaluation at that point.
(25)   Fairhaven Fine Furnishings also has openings available for a data entry clerk and a receptionist. Both positions require exceptional computer skills, and applicants will need to demonstrate adequate abilities
(30) prior to being hired. The receptionist must also have excellent communication and customer service skills, as he or she will be responsible for answering phone calls and greeting customers as they enter our
(35) showroom. Likewise, the data entry clerk must demonstrate strong communication skills, as this position requires interacting with company representatives from our various departments as well as

(40)   representatives from each of the companies
         that provide our products. However, the data
         entry clerk will not be communicating
         directly with Fairhaven's customers. The
         receptionist position is full-time and pays
(45) $10.50 per hour. The data entry position is
         20 hours per week and pays $12.35 per hour.
         Both positions include health insurance
         benefits following an acceptable 90-day
         performance evaluation. The company will
(50)   also contribute toward vision and dental
         benefits, making a greater contribution
         toward these benefits for full-time employees
         than those working part-time.
                 Applicants for any of these positions
(55)   must first submit a completed resume,
         including work and salary history, and a list
         of three professional references. After these
         documents have been reviewed by a
         department manager, qualified applicants
(60)   will be contacted for a telephone interview.
         The final step in the hiring process will be a
         personal interview with our hiring team.

16. Based on the passage, which of these statements
is a fact?
   a. Fairhaven Fine Furnishings would be a great
   place to work.
   b. The receptionist position is better suited for
   a woman than a man.
   c. All the available positions offer some health
   insurance benefits.
   d. The phone interview is the most important
   step in the hiring process.

17. What is the organizational structure of the first
paragraph?
   a. sequential
   b. description
   c. cause and effect
   d. problem and solution

18. Which is true about the second and third
paragraphs?
   a. The second paragraph uses classification to
   group similar ideas.
   b. The steps in the application process are
   listed in a random order.
   c. Signal words indicate a cause and effect
   structure in the paragraphs.
   d. Two job positions are compared and
   contrasted in the second paragraph.

19. Which inference can best be made, based on
the information in the passage?
   a. The data entry clerk is the most important
   position.
   b. Warehouse employees are valued very highly
   within the company.
   c. The company is likely to hire the first
   applicant for each of the jobs.
   d. The receptionist position will be the most
   difficult for the company to fill.

20. What is the main idea of the third paragraph?
   a. Some applicants will be invited to interview
   in person.
   b. There are several steps involved in the hiring
   process.
   c. Department managers will contact qualified
   applicants by phone.
   d. Only the most qualified applicants will meet
   with the hiring team.

Use the following passage to answer questions 21–23.

Imani P. Jones
421 Carroll Street
Franklin, NY 10821
(512) 555-4390

May 22, 2014

Shanice Childress-Harris
Owner
Luxalot Florists, Inc.
80 River Street
Franklin, NY 10821

Dear Ms. Childress-Harris:

I am writing to register a complaint about the floral displays that were prepared and delivered by Luxalot Florists for my son DeAndre Jones's wedding on May 18. After consulting with your assistant, Maurice Thomas, on February 13 and again on March 1, we thought that our desires were understood and that Maurice and the rest of the team had a clear plan for the wedding's floral designs.

We asked for Luxalot to deliver two standing bouquets for the entrance to the chapel, one larger standing bouquet for the altar, and 18 centerpieces for the tables at the reception. Maurice asked us what colors we preferred, and we told him that the wedding's color scheme was white, yellow, and fuchsia. He suggested that a beautiful combination in these colors would be First Snow tulips, Sunray roses, and Hot Pink ranunculus. He also wanted to add a few stems of filler flowers, such as baby's breath and Queen Anne's lace, which I thought was a good idea to reduce the overall cost.

I was shocked to see a completely different combination of flowers than the one we had discussed on the day of the wedding. The bouquets consisted primarily of baby's breath and Queen Anne's lace, and the other flowers were carnations, lilies, and irises. At the reception, we saw that the centerpieces had the same combination and also learned that only 14 centerpieces had been sent, so four tables were not adorned with flowers.

I am writing to you to request a refund of half ($2,700) of the amount I paid for the flower displays ($5,400). I would ask for a full refund, but the flowers that did arrive were very fresh and in the correct color scheme.

I await your prompt response to this matter.
Sincerely,

Imani P. Jones

21. In the first sentence of the letter, the word *register* means
  a. a machine that calculates and holds money at a store.
  b. registrar.
  c. formally submit.
  d. withdraw.

22. Based on the information in the second paragraph of the letter, we can infer that the definition of *fuchsia* is
  a. the color white.
  b. bright pink.
  c. a type of flower.
  d. none of the above.

23. Based on the letter, which is NOT a reason why the writer wants a refund?
  a. The flower displays contained too many inexpensive flowers.
  b. The flower displays contained the incorrect types of flowers.
  c. Luxalot did not send the correct number of flower displays.
  d. The flower displays were in the wrong colors.

Use the following passage to answer questions 24–27.

Is Your Drowsiness Dangerous?

Despite common misconceptions, anyone—regardless of gender, weight, or fitness level—can develop obstructive sleep apnea, a life-threatening condition characterized by episodes of complete or partial airway obstruction during sleep. As many as 12 million to 18 million American adults have untreated sleep apnea, and the experts at the American Academy of Sleep Medicine are recommending the following steps for diagnosis and treatment to significantly improve overall health, mood, and productivity.

First, be aware of the risk factors. Your risk of sleep apnea increases between middle and older age and with the amount of excess body weight you carry. In general, men have a greater likelihood of developing the disease. However, menopause is a risk factor for sleep apnea in women. Your risk is also higher if family members have been diagnosed with sleep apnea. Smoking is another significant risk factor, as well as being a detriment to your overall health.

In addition to these more commonly known risk factors, many people don't realize that they're in greater danger of developing sleep apnea if they already suffer from other common diseases. "Seven in ten type 2 diabetics and 30% to 40% of adults with hypertension also have obstructive sleep apnea," says Dr. M. Safwan Badr, president of the American Academy of Sleep Medicine. "As a result, patients with these conditions should pay close attention for potential symptoms and then seek necessary treatment."

(continues)

It's important to watch for symptoms. While the symptom most commonly associated with sleep apnea is snoring, not everyone who snores has the disease. However, when snoring is paired with choking, gasping, or pauses in breathing during sleep, it's a more likely indicator of sleep apnea. Sleep apnea symptoms also may appear during the daytime and include morning headaches, excessive sleepiness, trouble concentrating, memory or learning problems, and general moodiness, irritability, or depression.

"Sleep apnea can make you wake up in the morning feeling tired, even though you believe you've had a full night of sleep," says Badr. "During the day, you may feel incredibly fatigued because you're actually waking up numerous times throughout the night and your body isn't getting the rest it needs."

If you suspect that you have the risk factors and symptoms of sleep apnea, it's important that you are evaluated by a board-certified sleep-medicine physician right away. Left untreated, sleep apnea may have a serious impact on your overall health, even increasing your risk of death. The sleep-medicine physician will have the training and expertise to diagnose your condition. He or she will conduct a thorough physical examination and sleep evaluation, asking questions like whether symptoms began when you gained weight or stopped exercising, and whether your partner or roommate has complained that you snore or make choking noises in your sleep. If the sleep physician determines that you are at risk for obstructive sleep apnea, then you will be scheduled for a sleep study.

Once diagnosed, the recommended treatment for sleep apnea is continuous positive airway pressure (CPAP) therapy, which provides a steady stream of air through a mask to gently keep the patient's airway open throughout the night, making it easier to breathe. In patients with moderate or severe sleep apnea, it's estimated that CPAP therapy reduces the ten-year risk of heart attack by 49% and stroke by 31%.

"Treating sleep apnea provides all the benefits of improved sleep, including increased alertness during the day and improved memory and cognitive function," says Badr. "Clinical evidence also shows that sleep apnea treatment lowers blood pressure, thus decreasing your risk of cardiovascular disease, and improves nighttime glucose levels and insulin sensitivity among type 2 diabetics."

—*Adapted from an article published on Brandpoint.com.*

24. According to the passage, what are some of the symptoms of sleep apnea?

a. heartburn, nausea, and upper abdominal pain when awake

b. migraines, excessive eating, and chest pain at night

c. choking, gasping, and pauses while breathing during sleep

d. type 2 diabetes, menopause, and hypertension

25. Which statement best expresses the main idea of the passage?

a. Sleep apnea primarily affects people with hypertension and diabetes.

b. Everyone should be aware of the risk factors and signs of sleep apnea and get tested if there is reason for concern.

c. As many as 12 million to 18 million American adults are living with sleep apnea but have not been treated.

d. Sleep apnea is a condition that can be successfully treated with continuous positive airway pressure (CPAP) therapy.

26. How does the author present and develop the key ideas of this passage?

a. by listing facts and advice related to sleep apnea

b. by presenting a chronological order of the development of sleep apnea as a person ages

c. by describing the differences between people who have sleep apnea and those who don't

d. by giving examples of patients who have been treated successfully for sleep apnea

27. Based on the passage, we can infer that the author has which of the following viewpoints?

a. To accurately identify and treat sleep apnea, it's better to see a board-certified sleep-medicine doctor than to see another type of doctor.

b. The medical profession overdiagnoses sleep apnea, causing increased anxiety and irritability in patients.

c. It's a shame that sleep apnea is so difficult to diagnose, leaving many Americans untreated.

d. Screening for sleep apnea must be part of a person's annual checkup with one's primary-care physician.

Answers and Explanations

Chapter Practice

1. c. Madeline recognizes the family instinct to own a farm, but she calls it "fatal" and mentions other family members' bad experiences.

2. d. There are several lines in the passage that support this choice. The narrator says that she was *fitted by temperament . . . for farm and country living* and that her experiences on farms as a child *got in the blood*. Her father's sister made a similar observation: *You have in you that fatal drop of Pearce blood, clamoring for change and adventure, and above all, for a farm.* The narrator adds that *I see no reason for denying so fundamental an urge, ruin or no. It is more important to live the life one wishes to live, and to go down with it if necessary, quite contentedly, than to live more profitably but less happily.*

3. b. The second paragraph starts off with a reference to the Florida orange grove that the narrator purchases. She doesn't mention it by name at first, but she does in the last sentence. You can also assume that *the Creek* is short for *Cross Creek*, which is the name of the book.

4. b. In the sentence before this line, the author says that she was troubled by the hard work at the Creek and the difficulty of making a living on the grove. Relief came when someone named Martha *drew aside a curtain* and welcomed her into the group of people who had a history with the farm. This implies that by pulling back the curtain, Martha was clearing up some of the writer's confusion or angst by sharing information about the grove in the past.

Reading Comprehension Review

5. b. The first paragraph states that *arsenic is present in the environment as a naturally occurring substance.* We can infer that it is hazardous—or hurtful—to people's health because it is referred to as a *contaminant.* Another important reason is because officials are trying to keep apple juice safe by making sure that arsenic levels are very low; that implies that arsenic at higher levels makes food unsafe.

6. c. The term *parts per billion (ppb)* is mentioned in the third paragraph in the same context—discussing the amount of arsenic found in drinks.

7. c. There are several clues throughout the letter that Faye is Frances's husband, but the biggest one appears in the fourth paragraph: *When I told Faye about it, he looked vexed and said I must never laugh at an enlisted man—that it was not dignified in the wife of an officer to do so. And then I told him that an officer should teach an enlisted man not to snicker at his wife, and not to call her "Sorr," which was disrespectful. I wanted to say more, but Faye suddenly left the room.* We can infer that this was a private disagreement between a husband and a wife. Faye thought that Frances had not acted like a dignified wife, but Frances said that Faye should have stood up for her: *I told him that an officer should teach an enlisted man not to snicker at his wife, and not to call her "Sorr," which was disrespectful.* Faye may have taken this comment personally, because he suddenly left the room.

8. d. She seems interested in the ins and outs of army protocol—she describes details and tries to figure out the rules of rank—but she also questions why things are as they are.

9. c. The writer hints at this point when he notes that *all this—the mysterious, far-reaching hair-line trail, the absence of sun from the sky, the tremendous cold, and the strangeness and weirdness of it all—made no impression on the man.* The ideas presented in the last paragraph also support this theme.

10. b. Although the writer criticizes the man for not thinking deeply about his circumstances and about life in general, the man does seem knowledgeable. He knows about the path of the sun, he knows the exact temperature, and it's suggested that he knows the exact path of the trail he is on. *Matter-of-fact* is also a good description for the man. There are many reasons to think that the man focuses on the world around him in a straightforward way. For example, the writer notes that *He was quick and alert in the things of life, but only in the things, and not in the significances.* The last three sentences of the passage offer further evidence that he is matter-of-fact.

11. c. Not everyone would agree that a certain food is *yummy*, which makes this statement an opinion. The other answer choices all include statements that could be proven. Most people do know that a healthy lifestyle is important, and the information about whole grains and cheese could be verified in a health or science textbook.

12. b. The types of foods needed to stay healthy are classified by similarities. Each of the food groups discussed is a category. Information about the types of food in each category, as well as the number of servings needed daily, is included in that section of the text.

13. c. The importance of a balanced diet is the main point that the author wants readers to understand. Including plenty of dairy is a detail that supports the main idea. While it is

true that most foods can be grouped into five basic types, this is not the main point of the passage.

14. a. Choice **d** states the main idea of the third paragraph, and choice **a**, the statement that fruit smoothies are one way to get enough servings of fruit, supports this idea. Fruit snacks are mentioned in the passage, but nothing is said about them actually offering a serving of fruit. Choice **c** is also a statement from the passage; however, it does not support the main idea.

15. a. Choice **a** restates the main idea and the most important details from the passage. Choice **b** summarizes the third and fourth paragraphs, while choice **d** summarizes the second paragraph. The information in choice **c** is true; however, it includes information that was not mentioned in the paragraph.

16. c. By reading the job descriptions, we can prove that each position offers insurance benefits. Because the statement can be verified, it is a fact. Not everyone would agree with the other three answer choices, so they are opinions.

17. b. The topic of this paragraph is the warehouse employee position. This topic is introduced in the beginning of the paragraph, then the remainder of the sentences describe the position. The requirements, hours, salary, and benefits are all explained. The order of the information is not important, there is not a problem to discuss, and no events result in the occurrence of other events.

18. d. The words *both* and *likewise* indicate ways in which the two jobs are similar. *However, on the other hand,* and *greater* point out differences between the two positions. The third paragraph uses a sequential organizational structure, listing the steps in the order in which they will occur. *First, after,* and *final* are clues to the structure used in this paragraph.

19. b. Several clues help you read between the lines in this passage. Notice that the warehouse employee receives a much higher salary and more benefits than the others. Also, the passage states that the warehouse job "offers many opportunities for future advancement" and that "many of Fairhaven's current management team members began their careers working in the warehouse." Such advancement is not mentioned for either of the other available positions. These hints indicate that warehouse employees are valued highly within the company.

20. b. The main idea of this paragraph is implied rather than directly stated. Readers are able to infer this information by reading the entire paragraph. Although it is not the main idea, readers can also infer the idea that only the most qualified applicants will meet with the hiring team in person because the other steps seem to narrow down the field to only those best suited for the job. Choices **a**, **c**, and **d** are supporting details.

21. c. The letter writer is indeed submitting her complaint to the owner of Luxalot and writing it in a formal way. The word *register* has many meanings. One of them is a machine that calculates and holds money at a store (*cash register*), but that doesn't make sense in this sentence. We are looking for a different meaning of the word *register*. Also note that in the sentence, *register* is used as a verb, whereas a machine that calculates and holds money at a store is a noun. *Registrar* means an official record keeper (for instance, the person at a school or college who keeps records and helps to sign up students for classes). Finally, the letter writer is presenting her complaint to the owner of Luxalot and wants the owner to take action. She is not withdrawing, or removing, her complaint.

22. b. The word is used in the statement that *the wedding's color scheme was white, yellow, and fuchsia.* Then, in the next sentence, the writer mentions the types of flowers that would fit that combination of colors: *First Snow tulips, Sunray roses, and Hot Pink ranunculus.* We can deduce that First Snow tulips are white flowers (because snow is white), that Sunray roses are yellow flowers (because the sun is yellow), and that Hot Pink ranunculus are fuchsia-colored flowers. *Fuchsia* probably means hot—or bright— pink.

23. d. This is not a reason why the writer is dissatisfied. At the end of the letter, she explains, *I would ask for a full refund, but the flowers that did arrive were . . . in the correct color scheme.* Choice **a** is a reason why the writer is dissatisfied. She mentions that the original plan was to use *a few stems of filler flowers, such as baby's breath and Queen Anne's lace, which I thought was a good idea to reduce the overall cost.* We can assume that baby's breath and Queen Anne's lace are inexpensive flowers because Mrs. Jones calls them *filler flowers* and because if they are used, the cost goes down. Then, on the day of the wedding, *The bouquets consisted primarily of baby's breath and Queen Anne's lace*—not *a few stems*, as had been discussed. This all adds up to mean that the displays contained too many inexpensive flowers. Choice **b** is an incorrect choice because the writer says that the plan was to use mainly tulips, roses, and ranunculus. Instead, the company delivered mainly *baby's breath and Queen Anne's lace, and the other flowers were carnations, lilies, and irises.* Choice **c** is an incorrect choice because she says that she ordered 18 centerpieces, but only 14 were delivered.

24. c. All three of these symptoms are listed in the article as possible signs that a person suffers from sleep apnea. Migraines are a type of headache, and the article does mention that headaches could be a symptom, but it specifies *morning* headaches. Also, the article does not mention excessive eating or chest pains as signs of sleep apnea. (Sleep apnea may cause heart attacks—which can cause a person to feel chest pain—but that does not mean that chest pain is a sign of sleep apnea.) Choice **d** is incorrect because each of these is mentioned as a *risk factor* for developing sleep apnea—people who have type 2 diabetes or hypertension or who are going through menopause may be more likely to develop sleep apnea, but this doesn't mean that these conditions are *symptoms* of having sleep apnea. (If you don't quite understand this point, consider this everyday example: Standing outside in the freezing rain would be a *risk factor* for getting a cold. The *symptoms* of having indeed come down with a cold would be coughing, sneezing, and a runny nose.)

25. b. The writer starts off by saying that *anyone— regardless of gender, weight, or fitness level—can develop obstructive sleep apnea*, which suggests that everyone should be knowledgeable about the condition. At different points in the article, the author also states: *First, be aware of the risk factors*; *It's important to watch for symptoms*; and *If you suspect that you have the risk factors and symptoms of sleep apnea, it's important that you are evaluated by a board-certified sleep-medicine physician right away*. Choice **a** is incorrect because although, according to the article, a large portion of people who have hypertension and type 2 diabetes also have sleep apnea, that does not mean that sleep apnea primarily affects people with those conditions. In fact, the first paragraph of the article stresses that *anyone* can develop sleep apnea. Choices **c** and **d** are not main ideas of the passage.

26. a. The author presents facts about the symptoms, diagnosis, and treatment of sleep apnea, and advises readers to pay attention to risk factors and symptoms and to get tested if they think they may have sleep apnea. *Chronological* means ordered by time from start to finish, as in a time line. The author does not discuss the development of sleep apnea over time. The author also does not discuss specific people who have sleep apnea.

27. a. This choice is supported by these sentences in the article: *If you suspect that you have the risk factors and symptoms of sleep apnea, it's important that you are evaluated by a board-certified sleep-medicine physician right away. . . . The sleep-medicine physician will have the training and expertise to diagnose your condition. He or she will conduct a thorough physical examination. . . .* The author emphasizes the skill of board-certified sleep-medicine doctors when it comes to sleep apnea, never mentions other types of doctors (here or elsewhere in the article), and encourages readers to visit a board-certified sleep-medicine doctor if they think they may have sleep apnea. All of this suggests that when it comes to sleep apnea, the author probably thinks that it is better to see a board-certified sleep-medicine doctor than to see another type of doctor. Choice **b** is incorrect because overdiagnosis is not mentioned or implied in the article. Instead, the author discusses sleep-medicine doctors' ability to diagnose sleep apnea accurately. Choice **c** is incorrect because the author does not say or imply that sleep apnea is difficult to diagnose. Instead, one of the big messages of the article is that many people with sleep apnea are going untreated simply because they've never asked to be screened in the first place. The author does not imply choice **d** in the article.

REVIEW

In this chapter, you learned several strategies to help you better comprehend nonfiction reading materials:

1. The main idea is the central message of a passage. Supporting details help to strengthen readers' understanding of the main idea.

2. To summarize is to restate the most important information in your own words. Be sure to think about the main idea and the most important details when creating a summary.

3. Writers include both facts and opinions to express their ideas. Facts are provable and can be verified; opinions tell someone's personal thoughts or ideas, may vary from one person to another, and cannot be verified.

4. Organizational structure refers to the way ideas are arranged in a passage. Common structures include sequence, cause and effect, compare and contrast, problem and solution, classification, and description.

5. When sequence is used to organize a passage, ideas may be listed in time order or in order of importance. Writers may choose to begin with either the most important or least important idea.

6. A cause and effect structure points out how ideas or events are related. A cause is the reason another event occurs; an effect is the result of one or more causes.

7. To compare is to show how ideas, events, or objects are similar; to contrast is to point out ways in which the topics are different. A compare and contrast structure focuses on these similarities and differences.

8. A problem and solution structure introduces a problem, then discusses one or more possible ways to solve the problem.

9. When a writer uses classification as the organizational structure, he or she groups similar ideas together in categories.

10. A description introduces a topic, then provides information and details to explain the topic to readers.

11. To make an inference means to read between the lines and determine what the writer is telling readers without directly stating that information.

12. At times, readers will need to make multiple inferences to fully understand a passage. This may require putting together bits of information located throughout the text to figure out what the writer wants readers to understand.

5 ▶ LANGUAGE AND GRAMMAR: READING SKILLS

CHAPTER SUMMARY
This chapter will help you build the foundation you need to understand the fiction and nonfiction passages found on the GED® Reasoning through Language Arts test. You will learn to identify word parts, prefixes, suffixes, context clues, multiple word meanings, the author's point of view and purpose, and theme. It will also teach you to make predictions and synthesize what you read.

Many of the questions on the GED® RLA exam are designed to test your knowledge of grammar, word usage, and language mechanics. Make sure you are prepared by carefully reviewing this chapter and answering the practice questions. Answers and explanations for all practice questions are at the end of the chapter.

Word Parts

To understand what a passage is about, you have to be able to determine the meanings of its words. Words are formed from a combination of root words, prefixes, and suffixes. **Root words** are the foundation of words.

Prefixes are added to the beginning of words to change their meanings. **Suffixes** are added to the ends of words to change their meanings.

Look at the following example:

unexpected = un + expect + ed

In the word *unexpected*, *un-* is the prefix, *expect* is the root word, and *-ed* is the suffix. These parts work together to give the word meaning. Think about the differences in the meanings of the following sentences:

We <u>expect</u> her to call by 1:00 today.
We <u>expected</u> her to call by noon yesterday.
The fact that she did not call was unexpected.

Adding the suffix *-ed* to the end of the word changes it to past tense. Adding the prefix *un-* to the beginning tells that the event was *not* expected.

Mario is an <u>honest</u> man.

Let's look at the underlined word, *honest*. We know that honest means "truthful" or "trustworthy." So, the sentence lets us know that Mario can be trusted.

Mario is a <u>dishonest</u> man.

In this sentence, the prefix *dis-* has been added to the root word *honest*. This prefix means "not," so we know that *dishonest* means "not honest." Adding the prefix has changed the meaning of the sentence. Now we know that Mario cannot be trusted.

Emily handled the package with <u>care</u>.
Emily was <u>careless</u> with the package.

The first sentence tells that Emily was gentle with the package. However, when the suffix *-less* is added to the root word *care*, the meaning changes. This suffix means "without," so *careless* means "without care."

Emily was <u>careful</u> with the package.

This sentence uses the same root, *care*, but adds the suffix *-ful*. This suffix means "full of," so Emily was full of care when she handled the package.

Following are lists of some common prefixes and suffixes and their meanings. Knowing the meanings of these word parts can help you figure out meanings of words and help you better understand what you read.

Prefixes

- *co-*: with
- *de-*: to take away
- *dis-*: lack of, opposite of
- *ex-*: out of, previous
- *extra-*: outside, beyond
- *il-, in-, im-, ir-*: not
- *inter-*: between, among
- *mis-*: wrongly, badly
- *non-*: without, not
- *pre-*: before
- *post-*: after
- *re-*: again
- *sub-*: lower, nearly, under
- *super-*: above, over
- *trans-*: across
- *un-*: not

Suffixes

- *-able, -ible*: able to, can be done
- *-ant*: one who
- *-en*: made of
- *-er*: comparative, one who
- *-ful*: full of
- *-ive*: likely to
- *-ize*: to make
- *-less*: without
- *-ly*: in a certain way
- *-ment*: action, process
- *-ness, -ity*: state of
- *-or*: one who
- *-ous*: full of
- *-tion*: act, process

Now, use what you know about word parts to determine the meaning of the underlined word in the following sentence. Write the meaning of the word on the line underneath.

It seemed <u>illogical</u> for her to drop out of the campaign.

_____

Breaking the underlined word into word parts can help determine its meaning. The word *illogical* is made up of the prefix *il-*, meaning "not," and the word *logical*. If something is logical, it makes sense. So, if it is illogical, it does not make sense.

> **TIP**
>
> Keep in mind that groups of letters are considered a prefix or suffix only if they are added to a root word. For example, *mis-* is a prefix when added to the root word *spell* to create the word *misspell*. However, these letters are not a prefix in the words *mistletoe* or *misty*.

Sometimes, thinking of a word with a similar root can help you figure out the meaning of an unfamiliar word.

> *The captain watched the sails <u>deflate</u> as he attempted to guide the boat to the dock.*

Suppose you do not know the meaning of *deflate*. Ask yourself, "Do I know a word that has a similar root?" You probably already know that *inflate* means to fill something with air or to make something larger.

> *Dad will <u>inflate</u> the balloons before the party.*

Using what you know about the meanings of word parts, you can figure out that *deflate* means that the air has gone out of something, or it has gotten smaller.

Let's try another example:

> *Brian carries his <u>portable</u> CD player everywhere he goes.*

Portable contains the root *port* and the suffix *-able*. *Port* means "to move," so *portable* means that the CD player is "able to be moved."

> *The company plans to <u>export</u> 75% of its products overseas.*

Suppose you are unsure of the meaning of *export*. Do you know a word that has a similar root? *Portable* and *export* have the same root. You know that the prefix in *export*, *ex-*, means "out of" and *port* means "to move," so *export* means "to move out." So, the company plans to move its products out and send them overseas.

> *The island <u>imports</u> most of its fruit from other countries.*

If *export* means "to move out," what do you think *import* means? It means "to move in" or "to bring in."

Now you try. What words could help you determine the meaning of the underlined word in the following sentence? Write the words on the line underneath.

> *She tried to <u>visualize</u> the author's description of the animal.*

_____

Vision and *visible* both have roots that are similar to that of *visualize*. *Vision* is the sense of sight. If something is *visible*, it is able to be seen. So, to *visualize* means "to see something."

Here are a few sets of words with similar roots. Knowing sets of words with similar roots can help you determine word meanings. What other words could you add to each set in the list below? What other groups of words can you think of that have similar roots?

- adjoin, conjunction, juncture
- anniversary, annual, biannual

- audible, audience, audio
- benevolent, benefit, beneficial
- chronic, chronological, synchronize
- civic, civilian, civilization
- contradict, dictate, dictionary
- describe, prescribe, transcribe
- design, signal, signature
- empathy, pathetic, sympathy
- evacuate, vacancy, vacuum
- exclaim, exclamation, proclaim
- mystify, mystery, mysterious
- pollutant, pollute, pollution
- telescope, telephone, television
- terrain, terrestrial, territory

Parts of Speech

Verbs

Verbs are the heart of a sentence. They express the action or state of being of the subject, telling us what the subject is doing, thinking, or feeling. They also tell us when that action or state of being occurs—in the past, present, or future—and they can communicate more complicated ideas, for instance whether something happens often or whether there is a possibility that something will happen in the future.

Infinitive and Simple Present Tense

An **infinitive** is the base form of the verb plus the word *to*, such as *to go*, *to dream*, and *to eat*. The infinitive form can be used in many ways in a sentence.

Here are some examples:

Tong promises to return *by noon.*
To walk *was the most logical decision.*

One of the most common mistakes in English involves the infinitive. People often say *try and* do something rather than the correct *try to* do something. For example:

Incorrect: Try and *come to work on time tomorrow.*
Correct: Try *to come to work on time tomorrow.*

Incorrect: *I'll* try and *buy the tickets at the box office rather than online.*
Correct: *I'll* try *to buy the tickets at the box office rather than online.*

This may be tested on the GED® test, so make sure you know the difference.

Simple present tense is the verb form that communicates facts or indicates that something occurs on a regular basis. For example:

The assistants commute *to work on the subway, but their boss* takes *a limo.*
I commute *to work every morning on the subway.*
She speaks *English.*
I am *from Philadelphia.*
Dogs bark, *and cats* meow.
In the Caribbean, the water is *aqua blue.*
Marissa runs *five miles every weekend.*

The simple present tense of regular verbs is formed as follows, using the verb *to drive* as an example:

	SINGULAR	PLURAL
First person (I/we)	Base form (drive)	Base form (drive)
Second person (you)	Base form (drive)	Base form (drive)
Third person (he/she/they)	Base form plus -s or -es (drives)	Base form (drive)

Present Continuous Tense

Present continuous tense is the verb form that describes what is happening now, at this exact moment. It ends in *-ing* and is accompanied by one of the following helping verbs: *am*, *is*, or *are* (the present tense of the verb *to be*). For instance:

Adam is driving *to the fair.*
They are driving *to the picnic.*

Gerunds

Words that end in -*ing* don't always function as verbs. Sometimes they act as nouns and are called **gerunds**. They can also function as adjectives.

Examples:

> *Tracy enjoys* running *on the beach.*
> Here, *running* serves as a noun—it is the thing that Tracy enjoys.

> *The* loading *dock is outside the back door.*
> Here, *loading* serves as an adjective—it describes the dock.

Here is an example of how the same word can have three different functions:

verb:	*He is* screaming *loudly.*
gerund (noun):	*That* screaming *is driving me crazy.*
adjective:	*The* screaming *boy finally stopped.*

When correcting sentences on the GED® RLA test, do not assume that a word that ends in -*ing* is a verb. You will need to read closely to determine how the word functions in the sentence. Here are a few guidelines for identifying and using gerunds:

1. Gerunds are often used after a preposition.
   Keza thought that by taking *the train she would* save money *and time.*
   Noriel was afraid of offending *her host, but she couldn't eat dinner.*
2. Gerunds frequently follow these verbs:

admit	dislike	practice
appreciate	enjoy	put off
avoid	escape	quit
can't help	finish	recall
consider	imagine	resist
delay	keep	risk
deny	miss	suggest
discuss	postpone	tolerate

We should discuss buying *a new computer.*
I quit smoking.

Past Tense

Simple past tense is the verb form that expresses what happened at a specific moment in the past.

> *It* rained *for three hours yesterday.*
> *She* opened *the door and* welcomed *the guests.*

Past Participle

The **past participle** of a verb consists of its past form, accompanied by the helping verb *have, has,* or *had* (e.g., have cared, has forgiven, had thought, etc.). This is true of both regular and irregular verbs.

Past Continuous Tense

The **past continuous tense** indicates that an action happened in the past and continued for some time. It's used with the helping verb *was* or *were.*

> *She* was walking *when the rain started.*
> *While they* were singing, *the phone rang.*

Past Perfect Tense

Used with the helping verb *had,* the **past perfect tense** indicates that an action happened in the past before another action happened in the past. This may sound confusing, but it's a tense that you probably often use in everyday speech. Look at these examples:

> *Yesterday, Theresa told me that she thought Harry* had played *too much golf during their honeymoon.*

Notice that the sentence places us at one point in time—when Theresa was talking and thinking—and it uses the past perfect to look back at an earlier point in time, when something may have happened during her honeymoon.

> *Jack's vacation was cut short when he broke his ankle in London, but he* had had *the time of his life in Paris.*

In this sentence, we're placed at the time when Jack's vacation was cut short, and we're looking back at the time when he enjoyed himself in Paris.

> *Aisling's parents* had *always* wanted *her to become a doctor, but in college she decided to become an English major.*

The time that Aisling's parents wanted her to become a doctor happened before the time that she decided to become an English major.

Past Perfect and the Conditional

On the GED® test, you may be asked to use the past perfect in another situation: **conditional sentences** set in the past.

You probably use the conditional all the time in everyday life without knowing it. It follows this general pattern: *If this happens, then that happens.* Look at these examples:

> *I will go inside if you tell me to.*
> *If you don't know where those cookies came from, you shouldn't eat them.*

Now look at these examples of conditional sentences set in the past. They all include the past perfect:

> *I would have brought sunscreen if I had known it was going to be so hot and sunny.*

> *If you had really wanted to keep that job, you would have gotten to work on time.*
> *If someone had called to tell me that the doctor's office was closed, I would have stayed in bed.*

NOTE

Conditional sentences in the past often include the words *would have*.

Regular versus Irregular Verbs

Most English verbs are regular—they follow a standard set of rules for forming the simple past tense. Usually, add *-ed*.

> *He interrupted me when I was typing.*

If the verb ends with the letter *e*, just add *-d*.

> *The prisoners escaped.*

If the verb ends with the letter *y*, change the *y* to an *i* and add *-ed*.

> *I carried the water pitcher to the table.*

Irregular Verbs

About 150 English verbs are irregular—they don't follow the standard rules for changing tense.

Many irregular verbs form the past tense by changing the vowel to *a*. For example:

Present	Simple Past
begin	began
sing	sang
spring	sprang
come	came
overcome	overcame
run	ran

Other irregular verbs are more "irregular," such as these:

Present	Simple Past
bite	bit
bring	brought
dig	dug
hear	heard
leave	left
plead	pled
send	sent

In English, as in many other languages, the essential verb, *to be*, is highly irregular:

Subject	Present	Simple Past
I	am	was
you	are	were
he, she, it	is	was
we	are	were
they	are	were

Using a Consistent Tense

A common writing mistake is to jump between verb tenses when it is not necessary or correct to do so. You may be asked to spot this mistake on the GED® RLA test.

If a writer indicates that a certain action takes place at a certain time, he or she should be consistent in the use of verb tense when writing about that action elsewhere in the sentence (or paragraph or story). Review the following examples:

Incorrect: *She* left *the house and* forgets *her keys in the kitchen.*

Correct: *She* left *the house and* forgot *her keys in the kitchen.*

Incorrect: *Jon* signed up *to run the marathon, but after talking to his doctor, he* decides *it would be too strenuous.*

Correct: *Jon* signed up *to run the marathon, but after talking to his doctor, he* decided *it would be too strenuous.*

Subject–Verb Agreement

In grammar, agreement means that verbs should agree with their subjects. If the subject is singular, the verb should be singular. If the subject is plural, the verb should be plural. Because we often use incorrect grammar when we speak, identifying correct subject–verb agreement can be challenging.

Read the following examples, which highlight common agreement errors:

Incorrect: The president, *along with his wife and two daughters,* are *going to Hawaii on vacation.*

Correct: The president, *along with his wife and two daughters,* is *going to Hawaii on vacation.*

Although we know that four people are going on vacation—the president, his wife, and their two daughters—the sentence really has only one subject: *the president.* The phrase *along with his wife and two daughters* is just a side point; it is set off with commas and is not essential to the grammar of the sentence. Since the real subject, *the president,* is singular, the verb should be singular too: *is.*

NOTE

It's easy to read sentences such as the first example and think that they are correct. That is because a plural word—in this case, *daughters*—is the word that comes right before the verb. The phrase *two daughters are* sounds natural, even though in this sentence it is not correct. Make sure to keep in mind what the real subject of a sentence is, so you know what verb form is necessary.

Incorrect: *The jury* have *left the courtroom to make* their *decision.*

Correct: *The* jury has *left the courtroom to make* its *decision.*

Although *jury* refers to a group of people, the actual word *jury* is a singular noun—it means all of the jury members taken as a whole.

Here are examples of other nouns that may seem plural at first but are usually treated as singular and take a singular verb: *team, family, group, band, committee, tribe, audience,* and *flock.*

Incorrect: *That* boxer don't *have a chance against Carl.*

Correct: *That* boxer doesn't *have a chance against Carl.*

Although the first sentence may sound correct in casual speech, the word *boxer* is singular, so it should be followed by a singular verb form. *Don't* is a plural form.

How to Get Subject–Verb Agreement Right

Your main challenge when deciding if a sentence has correct subject–verb agreement will probably be determining who or what serves as the subject of the sentence.

In most cases, this should be simple and will come naturally to you. But as you saw in the previous examples, sometimes the real subject is not immediately obvious.

Here is another example. Can you identify the subject of the sentence?

Only one of the students was officially registered for class.

In this sentence, the subject is *one*, not *students*. Although it may seem as if the students are perform-

ing the action, the true subject of the sentence is the *one* student—whoever that person may be—meaning that the sentence requires the singular verb *was.*

Here's another example:

Vanessa and Erin are going to join the committee.

It's easy to see that there are two subjects in this sentence: *Vanessa* and *Erin*. The verb is correctly plural: *are.*

Now review these similar sentences:

Either Vanessa or Erin is going to join the committee.
Neither Vanessa nor Erin is going to join the committee.

In both cases, even though there are still two names—*Vanessa* and *Erin*—the subject is singular. In the first case, only one of them is going to join the committee (we don't know who, but it will be only one of them). In the second case, neither one will; *neither* also requires a singular verb.

NOTE

If one plural and one singular subject are connected by *or* or *nor*, the verb form must agree with the closer subject. For instance:

Neither Vanessa nor the teachers want to join the committee.
Neither the teachers nor Vanessa wants to join the committee.

Let's go back to our original example:

Vanessa and Erin are going to join the committee.

There are two nouns at the start of the sentence, and it is clear that there are two subjects: *Vanessa* and *Erin*.

LANGUAGE AND GRAMMAR: READING SKILLS

Now take a look at this example:

Peanut butter and jelly is my favorite type of sandwich.

Although the phrase *peanut butter and jelly* is made up of two nouns, we know that the term *peanut butter and jelly* refers to one thing: a particular type of sandwich filling. In this case, you'd treat the whole phrase as one subject, so you would use a singular verb form (*is*).

Here are other examples of subjects that may look plural at first glance but are really singular:

Spaghetti and meatballs *was my grandmother's favorite dish.*
The New York Times *is delivered to my door every morning.*
The United States *has never won the Olympic gold in that sport.*

Here is one last type of sentence that often causes subject–verb agreement problems: sentences that start with words such as *There's*, *Here's*, and *What's*. Note that in these sentences, the subject comes *after* the verb. For example:

There's my dog, playing by the park bench.

The subject of the sentence is *my dog*.

Incorrect: There's *still three empty seats.*
Correct: There are *still three empty seats.*

Don't forget that *There's* is really a shorthand (or contraction) of the phrase *There is*. Since the subject of this sentence—*seats*—is plural, the sentence requires a plural introduction: *There are*.

Incorrect: What's *the side effects of this medication?*
Correct: What are *the side effects of this medication?*

Similarly, *What's* is a contraction of *What is*, which is incorrect here because the subject of this sentence is plural: *side effects*.

Practice
For each sentence, fill in the blank with either *is* or *are*.

1. Red Rocks _____ their favorite concert venue in Colorado.

2. Julio, as well as the rest of the band, _____ excited about performing at Red Rocks.

3. Two members of the band _____ still back at the hotel.

4. Everyone _____ supposed to be onstage right now!

5. Where _____ Julio and the guitar player?

For the following three questions, select the best revision of the underlined part of the sentence.

6. Catherine <u>is gone</u> to the store later today.
   a. go
   b. will go
   c. went
   d. has gone

7. Gerald and Yolanda <u>have visited</u> me yesterday.
   a. visited
   b. are visiting
   c. visits
   d. had visited

8. Neither you nor your cousins <u>appearing</u> in the photograph.
   a. appears
   b. is appearing
   c. appear
   d. to appear

Pronouns

In order to understand the correct use of pronouns, you must first have a clear understanding of what a noun is. **Nouns** are words that identify objects.

> **People:** students, brother, David, neighbor
> **Places:** New York City, ocean, university, Jupiter
> **Things:** books, Saturday, bathing suit, the U.S. Navy
> **Ideas and qualities:** beauty, faith, anger, justice

A **pronoun** is a word that replaces or refers to a noun. Consider the following examples:

> Sheldon *prefers cereal to toast and jam.*

This can be rewritten with a pronoun as:

> He *prefers cereal to toast and jam.*

> *Last Friday,* Josh *drove to* Kathy *and* Tina's *cabin.*

This can be rewritten with pronouns as:

> *Last Friday,* he *drove to their cabin.*

> Jackson *doesn't care about anyone except* Jackson.

This can be rewritten with pronouns as:

> He *doesn't care about anyone except* himself.

There are many pronouns in the English language, depending on what type of noun the pronoun is replacing and how the pronoun functions in a sentence. Here are some examples of pronouns: *I, you, she, he, we, they, it, this, that, myself, ourselves, whoever, whomever, mine, yours.*

Pronouns and Antecedents

When a pronoun is used in a sentence, it should be clear what noun(s) it is substituting for or referring to. That noun is called an **antecedent**. For example:

> Adam *had fun while* he *was on vacation in Puerto Rico.*

The pronoun *he* is another way of saying the word *Adam. Adam* is the antecedent of *he.*

Here is another:

> My grandparents *first met when* they *were in college.*

The plural pronoun *they* stands in for the plural noun *grandparents,* which is the antecedent.

This may seem simple enough, but confusion over pronouns and antecedents can arise in more complicated sentences. You may be asked to spot or correct this type of problem on the GED® RLA test.

Consider this incorrect sentence:

> *Despite what the president told the reporters,* they *are not going to authorize military action.*

The sentence may sound correct to the ear, but if we give it some thought, do we really know what is meant by the pronoun *they*? (To put it another way: Do we know what the antecedent is of *they*?)

They is a plural pronoun, so it can't refer to *the president,* which is a singular noun. It could refer to *the reporters,* which is a plural noun, but that doesn't make sense logically—reporters are not in charge of the military.

Does *they* mean some other group of people (members of a committee or army generals)? Or should it be changed to *he,* to mean *the president*?

As you can see, when there is no obvious antecedent to a pronoun, the meaning of an entire sentence can be unclear.

Beware of *They*

Another common pronoun problem arises when the writer is discussing a person (singular) but isn't sure what gender to use—*she/her/her* or *he/him/his*—so tries to keep things vague by using a plural pronoun (*they/them/their*) instead. Consider this example:

> *If* a student *is late to class three times,* they *will be reported to the principal.*

The pronoun *they* doesn't work here because it's plural but its antecedent is the singular noun *student*. Here is a correct way to rewrite the sentence:

> *If* a student *is late to class three times,* he or she *will be reported to the principal.*

Or you could rephrase the sentence this way:

> *If* students *are late to class three times,* they *will be reported to the principal.*

Subject Pronouns and Object Pronouns

When editing sentences for correct pronoun use, you will need to determine whether the pronoun is the subject or the object of the sentence. Consider the following sentence:

> *Jane brought Jack to the dentist.*

Jane is the subject of the sentence—the person who is acting out the verb *brought*. *Jack* is the object—the person who is receiving the action of the verb.

If we wanted to swap out the words *Jane* and *Jack* with pronouns, we would need to use a subjective pronoun for *Jane* and an objective pronoun for *Jack*. Note the correct sentence, after a couple of incorrect tries:

> **Incorrect:** She *brought* he *to the dentist.*
> **Incorrect:** Her *brought* him *to the dentist.*
> **Correct:** She *brought* him *to the dentist.*

Here is a list of subject and object pronouns. Make sure you know the difference:

Subject	Object
I	me
you	you
he	him
she	her
it	it
we	us
who	whom
they	them

Who versus Whom

This brings us to one of the most common grammar problems in the English language: using the word *who* (a subjective pronoun) when the word *whom* (an objective pronoun) is called for. This error could appear on the GED® RLA test, so make sure you know how to spot it.

Consider the following examples:

> Who *made dinner last night?*

Who is the subject of this sentence. Whoever that mysterious meal-preparing person is, he or she performed the action of the sentence (making dinner).

> Whom *should John invite to your party?*

Here, *John* is the subject of the sentence. John is going to perform the action of the sentence (inviting one or more guests). *Whom* is the object of the sentence: it refers to one or more persons who will receive the action of the sentence (John's invitation).

An easy way to test whether you should use *who* or *whom* in a sentence is to swap it for another pronoun that you're more familiar with and check to see if that makes sense.

Let's try out this trick on the following sentence:

[Who/Whom] *is Jake going to marry?*

First, let's try to answer the question with the word *she.* It is a subjective pronoun, so it will test whether the subjective pronoun *who* would work in the sentence.

[Who/Whom] *is Jake going to marry? Jake is going to marry* she.

That is clearly not grammatical. Now let's try an objective pronoun, *her:*

[Who/Whom] *is Jake going to marry? Jake is going to marry* her.

That makes sense, so we know that we need another objective pronoun—*whom*—for the question:

Whom *is Jake going to marry?*

Here is another example:

Incorrect: *Ms. Dee is the teacher* who *I always ask for advice.*
Correct: *Ms. Dee is the teacher* whom *I always ask for advice.*

When deciding whether to use *who* or *whom,* look at the core phrase: *I ask* _____.

I ask her would be grammatical, not *I ask she.* Therefore, in our sentence, we need to use the same type of pronoun as *her* (objective). That means we need to use *whom.*

Incorrect: *Gordon is the man* whom *lives down the street.*
Correct: *Gordon is the man* who *lives down the street.*

To determine *who* versus *whom,* the core phrase is: _____ *lives down the street.*

Let's test it:

Him *lives down the street.*
He *lives down the street.*

The second sentence, with the subjective pronoun *he,* is correct, so we should use *who* in our sentence.

Now take a look at these more advanced examples to prepare for the GED® RLA test.

The same rules for *who* and *whom* apply to *whoever* and *whomever.*

Incorrect: *I'll play chess with* whoever.
Correct: *I'll play chess with* whomever.

The core phrase here is: *I'll play with* _____. The missing word is an object of the preposition *with,* so we need to use the objective pronoun *whomever.*

Let's do that test again, just to be sure. Let's try the sentence with a subjective pronoun, *she:*

I'll play chess with she.

That is clearly not correct. The subjective pronoun *whoever* is therefore not correct. Now let's try the objective pronoun *her:*

I'll play chess with her.

That's a perfect fit, so the objective pronoun *whomever* must be right.

Practice

For each of the following questions, fill in the blank with *who, whom, whoever,* or *whomever.*

9. _____ are you taking to the dance?

10. _____ is making that noise had better quiet down!

11. That man over there is the customer _____ complained about me to my boss.

12. _____ is taking you to the dance?

Possessive Pronouns

Like possessive nouns (such as *Carla's, the house's, the three players'*), possessive pronouns show ownership. However, possessive pronouns do *not* use apostrophes.

> **Incorrect:** *The purple and green balloons were their's.*
> **Correct:** *The purple and green balloons were theirs.*
> **Incorrect:** It's *tail was long and furry.*
> **Correct:** Its *tail was long and furry.*

Note that some possessive pronouns function as adjectives and are used to describe a noun. For instance: *my* car (*my* describes the noun *car*), *her* tennis shoes (*her* describes the noun *tennis shoes*), and *your* strawberries (*your* describes the noun *strawberries*).

Other possessive pronouns function as nouns themselves, for instance:

> *The blue car is* mine.
> *Those tennis shoes are* hers.
> Yours *are sweeter than* ours.

Make sure you are familiar with the spelling of both types of possessive pronouns:

Possessive (adjective)	Possessive (noun)
my	mine
your	yours
his	his
her	hers
its	its
our	ours
whose	whose
their	theirs

Read the following sentence. Then replace the underlined words with the correct pronouns:

> When Lisa and Jim's friend Tony arrived home from Iraq, <u>Lisa and Jim</u> took <u>Tony</u> to <u>Tony's</u> favorite restaurant and told <u>Tony</u> to order whatever <u>Tony</u> liked.
> When Lisa and Jim's friend Tony arrived home from Iraq, *they* took *him* to *his* favorite restaurant and told *him* to order whatever *he* liked.

Lisa and Jim translates to *they* because *Lisa and Jim* serves as a subject of the sentence (Lisa and Jim are the people who are performing the main action—taking Tony to dinner).

Tony's is a possessive noun, which translates to the possessive pronoun *his*.

To figure out the rest of the answers—pronouns that replace the word *Tony*—ask yourself whether *Tony* is a subject (performing an action) or an object (receiving an action). If he's the subject, make it *he*. If he's the object, make it *him*.

Pronouns Combined with Other Nouns

Often pronouns are combined with other subjects or objects in a sentence. For instance, in the following sentence, there is one subject (*Ruth*) and two objects (*Peter* and _____):

> *Ruth drove Peter and* _____ *to the football game.*

Do you know which pronoun should fill in the blank?

> Ruth drove Peter and *me* to the football game.
> Ruth drove Peter and *I* to the football game.

Although the second sentence may sound correct, it is not. (It may sound correct to you because we hear this type of phrasing all the time. Many people use it because they think it sounds more proper or formal, but in reality it is poor grammar.)

The first sentence is right. The word *me* is an objective pronoun, which is what is needed in the grammar of this sentence. *I* is a subjective pronoun, which is incorrect here.

There's an easy trick for finding the correct pronoun in situations such as this (when a pronoun is combined with another noun and you want to know what type of pronoun to use): **Cross out the other phrase**—here, *Peter and*—**and then see what pronoun you need.** Here it would be:

Ruth drove me *to the football game.*

You would never say:

Ruth drove I *to the football game.*

Practice

For each of the following questions, choose the pronoun that fits best.

13. Joe had _____ temperature taken at the doctor's office on Tuesday.
   a. its
   b. his
   c. him
   d. none of the above

14. Someone forgot to lock up _____ shoes and gym bag.
   a. his or her
   b. his or hers
   c. their
   d. there

15. The closet is so dark! I can't tell which coat is _____ and which is _____.
   a. your, my
   b. yours, mine
   c. our, their
   d. our, they're

Dangling and Misplaced Modifiers

A **dangling modifier** is a misplaced word or phrase. If a word or a phrase is placed incorrectly in a sentence, the meaning of the sentence can be misinterpreted.

How to Spot Dangling Modifiers

Incorrect: *Running for the bus, my backpack fell in the street.*

This suggests that the subject of the sentence—*my backpack*—was running for the bus, which we know is not correct!

The phrase *Running for the bus* is a **dangling modifier** because it describes the action of the person speaking, but that person is not mentioned in the sentence.

Here is the sentence written correctly:

Correct: *As I was running for the bus, my backpack fell in the street.*

When editing sentences for dangling modifiers, pay attention to words that end in *-ing* and appear at the beginning of the sentence. This can signal a sentence that has a dangling modifier. For example:

Incorrect: *Searching the entire house, the key was under the table.*

This sentence says that the key searched the entire house, which doesn't make sense.

Correct: *After searching the entire house, he found the key under the table.*

NOTE

Most dangling modifiers occur at the beginnings of sentences, but they can appear at the ends of sentences, too.

How to Spot Misplaced Modifiers

Now let's look at a similar type of error: **misplaced modifiers**. These are phrases or clauses that appear in the wrong spot in a sentence, so it seems as if they describe one thing when they really are intended to describe something else.

For example:

Incorrect: *Ten minutes later, a sad-looking man in a dirty suit with yellow teeth entered the room.*

Correct: *Ten minutes later, a sad-looking man who wore a dirty suit and had yellow teeth entered the room.*

The suit didn't have yellow teeth—the man did.

Incorrect: *She gave homemade treats to the kids wrapped in tinfoil.*

Correct: *She gave the kids homemade treats wrapped in tinfoil.*

The kids weren't wrapped in tinfoil—the treats were.

Only, Just, Barely, and Nearly

The words *only, just, barely, nearly,* and *almost* should appear right before the noun or verb being modified. Their placement determines the message of the sentence.

Only Peter ran to the store. (No one else but Peter went.)

Peter only ran to the store. (He didn't walk.)

Peter ran only to the store. (He didn't go anywhere else.)

Peter ran to the only store. (There was no other store around but that one.)

Peter ran to the store only. (He ran to the store and did nothing else.)

Practice

For each of the following sentences, select the best revision.

16. Moving to Nevada, Shira's truck broke down.
    a. While Shira was moving to Nevada, her truck broke down.
    b. Shira's truck, moving to Nevada, broke down.
    c. Shira's truck broke down while moving to Nevada.
    d. The sentence is correct as is.

17. Exhausted after a long day at the office, Tom only used the treadmill for ten minutes before heading home from the gym.
    a. After Tom's exhausting day at the office, he only used the treadmill for ten minutes before heading home from the gym.
    b. Exhausted after a long day at the office, Tom headed home from the gym after only using the treadmill for ten minutes.
    c. Exhausted after a long day at the office, Tom used the treadmill for only ten minutes before heading home from the gym.
    d. The sentence is correct as is.

18. Historians have wondered whether General Thomas Herald was really a woman in disguise for more than 200 years.
    a. For more than 200 years, historians have wondered whether General Thomas Herald was really a woman in disguise.
    b. Historians have wondered, Was General Thomas Herald really a woman in disguise for more than 200 years?
    c. Historians have wondered whether General Thomas Herald, in disguise, was really a woman for more than 200 years.
    d. The sentence is correct as is.

Context Clues

Even great readers will come across unfamiliar words in a text at times. One way to figure out the meanings of these words is to use **context clues**. These are hints that are included in the sentence or passage that help readers understand the meanings of words.

Authors often use **synonyms**, or words with similar meanings, to help readers understand unfamiliar terms.

> *Beginning this semester, students will have an <u>abbreviated</u>, or shortened, day every Wednesday.*

In this sentence, the author included the synonym *shortened* to explain what he or she means by *abbreviated*. This context clue helps readers determine the meaning of a word that might be unfamiliar.

An author might also include **antonyms**, or words with opposite meanings, to clarify the definition of a word.

> *Please be advised that both <u>residents</u> and visitors are expected to park their cars on the west side of the apartment building.*

This sentence talks about *residents* and *visitors*. So, we can conclude that residents are different than visitors. Because you probably know that visitors are people who do not live in the building, we can figure out that *residents* are people who do live there.

Definitions or **explanations** are often used as context clues.

> *The <u>reluctant</u> child was not eager to share his project with the class.*

In this sentence, the author explained the meaning of *reluctant* by saying that the child was *not eager*.

Examples are another type of context clue that can be used to determine the meaning of unknown words.

> *Ms. Greene pointed out pictures of several <u>monuments</u> in the students' history books, including the Statue of Liberty, the Lincoln Memorial, and the Liberty Bell.*

This sentence includes three examples of monuments: the Statue of Liberty, the Lincoln Memorial, and the Liberty Bell. From these examples, we can figure out that a *monument* must be a famous place or structure that has a special importance.

TIP

When looking for context clues, be sure to check sentences surrounding the unfamiliar word. These clues might be contained in the sentences before or after the sentence that includes the word in question, or they may even be in another part of the paragraph.

As you read the following sentences, look for context clues that could help you determine the meanings of the underlined words. Then, answer the questions that follow.

> *We climbed all day before reaching the <u>apex</u>, or top, of the mountain. We hadn't eaten anything in several hours and were all <u>famished</u>. I was so extremely hungry that I couldn't wait for lunch. As we ate our picnic, we talked about many topics, some <u>frivolous</u>, others serious. After an hour of eating, relaxing, and enjoying the gorgeous view, we began our hike back down the trail.*

1. What is the meaning of *apex*?

_____

2. What clues helped you determine the meaning?

_____

The synonym *top* probably helped you figure out that *apex* means the top, or the highest point, of the mountain.

3. What is the meaning of *famished*?

_____

4. What clues helped you determine the meaning?

_____

The sentence explains that the hikers hadn't eaten anything in several hours. The following sentence includes the definition "extremely hungry." These context clues probably helped you figure out that *famished* means "extremely hungry" or "starving." Notice that some of the clues were in the sentence following the underlined word. Also, notice that clues were found in more than one place. Be sure to look throughout the entire paragraph for clues that can help you determine meaning.

5. What is the meaning of *frivolous*?

_____

6. What clues helped you determine the meaning?

_____

The paragraph states that some of the topics the hikers discussed were *frivolous* and others were *serious*.

This use of an antonym tells us that something that is *frivolous* is not serious.

Multiple Meaning Words

Many words have more than one meaning. As we read, it is important to know which meaning the author intends to use. Consider the use of the word *stoop* in the following sentences:

Li sat on the front <u>stoop</u>, waiting for her neighbor to come home.

David had to <u>stoop</u> to fit into the tiny door of his little brother's clubhouse.

The other candidate is constantly telling lies, but I would never <u>stoop</u> so low.

In the first sentence, *stoop* means "a small porch." In the second sentence, *stoop* means "to bend forward." In the third sentence, *stoop* means "to do something unethical."

So, if words have more than one meaning, how are you supposed to figure out which is correct? You'll have to use context clues. Think about which definition makes sense in that particular sentence.

Read the following sentence.

The detective said the intruders left without a <u>trace</u>.

Which is the meaning of *trace* in this sentence?
  a. a tiny amount
  b. a remaining sign
  c. a type of drawing
  d. to find something

In the sentence, the detective could not find any remaining sign that the intruders had been there.

Although each of the answer choices is a definition of *trace*, only choice **b** makes sense in the context of the sentence.

Frequently Confused Words and Homonyms

Quick—what's the difference between *it's* and *its*? *Know* and *no*? *To* and *too*?

Like many words in the English language, these words often confuse people because they sound the same but have very different meanings. Other frequently confused words have the same *spelling* but different meanings. All of these are called **homonyms**.

To help avoid confusion on the GED® test—and in everyday life—familiarize yourself with the following homonyms and other words (such as *affect* and *effect*) that people often mix up.

Words to Remember
affect/effect

Here are the two definitions of *affect* and *effect* that people often confuse:

> to *affect* (verb): to influence
>> Eric's childhood in rural Arkansas *affected* how he viewed the world.
>
> *effect* (noun): the result of influence
>> Eric's childhood in rural Arkansas had an *effect* on how he viewed the world.

Both words also have other meanings, which you should try not to confuse:

> to *effect* (verb): to cause something to happen, accomplish
>> Over time, the union's efforts *effected* change at the factory.

> to *affect* (verb): to pretend or make a display of
>> The designer sometimes *affected* a British accent when he went to parties, which was ridiculous because he had been born and raised in New Jersey.
>
> *affect* (noun): a feeling or emotion, or the way that a feeling or emotion is expressed physically
>> He had a calm, cool *affect*, which was disturbing because his son had just gone missing.

its/it's

> *its*: belonging to a certain animal or thing
>> The dog wants *its* bone.
>
> *it's*: the contraction of *it is*
>> *It's* too hot to go outside.

lie/lay

> *lie*: to make an untrue statement (verb); an untrue statement (noun)
>> Never *lie* on a job application, because if *the lie* is detected, you probably won't get hired.
>
> *lie, lay*: the present and past tenses of the verb *to lie*, meaning to recline or rest in a horizontal position
>> Every Sunday afternoon, I *lie* on the couch and watch movies.
>> Last Sunday afternoon, I *lay* on the couch and watched movies.
>
> *lay, laid*: the present and past tenses of the verb *to lay*, meaning to put something down
>> You can *lay* the baby down in Sarah's old crib.
>> He *laid* the baby down in Sarah's old crib.

know/no; knew/new

> *know*: to be well informed, to recognize
>> I *know* a lot about growing tomatoes.
>
> *no*: zero, none
>> I have *no* idea how to grow tomatoes.

knew: past tense of the verb *to know*

    I *knew* how to grow tomatoes when I was younger.

new: appearing or made for the first time

    I will need to buy *new* tomatoes.

through/threw

through: a preposition meaning into one side and out the other

    Don't worry—I know you will make it *through* this difficult period.

threw: past tense of the verb *to throw*

    He *threw* out his house keys by mistake!

NOTE

You may see the word *thru* in everyday life (for instance, at a fast-food restaurant's "drive-thru"), but it's an informal spelling that is usually not appropriate in school or work settings. You should also avoid using it on the GED® test!

then/than

then: after something has happened, next

    First I will do my laundry, and *then* I will wash the kitchen floor.

than: a word used when comparing two things

    I would rather go to Florida this winter *than* stay in Wisconsin.

Practice

Select the word that best fits each sentence.

19. Jill, go rest while I _____ out the silver and get the table ready for the party.
  a. lie
  b. lay

20. Mira _____ the congregation in song at the memorial service yesterday.
  a. lead
  b. led

21. I plan to pick up my paycheck this afternoon and _____ cash it at the bank on the corner.
  a. than
  b. then

22. It's a shame that Tim and Jean and _____ children won't be at the reunion on Saturday.
  a. their
  b. there

Literary Devices

Metaphors

Before we explain what it is, look at this example of a metaphor:

Janie was <u>the heart</u> of the organization: all ideas came from her and circulated back to her for her feedback.

Here *the heart* is a metaphor—Janie was not literally a human heart, but she acted as a heart at the organization. All ideas flowed through her, just as blood is pumped out from and flows back to the heart in the human body.

    A **metaphor** is a word or phrase for one thing that the writer uses to refer to another thing, showing that they are similar.

    Here is another example:

His smile is <u>a ray of sunshine</u> that makes people feel happy, no matter how down they are.

Of course, the smile is not literally made of sunshine. The writer is using the metaphor *a ray of sunshine* to express the positive effect of the person's smile on the people around him.

Similes

Similes are similar to metaphors, but they use the word *like* or *as*. For example:

> His smile is <u>like a ray of sunshine</u>.
> My puppy Waldo is <u>as sweet as a teddy bear</u>.
> Running errands for my boss is <u>as much fun as going to the dentist</u>.

Here's a fourth example, which comes from a very descriptive paragraph in the short story "A Rose for Emily," by William Faulkner:

> Her eyes, lost in the fatty ridges of her face, <u>looked like two small pieces of coal pressed into a lump of dough</u> as they moved from one face to another while the visitors stated their errand.

A Closer Look at Figurative Language

In some passages, the use of figurative language can be much more complicated than in the sentences in the preceding section, but if you break it down, you'll see the hidden meaning.

John F. Kennedy's 1961 inaugural address used figurative language to discuss sophisticated ideas with the audience. In the second paragraph, reprinted here, you can see several examples.

EXCERPT

We dare not forget today that we are the heirs of that first revolution. Let the word go forth from this time and place, to friend and foe alike, that the torch has been passed to a new generation of Americans—born in this century, tempered by war, disciplined by a hard and bitter peace, proud of our ancient heritage—and unwilling to witness or permit the slow undoing of those human rights to which this nation has always been committed, and to which we are committed today at home and around the world.

Let's look at the first sentence:

> We dare not forget today that we are the heirs of that first revolution.

By using the word *heirs*, President Kennedy communicates a deep sense of obligation to the American public listening to him. Hearing that word makes an audience think of family history and connection.

Now, let's look at the second sentence:

> Let the word go forth from this time and place, to friend and foe alike, that the torch has been passed to a new generation of Americans—born in this century, tempered by war, disciplined by a hard and bitter peace, proud of our ancient heritage—and unwilling to witness or permit the slow undoing of those human rights to which this nation has always been committed, and to which we are committed today at home and around the world.

In this (very long) sentence, the image of a flame in the torch suggests the power and intensity of Kennedy's call to action. The metaphor gains even more intensity and atmosphere from the image of an Olympic marathon—the torch has been passed—in which a runner literally passes a lighted torch to the next runner in the relay team.

Before you take the GED® test, practice your grammar skills by building sentences and reviewing how the parts fit together. Engage in active reading, ask yourself questions, and review the language mechanics present in the passages you read. The more you review the information presented in this section, the more successful you will be on the GED® RLA test.

Language and Grammar Review

For questions 23–27, select the correct version of the underlined sentence or portion of a sentence in the passage.

Millennials Take New Approach to Work-Life Balance
—Adapted from an article published on Brandpoint.com

23. More and more, Millennials are on the road for work. In an average month, one in four business-traveling Millennials travels overnight for work at least once per week. As the line between "personal" and "business" grows thinner and thinner for this generation, <u>Millennials are increasingly finding adventure thru business.</u>

  a. Millennials are increasingly finding adventure threw business.

  b. Millennials are increasingly finding adventure through business.

  c. Millennials are increasingly found to have adventure through business.

  d. This is correct as is.

24. More than any other group, Millennial business travelers are likely to add on extra days to their work-related trips for leisure travel (84%), according to the Hilton Garden Inn Discovery and Connection Survey.

  <u>As the economy improves business travel across the nation is on the rise.</u> According to the Global Business Travel Association, U.S. business travel is expected to grow 5.1% in 2013.

  a. As the economy improves, business travel across the nation is on the rise.

  b. As the economy improves business travel, the nation is on the rise.

  c. As the economy improves, business travel across the nation rose.

  d. The sentence is correct as is.

25. As more Millennials hit the road for work, they are keeping top of mind a few simple business travel perks to fulfill their appetite for personal adventure and discovery:

  Fly for free. <u>Those flying for business can earn airline miles in they're name.</u> These business miles quickly add up, allowing travelers to upgrade seats or add another destination without accruing additional cost. Business travelers can then use these miles to bring a friend or loved one on the trip with them—quickly transitioning from business to family vacation or romantic getaway once the weekend hits.

  a. Those flying for business can earn airline miles in there name.

  b. Those flying for business can earn airline miles in your name.

  c. Those flying for business can earn airline miles in their name.

  d. The sentence is correct as is.

26. Earn hotel perks. Frequent stays in hotels offering rewards programs can grant business travelers <u>benefits such as free overnight stays late checkout and complimentary breakfast</u>. These extras turn a business trip into much more, especially when additional nights are used to extend a business trip into a vacation.

   a. benefits such as free overnight stays, late checkout and complimentary breakfast.

   b. benefits such as free overnight stays, late checkout, and complimentary breakfast.

   c. benefits such as free, overnight stays, late checkout, and complimentary, breakfast.

   d. This is correct as is.

27. Millennials continue to be at the forefront of achieving work-life balance <u>by using business travel to discover new cities, taste authentic cuisines, explore different cultures, and connecting with new people across the globe.</u>

   a. by using business travel to discover new cities, taste authentic cuisines, explore different cultures, and connect with new people across the globe.

   b. by using business travel to discover new cities, taste authentic cuisines, explore different cultures, while connecting with new people across the globe.

   c. by using business travel to discovering new cities, tasting authentic cuisines, exploring different cultures, and connecting with new people across the globe.

   d. This is correct as is.

28. Choose the sentence that contains correct capitalization.

   a. She and i are really hoping the Brooklyn Nets do well this year.

   b. She and I are really hoping the Brooklyn Nets do well this Year.

   c. She and I are really hoping the Brooklyn nets do well this year.

   d. She and I are really hoping the Brooklyn Nets do well this year.

29. Select the answer choice that contains correct punctuation.

   a. "I married him because I thought he was a gentleman. I thought he knew something about breeding, but he wasn't fit to lick my shoe." Says Catherine, a character in *The Great Gatsby*.

   b. "I married him because I thought he was a gentleman," Catherine, a character in *The Great Gatsby*, says, "I thought he knew something about breeding, but he wasn't fit to lick my shoe."

   c. "I married him because I thought he was a gentleman," Catherine, a character in *The Great Gatsby*, says. "I thought he knew something about breeding, but he wasn't fit to lick my shoe."

   d. None of the above is correct.

For questions 30 and 31, select the word that best completes the sentence.

30. Melissa's friend asked _____ for a ride home.
   a. they
   b. hers
   c. she
   d. none of the above

31. To _____ are you speaking?
   a. who
   b. whom
   c. when
   d. none of the above

Answers and Explanations

Chapter Practice

1. b. Jill, go lie down while I *lay* out the silver and get the table ready for the party.

2. b. Mira *led* the congregation in song at the memorial service yesterday.

3. b. I plan to pick up my paycheck this afternoon and *then* cash it at the bank on the corner.

4. a. It's a shame that Tim and Jean and *their* children won't be at the reunion on Saturday.

5. Red Rocks *is* their favorite concert venue in Colorado. By itself, the word *rocks* is plural, of course, but *Red Rocks* is a proper noun—it's the name of one specific place in Colorado. Since *Red Rocks* is a singular noun, we need to use *is*.

6. Julio, as well as the rest of the band, **is** excited about performing at Red Rocks. The subject of this sentence is *Julio*, not *Julio, as well as the rest of the band*. Why? The phrase *the rest of the band* is set off with commas as a side point. Since the subject of the sentence, *Julio*, is a singular noun—one person—we need to use *is* (the singular form of the verb *to be*).

7. a. *Visited* is the simple past tense form of the verb *to visit*, which makes sense in this sentence because we know this happened yesterday, not last week or right now.

8. c. When a singular subject and a plural subject are connected by *nor*, the verb must agree with the closer subject—in this case, the plural *cousins*. This choice, *appear*, is the correct verb form for a plural subject.

9. *Whom* are you taking to the dance? Here, the mystery person will be taken to a dance—an action will be performed on him or her. Therefore the mystery person is an object, and we need to use a pronoun that works with objects: *whom*.

10. *Whoever* is making that noise had better quiet down! When deciding whether to use *who/whoever* or *whom/whomever*, you need to ask if the person in question is the subject of the sentence (performing the action) or the object (receiving the action). Here, the mystery person being yelled at is the subject of the sentence—he or she is making the noise—so we need to use *whoever*, a pronoun for subjects. If the person were the object, we'd need to use *whomever*, a pronoun for objects.

11. That man over there is the customer *who* complained about me to my boss. In the second part of the sentence, the customer performed the action—*complained*—so he or she is the subject. We need to use *who*, a pronoun for subjects.

12. **Who** is taking you to the dance? The mystery person here is performing the action—taking you to the dance. Therefore, he or she is the subject. We need to use a pronoun that works with subjects: *who*.

13. b. We need a possessive pronoun that fits with *Joe*—a singular male noun. That is *his*.

14. a. We don't know the gender of the person who forgot to lock up the shoes and gym bag, but we know it is one person (*someone* is singular). As a result, we need to use *his or her* (singular possessive pronouns).

15. b. These possessive pronouns are used correctly and make sense in this sentence.

16. a. *Moving to Nevada* is a dangling modifier. We all know that it was *Shira* who moved to Nevada—the truck didn't move to Nevada. But based on the structure of this sentence, *moving to Nevada* modifies *Shira's truck*. The revision in this choice corrects that problem.

17. c. In the original sentence, the word *only* is in the wrong spot, and this choice moves it to where it belongs, right before *ten minutes*. What's wrong with the original sentence? The word *only* modifies the wrong thing; the sentence says that Tom *only used the treadmill* at the gym. We know that this is not correct, of course. Tom surely did many things at the gym: he must have opened the front door, walked over to the machines, and selected a treadmill; maybe he changed into his gym clothes, drank some water, and said hello to a friend, too.

18. a. The problem with the original sentence is that the phrase *for more than 200 years* modifies the wrong thing—it suggests that the general may have been in disguise for 200 years. This doesn't make any sense—people don't live for 200 years! This choice correctly places *for more than 200 years* right before *historians have wondered*—it's the wondering that's been happening for 200 years.

19. Two members of the band *are* still back at the hotel. What is the subject of this sentence—*Two members* or *the band*? It is *two members*. As a result, we need to use the verb *are*.

20. Everyone *is* supposed to be onstage right now! The word *everyone* may refer to a lot of people, but the word itself is singular. Therefore we need to use *is*.

21. Where *are* Julio and the guitar player? There are two subjects in this sentence: *Julio* and *the guitar player*. Therefore we need to use *are* (the plural form of the verb *to be*).

22. b. Because the sentence includes the phrase *later today*, we know that we need a future verb form. The sentence should read: *Catherine will go to the store later today*.

Language and Grammar Review

23. b. This sentence correctly changes *thru* to *through*, which is the proper spelling.

24. a. It is hard to tell because the underlined sentence is not punctuated properly, but there are really two clauses here. The first clause (*As the economy improves*) is a dependent clause, so it should be joined with a comma to the independent clause that follows (*business travel across the nation is on the rise*).

25. c. The word *they're* should be changed to the possessive pronoun *their*. *They're* is a contraction meaning *they are*.

26. b. This sentence includes a list of three things: (1) *free overnight stays*, (2) *late checkout*, and (3) *complimentary breakfast*. In a series, there should be commas (or semicolons, in special situations) after every item except for the last one. This revision follows that rule.

27. a. The problem with the sentence in the passage is that it contains a series that is not parallel. There is a list of four items, and the first three items are worded in a similar way (*discover . . .* , *taste . . .* , *explore . . .*), but the fourth item is different (*connecting . . .*). This revision corrects the problem. It changes the fourth item, *connecting with new people*, to *connect with new people*, which matches the verb form in the other items. The phrase *connect with new people* also fits grammatically with the first part of the sentence. The phrase *connecting with new people* didn't work. Why? Remove the first three items of the series to see what we were really saying with *connecting*. The sentence would read: *Millennials continue to be at the forefront of achieving work-life balance by using business travel to . . . connecting with new people across the globe*, but this doesn't make any sense.

28. d. The pronoun *I* and the proper noun *Brooklyn Nets* are both correctly capitalized.

29. c. This is correct punctuation and organization of a quote.

30. d. This sentence calls for an object pronoun, explaining whom Melissa's friend asked for a ride. None of the choices are appropriate pronouns.

31. b. Let's rewrite this sentence: *You are speaking to _____.* The speaker (*you*) is the subject—he or she is performing the action of the sentence (talking to someone). What we need here is an object pronoun, for the person being spoken to. *Whom* is an object pronoun and makes sense in this sentence.

REVIEW

In this chapter, you have learned two strategies to help you better comprehend reading materials:

1. Breaking unfamiliar words into word parts, such as prefixes, suffixes, and root words, can be helpful in determining a word's meaning. Thinking of words with similar roots can also help readers figure out the meaning of unknown words.

2. Context clues such as synonyms, antonyms, definitions, and examples can be helpful in figuring out the meanings of unknown words. These clues may be in the same sentence as the unfamiliar word or in the surrounding sentences and paragraph.

C H A P T E R

6 ▶ LANGUAGE AND GRAMMAR: GRAMMAR SKILLS

CHAPTER SUMMARY
This chapter covers GED® test writing tips and strategies that will help you be successful on exam day. You'll learn to recognize and correct errors in sentence structure, usage, mechanics, and organization, as well as identify the purpose of various parts of an essay.

As you've seen in previous chapters, the GED® Reasoning through Language Arts exam tests both reading and writing skills. Don't let that get you worried—the good news is that preparing for one part helps you to prepare for the other. And of course, the more you practice, the better your score will likely be.

GED® Test Strategies

In this chapter, we focus on basic grammar and writing skills. The topics covered include:

- sentence structure
- usage
- mechanics
- organization

In addition, we also go over some GED® test tips and strategies. Together with the information provided in previous chapters, these proven tools for exam success will help you prepare for and excel on test day.

Sentence Construction

Sentence construction refers to the way sentences are created: how we join together subjects, verbs, objects, and other elements to express a complete thought.

Complete Sentences

You can't just string words together to create a sentence. To form a complete sentence, you need to have three basic elements:

1. A **subject**: This is who or what the sentence is about.
2. A **predicate**: This states what the subject is or does.
3. The sentence must express a **complete thought**.

Look at this example:

The phone is ringing.

This is a short but complete sentence. Why? It satisfies the three requirements:

1. It has a subject: *the phone.*
2. It has a predicate: *is ringing.* It explains what the subject is doing.
3. It expresses a complete thought. We know what happened and what was involved.

Now look at these examples:

Sit down.
Don't run.
Give me a break.

Are they complete sentences? Yes. These are very short, complete sentences that command, or tell, someone to do something. You can see that each has a predicate, but where is the subject? When it comes to commands, grammar experts think of the subject as being built into the command—the subject is the person being spoken to. What's important to remember is that commands can stand on their own as real sentences.

If a string of words doesn't have a subject or a predicate, it is a **sentence fragment**. Sentence fragments cannot stand on their own.

Practice

Identify the subject and the predicate of the following sentences.

1. The woman in the lobby is waiting for Mr. Williams.
   Subject: _____
   Predicate: _____

2. Mr. Williams went downstairs.
   Subject: _____
   Predicate: _____

Independent and Dependent Clauses

One of the building blocks of writing is the **clause**: a string of words that includes a subject and a predicate. Some clauses express a complete thought and can stand on their own as sentences. These are called **independent clauses**.

Other clauses, however, express an incomplete thought and cannot stand on their own. These are called **dependent clauses**. They need to be attached to an independent clause in order to fully make sense.

Here are some examples of both types:

Independent clause: *It started snowing.*
Dependent clause: *After Emily won the contest.*

Notice that the first clause expresses a complete idea (it began to snow) and that it is a grammatically correct sentence on its own.

But the dependent clause is incomplete—it's begging for a resolution. (After Emily won the contest, *what happened?*) As is, this clause is not a sentence; it's a sentence fragment. To create a grammatically correct sentence in this case, you can do two things:

- Simply remove the word *after*:
  Emily won the contest.
- Attach the dependent clause to an independent clause using a comma:

After Emily won the contest,	*she jumped up and down in excitement.*
dependent clause	independent clause

Here's another example:

Dependent clause: *That you should avoid eating in order to lose weight.*

As is, it's not a real sentence. To create a real sentence in this case, you can:

- Remove the word *that*:
  You should avoid eating in order to lose weight.
- Attach the dependent clause to an independent clause; for instance:

Potato chips and cookies are two foods	*that you should avoid eating in order to lose weight.*
independent clause	dependent clause

Coordinating Conjunctions

You probably use **coordinating conjunctions** all the time without realizing that they have a name; they are words that are used to connect independent clauses together to create one longer sentence. There are seven coordinating conjunctions: *for, and, nor, but, or, yet,* and *so.* You can use the acronym FANBOYS to remember them.

Here's an example of how they're used:

Independent clause: *It's going to rain this afternoon.*
Independent clause: *I still want to go to the game.*

We can use the coordinating conjunction *but* (plus a comma) to join them together:

It's going to rain this afternoon, but *I still want to go to the game.*

Subordinating Conjunctions

Another way to connect clauses is to use a **subordinating conjunction**—words such as *after, because,* and *unless.*

As an example, let's join together these two independent clauses:

Independent clause: *No one takes out the garbage.*
Independent clause: *It smells horrible in the garage.*

Depending on which conjunction we choose, we'll communicate additional information about the situation in the garage. For example:

It smells horrible in the garage because *no one takes out the garbage.*

By using *because,* we're making the point that the odor is caused by the fact that no one takes out the garbage. If we choose a different conjunction, we'll describe a different scenario and make a different point. For instance:

Even though *it smells horrible in the garage, no one takes out the garbage.*

Here's another example of two independent clauses and ways to connect them:

> **Independent clause:** *Jonathan quit.*
> **Independent clause:** *I had to work overtime.*
> *I had to work overtime* after *Jonathan quit.*
> Because *Jonathan quit, I had to work overtime.*

You may have noticed that when you add a subordinating conjunction to an independent clause, you create a **dependent clause**. For example, in the example just given, *Jonathan quit* is an independent clause. Even though it's just two words, it can function as a real sentence all by itself. But if you add a subordinating conjunction, it no longer can stand on its own as a real sentence. For example, *Because Jonathan quit* is not a complete thought. It prompts the reader to ask, *Because what?*

Here's a list of common subordinating conjunctions:

SUBORDINATING CONJUNCTION	USE	EXAMPLE
because since so that in order that	to show cause and effect or purpose	• We are attending class *because* we want to pass our GED® test. • *Since* I no longer work at Cost Club, I can't receive an employee discount. • I lived next to Beekman Junior College *so that* I could walk to school every day.
before after while when whenever until once as soon as as long as	to show time or time sequence	• *Before* I lived in Mason City, I lived in Des Moines. • I break out in hives *whenever* I eat strawberries. • I can handle the stress at work *as long as* I exercise daily.
though although even though whereas	to show contrast	• Peter passed the test *even though* he was very nervous. • Wendy loves to read books for school, *although* she gets distracted easily. • Jake was horrible at keeping a budget, *whereas* Bob always had his money in order.
if unless whether	to show a condition	• *If* you study hard and come to class, you will succeed. • You cannot take the exam *unless* you have proper identification.
as though as if as much as	to show similarity	• She looked *as though* she had seen a ghost. • *As much as* I want to visit my daughter, I don't think I'll be able to until next year.
where wherever	to show place	• The children want to know *where* their parents used to live.

Practice

Read the two clauses, and then choose which sentence does NOT combine them correctly.

3. **Independent clause:** *I moved to Paris.*
    Independent clause: *I learned how to speak French.*
    a. I moved to Paris, so I learned how to speak French.
    b. After I moved to Paris, I learned how to speak French.
    c. I learned how to speak French after I moved to Paris.
    d. I moved to Paris, wherever I learned how to speak French.

Run-On Sentences

A **run-on sentence** occurs when one independent clause runs right into another independent clause without proper punctuation. Sometimes no punctuation is used at all, while other times there is just a comma between the two thoughts.

Here are some examples of run-on sentences:

> *Terri wants to leave now, she's tired.*
> *Whether or not you believe me it's true I did not lie to you.*

There are several ways to correct this type of error. You can:

- Add a *period*, a *question mark*, or an *exclamation point* to create separate sentences.
- Add a *conjunction* (and a comma, if needed) to join the clauses together.
- Add a *semicolon*, *colon*, or *dash* to join the clauses together.
- *Rewrite* one or more of the clauses.

Here are a few ways to correct the earlier examples:

> *Terri wants to leave now—she's tired.*
> *Terri wants to leave now because she's tired.*
> *Whether or not you believe me, it's true. I did not lie to you!*
> *Whether or not you believe me, it's true; I did not lie to you.*
> *Whether or not you believe me, it's true—I did not lie to you.*

Practice

Select the revision that is NOT a good way to correct the run-on sentence.

4. Greenville is in the middle of nowhere, it's a really boring place to grow up.
    a. Greenville is in the middle of nowhere. It's a really boring place to grow up.
    b. Greenville is a really boring place to grow up; in the middle of nowhere.
    c. Greenville is a really boring place to grow up because it's in the middle of nowhere.
    d. Greenville is a really boring place to grow up—it's in the middle of nowhere.

Complex Sentences

As you learned before, many sentences contain both a dependent clause and an independent clause (they're joined together by the subordinating conjunction that's built into the dependent clause). This type of sentence is called a **complex sentence**. A complex sentence can begin with either the independent clause or the dependent clause. Comma placement depends on how the sentence is constructed.

> *While you were sleeping / , / the thunderstorm came through the city.*
> **Dependent clause / comma / independent clause**

The thunderstorm came through the city / while you were sleeping.

Independent clause / no comma / dependent clause

Because the city received so much snow / , / school will be canceled today.

Dependent clause / comma / independent clause

School will be canceled today / because the city received so much snow.

Independent clause / no comma / dependent clause

Did you notice a pattern with the commas? When the dependent clause is tacked onto the beginning of the independent clause, a comma is needed between the two clauses. When the dependent clause is tacked onto the end of the independent clause, no comma is needed.

You can use this rule when correcting sentences on the GED® test. Be careful to understand what is being said in the sentence you are correcting, however; sometimes the meaning of the sentence or other grammar rules will affect whether you should use a comma.

Which of the following sentences is NOT correctly punctuated?

    a. Even though I ate a huge dinner, I still want to try your macaroni and cheese.
    b. I know it will be really delicious because the chef used so much cheese and cream.
    c. Please don't finish it, before I get to try a spoonful.
    d. If you don't want me to have any, just tell me.

Choice **c** is not correctly punctuated. Here, the sentence starts off with an *independent* clause. There should not be a comma.

Parallel Construction

Before we explain this idea, look at the following example:

> *When Jim was dieting, he would usually eat just brown rice, grilled chicken, salad, and treat himself to nonfat ice cream for dessert.*

Did you notice a problem with this sentence? The problem is that the elements are not all parallel. **Parallelism** is a grammar rule that says that similar elements in a sentence should be written in a similar way.

Here, the similar elements are the four things that Jim WOULD eat when he was dieting. Let's look at them:

    1. brown rice
    2. grilled chicken
    3. salad
    4. treat himself to nonfat ice cream for dessert

You may have noticed that the first three items are parallel—they're all nouns—but the fourth item is different—it's a long phrase that starts off with a verb (*treat*).

There's another problem, too. Look at the words that introduce those four items:

> *When Jim was dieting, he would usually eat just . . .*

Each of the items needs to make sense after that introduction. To test this, just plug in each of the items after the introduction.

For example, the first item makes sense:

> *When Jim was dieting, he would usually eat just brown rice.*

The second item is grammatical, too:

When Jim was dieting, he would usually eat just grilled chicken.

The third item is also grammatical:

When Jim was dieting, he would usually eat just salad.

But the fourth item doesn't make sense after the introduction:

When Jim was dieting, he would usually eat just treat himself to nonfat ice cream for dessert.

There are many ways to fix the original sentence, but here is the most obvious way:

When Jim was dieting, he would usually eat just brown rice, grilled chicken, salad, and nonfat ice cream for dessert.

We deleted *treat himself to.* Now all four items are parallel—they're all nouns.

Practice

5. Select the best revision of this sentence:
   After Tina got her GED, she had to decide whether she was going to apply to colleges, look for a better job, or staying in her current job.
   a. After Tina got her GED, she had to decide whether she was going to apply to colleges, looking for a better job, or staying in her current job.
   b. After Tina got her GED, she had to decide whether she was going to apply to colleges, look for a better job, or in her current job.
   c. After Tina got her GED, she had to decide whether she was going to apply to colleges, look for a better job, or stay in her current job.
   d. The sentence is correct as is.

6. Identify the subject of the following sentence:
   They intend to buy the company this year.
   a. company
   b. this year
   c. They
   d. intend

7. Identify the dependent clause in the following sentence:
   If you think it is a good team, go see the Heat.
   a. If you think it is a good team
   b. go see the Heat
   c. a good team
   d. This sentence has no dependent clause.

8. Identify which of the following is a sentence fragment:
   a. I went.
   b. Who wrote this?
   c. Not going to happen today.
   d. Go away.

9. Select the best revision of the following run-on sentence:
   I'm going away on business, could you please watch the house, I'll be gone this weekend and I'd be most grateful.
   a. I'm going away on business this weekend. Could you please watch the house? I'd be most grateful.
   b. I'm going away on business, could you please watch the house? I'll be gone this weekend, and I'd be most grateful.
   c. I'm going away on business. Could you please watch the house. I'll be gone this weekend. I'd be most grateful.
   d. Could you please watch the house this weekend? I'm going away on business, I'd be most grateful.

10. Select the sentence that is NOT correctly punctuated.
   a. Since I started my new job last year, my life has changed dramatically.
   b. As long as I've been working, I've never really enjoyed what I was doing until now.
   c. It's less about the pay than it is about the people—I get along great with my coworkers.
   d. I'm going to try to keep this job, until I'm old and gray.

Capitalization

After you read certain passages on the GED® test, you'll be asked to fix grammar errors contained in some of the sentences. One of the things you may need to correct is capitalization, so it's important that you learn the rules of when to use capital letters and when to use lowercase letters.

You probably already know that the first letter of the first word of every sentence must be capitalized and that the pronoun *I* should always be a capital letter, but there are many other times when you should use uppercase letters, too.

Titles and Names

Titles such as *Ms.*, *Mrs.*, *Miss*, *Mr.*, and *Dr.* are always capitalized.

Many other words in the English language—nouns such as *mayor*, *judge*, *princess*, and *chairperson*—can serve as a title when placed in front of a person's name. When they are used this way, these words should be capitalized. For example:

> *Secretary of State* John Kerry
> *President* Barack Obama
> *Aunt* Jane

> *Uncle* Tim
> *Queen* Elizabeth
> *Prince* Harry
> *Pope* Francis
> *Judge* Judy
> *Ambassador* Jackson
> *General* Jack Kurutz
> *Private* Benjamin

These words do double duty in the English language. As you can see in the list, they can serve as titles when placed in front of a person's name. But they also often serve as plain old nouns. On the GED® test, don't automatically capitalize words like *president*, *general*, or *king* when you see them. In many cases, they are simply being used as common nouns and should be lowercase. Look at these examples:

> **Used as a title:** *President* Barack Obama
> **Used as a noun:** The *president* of the United States is Barack Obama.
> **Used as a title:** *General* Jack Kurutz
> **Used as a noun:** Jack Kurutz was a heroic *general* in World War II.
> **Used as a noun and as a title:** My favorite *aunt* is *Aunt* Jane.

Proper Nouns

A **proper noun** is a specific person, place, or thing. The names of these people, places, and things should always be capitalized.

Here are some examples of proper nouns and how they should be capitalized:

People	Places	Things/Events/Etc.
Eleanor Roosevelt	United States of America	Philadelphia Eagles
Lady Gaga	China	United Airlines
John F. Kennedy	Los Angeles	Crest
George Bush Sr.	North Fourth Street	Oscar Mayer
Uncle Tim	Central Park	ESPN
Mayor Ed Koch	Union Station	NASA
Queen Elizabeth	Eiffel Tower	Saturn
	Woodside Hospital	Battle of Bunker Hill
		St. Patrick's Day
		Fourth of July
		Car and Driver (the magazine)
		Modern Family (the TV show)
		In the Name of the Father (the movie)
		"Livin' on a Prayer" (the song)

You may have noticed that some of the words in these names—such as *the* and *of*—are *not* capitalized, although we stated earlier that proper nouns should always be capitalized. Why is this?

The rules of capitalization are very detailed—and sometimes the experts differ on what they should be—but in general, in proper names the following words should be lowercase unless they are the first word of the name.

- *the, a, an* (articles)
- *to, from, on, in, of, with*, and other prepositions (some experts capitalize prepositions that have four or more letters)
- *and, but, or, yet* (conjunctions)

Remember that when these words start off the proper noun, they are capitalized, not lowercase. For example: *In Touch* (the magazine), *A Beautiful Mind* (the movie), *For Whom the Bell Tolls* (the book).

Geographical Words

As with other proper names, the names of countries, states, cities, regions, and the like—and the words that are based on them—should be capitalized. For example:

Asia, Asian
Portugal, Portuguese
France, French, Frenchwoman, Frenchman
Great Britain, British
Middle East, Middle Eastern
the South, Southern (referring to those states in the United States)
Antarctica
Rome, Roman
New York City, New Yorker
Morris County

Movies, Books, Songs, and So On

The names of books, movies, plays, TV shows, songs, albums, and the like are another type of proper noun and should be capitalized. The same goes for newspaper headlines, the titles of magazine articles, the titles of essays you write, and more. For example:

> *Romeo and Juliet* (play)
> *Back to the Future* (movie)
> *The Big Bang Theory* (TV show)
> *The Wind in the Willows* (book)
> "Mayor Vows: City Will Bounce Back from Hurricane Sandy" (newspaper headline)
> "Why Violence Is Never the Answer" (magazine article)

Events and Time Periods

As with other proper nouns, specific historical periods and events should be capitalized. Centuries should not be capitalized when used as a regular noun in a sentence, though. Look at these examples:

> the Revolutionary War
> the Great Depression
> the Middle Ages
> The twentieth century marked a turning point in technology.

Directions

Directions on the compass (*west*, *south*, *northeast*, etc.) are considered to be common nouns and are not capitalized.

Directions also sometimes serve as proper names of specific places, however. When used in this way, they should be capitalized, as all proper nouns should be.

For example:

> *The Grand Canyon is one of the biggest tourist attractions in the* Southwest.

Here, *Southwest* means a specific region of the United States—the southwest corner of the country that includes Arizona and New Mexico.

> *The school is five miles* southwest *of Santa Fe.*

Here, *southwest* means the compass direction, so it should be lowercase.

Calendar Items

The days of the week, the months of the year, and holidays all need to be capitalized. (Do not capitalize the seasons unless they are used in a proper name, in a title, or in another way that would require a noun to have an uppercase letter.) Examples:

> *Monday*
> *January*
> *Easter*
> *Fourth of July*
> *summer, fall, winter, spring*

Note this example:

> *The club's Tenth Annual* Winter *Showcase will be held in January.*

In this case, *Winter* is capitalized because it is part of a proper name—the name of a specific event—not because it's a season. The name of the event could just as easily be *Tenth Annual* Talent *Showcase.*

Proper Nouns versus Common Nouns

Here is one more important thing to think about with proper nouns: You'll often find them blended with common nouns—for example, *Crest toothpaste* or *Oscar Mayer hot dogs.*

Notice that *toothpaste* and *hot dogs* are lowercase. Why?

The word *Crest* is a proper noun—it's a brand name—but *toothpaste* is a regular old noun. It should stay lowercase. Similarly, *Oscar Mayer* is a brand name, but *hot dogs* is a common noun, so it should be lowercase.

What if you encounter an example like *United Airlines*? Should *Airlines* be capitalized? Well, this depends on whether or not it is part of the official name of the company. In this case, it is—*United Airlines* is the full, proper name of the business, so *Airlines* should be capitalized.

Just remember: if you know (or can figure out from the passage you're reading) that a word is part of a proper name, it should be capitalized. If it is just a common noun, it should be lowercase.

Now look at these examples of proper nouns blended with common nouns. Note which words are capitalized (the proper noun) and which are lowercase (the common noun):

The Supreme Court *justice gave a speech at the school.*

I have a coupon for a free McDonald's *hamburger.*
The NASA *space shuttle will blast off on Sunday.*

Capitalization in Quotations

When a direct quote is included in a sentence and it's paired with a phrase like *she said*, *they shouted*, *he replied*, or *I wrote* to explain who is doing the talking (or the shouting, replying, or writing), the first word of the quotation should be capitalized.

Here are some examples:

Incorrect: *After dessert, he said quietly, "this was the worst meal of my life."*
Correct: *After dessert, he said quietly, "This was the worst meal of my life."*

Incorrect: *The chef told his assistant, "when you learn how to bake wedding cakes, you will get a raise."*

Correct: *The chef told his assistant, "When you learn how to bake wedding cakes, you will get a raise."*

Incorrect: *When I asked what her costume was, Erica replied, "a scary clown."*
Correct: *When I asked what her costume was, Erica replied, "A scary clown."*

While *A scary clown* is not a complete sentence, it is a complete quote, and it is introduced by the phrase *Erica replied*. Therefore, the first word of the quote should be capitalized.

NOTE

When a quoted sentence is split in two in a sentence, do not capitalize the first word of the second part, unless there is another reason to do so.

To explain this point, let's go back to one of the previous examples:

The chef told his assistant, "When you learn how to bake wedding cakes, you will get a raise."

The sentence can be reworked by splitting the quote in two:

"When you learn how to bake wedding cakes," the chef told his assistant, "you will get a raise."

Note that *you* should still be lowercase. This is because it is a word that is a continuation of a quoted sentence (*"When you learn how to bake wedding cakes, you will get a raise"*); it is not the first word of the quoted sentence.

Here are two more correct examples that make the same point:

> *"When you go on the boat," Carlos told us, "do not feed the sharks."*
> *Carlos told us, "Do not feed the sharks."*

Now look at this final example, to avoid confusion on the GED® test:

> *"Mia is on her way," Mike said. "She just arrived at the bus station."*

Why should *She* be capitalized? Because this is not a case of a quoted sentence being split up. Instead, there are two complete, separate sentences.

Note that the first sentence ends in a period.

> *"Mia is on her way," Mike said.*

and

> *"She just arrived at the bus station."*

She should be capitalized because it's the first word of a sentence, even though that sentence happens to be a quote.

Using Apostrophes to Create Possessive Nouns and Contractions

In English, apostrophes are an important tool that can help you create possessive words (*the dog's house, Aunt Jane's car*) as well as contractions (*they're, it's*). This lesson explains how and when to use apostrophes.

Possessive Nouns

A **possessive noun** shows the ownership that the noun has over something else. To make a noun possessive, add the following to the end of the word:

- **For most singular nouns:** Add an apostrophe and the letter *s*.
- **For most plural nouns:** Add just an apostrophe.

Look at these examples:

> Anthony's office
> the child's blanket
> the two brothers' toys
> the ladies' room
> the dog's bones [one dog has bones]
> the dogs' bones [two or more dogs have bones]

NOTE

Some plural nouns do not end in *s*, such as *children*, *women*, *mice*, and *deer*. In these cases, add an apostrophe and an *s*:
> the children's books
> the mice's cheese

When you are editing a sentence that contains a possessive noun, you will need to decide if it is singular or plural. The best way to do this is to read the entire sentence for clues.

A Mistake to Avoid

Here are some examples of a basic grammar mistake that many people make and that may be tested on the GED® test:

> **Incorrect:** *The* boy's *are building a treehouse.*
> **Incorrect:** *I just adopted two* puppy's.

What's the problem with these sentences? In each, the writer tried to make a plural word by using an apostrophe and the letter *s*. Look at the correct versions:

Correct: *The* boys *are building a treehouse.*
Correct: *I just adopted two* puppies.

There is no need for an apostrophe when a noun is plural. Use apostrophes when you make nouns possessive (for instance, *the* boys' *treehouse, the* puppies' *adoption*), not when you simply make nouns plural (*the* boys *have a treehouse, the* puppies *were adopted*).

Contractions

A **contraction** refers to the process of joining together two words to create one shorter word. An apostrophe replaces the letter(s) removed in the process.

The following is a list of common contractions:

aren't = are not	let's = let us	weren't = were not
can't = cannot	mightn't = might not	what'll = what will; what shall
couldn't = could not	mustn't = must not	what're = what are
didn't = did not	shan't = shall not	what's = what is; what has
doesn't = does not	she'd = she had; she would	what've = what have
don't = do not	she'll = she will; she shall	where's = where is; where has
hadn't = had not	she's = she is; she has	who'd = who had; who would
hasn't = has not	shouldn't = should not	who'll = who will; who shall
haven't = have not	that's = that is; that has	who's = who is; who has
he'd = he had; he would	there's = there is; there has	who've = who have
he'll = he will; he shall	they'd = they had; they would	won't = will not
he's = he is; he has	they'll = they will; they shall	wouldn't = would not
I'd = I had; I would	they're = they are	you'd = you had; you would
I'll = I will; I shall	they've = they have	you'll = you will; you shall
I'm = I am	we'd = we had; we would	you're = you are
I've = I have	we're = we are	you've = you have
isn't = is not	we've = we have	

For practice, replace the underlined words with the correct contractions.

<u>Do not</u> forget that <u>we are</u> right around the corner if you <u>cannot</u> find the keys.

Answer: *Don't* forget that *we're* right around the corner if you *can't* find the keys.

The contraction of *do not* is *don't*, the contraction of *we are* is *we're* (NOT *were*!), and the contraction of *cannot* is *can't*.

Contractions versus Possessive Pronouns

In English, there are a few contractions that are pronounced the same as a few possessive pronouns, and many people mistake these words. You may see questions on the GED® test that assess whether you know the difference.

Here's an example:

Correct: *The dog hurt its paw.*
Incorrect: *The dog hurt it's paw.*

The second sentence is incorrect because *it's* is a contraction of *it is*. That means that the sentence really says *The dog hurts it is paw*, which does not make any sense.

Here are some words that people commonly confuse:

Contraction	Possessive Pronoun
it's (it is)	its
you're (you are)	your
they're (they are)	their
who's (who is)	whose

REMEMBER

Contractions *always* use apostrophes. Possessive pronouns *never* use apostrophes.

An easy way to remember this is to think about what a contraction really is: in casual speech, we sometimes slide two words together, making one word. (*You are* becomes *you're*; *would not* becomes *wouldn't*; and so on.) In the process of sliding the words together, we drop out one or two of the letters. The apostrophe replaces the letter(s) that dropped out. (When we contract *you are* to make *you're*, we drop the *a*. The apostrophe replaces that *a*.)

Practice

11. Select the grammatically correct sentence.
    a. We're going to stay at my familys house.
    b. We're going to stay at my family's house.
    c. We're going to stay at my families house.
    d. Were going to stay at my family's house.

12. Select the grammatically correct sentence.
    a. Toms sister wasn't planning to come to his childrens' graduation.
    b. Tom's sister wasnt planning to come to his childrens' graduation.
    c. Tom's sister wasn't planning to come to his children's graduation.
    d. none of the above

13. Select the grammatically correct sentence.
    a. You're not going to fix that cars problems without the proper tools.
    b. Your not going to fix that cars problem's without the proper tools.
    c. You're not going to fix that cars' problems without the proper tools.
    d. none of the above

Sentence Punctuation

Proper punctuation marks are necessary when writing complete and correct sentences.

End Marks

A complete sentence must end with correct punctuation. The punctuation at the end of the sentence depends on what type of sentence it is.

1. A statement ends with a period.
   Minnesota is known for its cold winters.
2. A question ends with a question mark.
   Do you think it will snow tonight?
3. An exclamation—that is, a sentence with strong emotion—ends with an exclamation point.
   Call the police!

Commas

Commas are used to indicate breaks in different parts of a sentence. People are often confused about when to use a comma—it is common to place too many commas in a sentence. The following list outlines comma rules for standard English:

1. Use commas to separate three or more items in a **series** that includes the word *and* or *or*.
   > *I lost my wallet, my gloves, and my car keys all on one day.*
   > *Add ketchup, mayonnaise, or mustard to the sandwich.*
   > *Bring the paperwork, three forms of ID, and a photo to the office.*

   Note that the comma is placed **before** *and* or *or*, not after it.

   Do not use a comma when only two items are joined by *and* or *or*. That is not a series, so it doesn't need a comma.

   Incorrect: *Bring the paperwork, and three forms of ID to the office.*
   Correct: *Bring the paperwork and three forms of ID to the office.*

2. Use a comma after an introductory phrase. An **introductory phrase** can be a prepositional phrase that begins a sentence.
   > *In the end, Jamie was glad she had worked all weekend painting her room.*
   > *After hearing the weather report, the boss moved the company picnic indoors.*

3. Use a comma before a coordinating conjunction that joins two independent clauses. An **independent clause** contains a subject and a verb and would function as a grammatically correct sentence if it stood alone. Examples of coordinating conjunctions that join independent clauses are *and, but, or, nor, for, so,* and *yet.*
   > *I wanted to go to the movies,* but *I didn't have enough money to pay for the ticket.*

   > *William completed the computer training, so* he decided to apply for a new job.

4. Use commas to separate an appositive from the rest of the sentence if it is a **nonrestrictive appositive** that gives information about something mentioned in the sentence but it is not essential to the core meaning or grammar of the sentence. Do not use commas with restrictive appositives (e.g., *the poet Robert Burns*).
   > *Renita, the tall girl down the hall, will pick up my mail while I am on vacation.*
   > *The office will be closed on Friday, the last day of the month.*

5. Use a comma when a dependent clause comes before the independent clause.
   > *After I complete my degree, I plan to move to Los Angeles.*
   > *If you are sick, you must contact your supervisor.*

6. Use a comma to separate the year in a date.
   > *March 14, 2008, is my daughter's birthday.*

7. Use commas to separate a state name from a city name (or a country name from a city name, etc.).
   > *Kansas City, Kansas, is my birthplace.*
   > *I'd love to visit my friends in Alberta, Canada, next year.*
   > *The flight began in Beijing, China, stopped in Osaka, Japan, and arrived 12 hours later in San Francisco, California.*

Practice

14. Select the best revision of the sentence below:
    Larry my friend from high school lives next door.
    a. Larry, my friend from high school lives next door.
    b. Larry, my friend from high school lives, next door.
    c. Larry, my friend from high school, lives next door.
    d. The sentence is correct as is.

Semicolons and Colons

A **semicolon** (;) can be used to join two independent clauses. Joining two independent clauses this way suggests that the two clauses are related in meaning and of equal importance.

> *Every Friday we go out for dinner and see a movie; it is our reward for a long week at work.*

There are several instances when a **colon** (:) can be used in a sentence.

1. Use a colon after an independent clause to introduce a list.
   > *Travis requested his favorite meal for his birthday: pizza, cheese bread, and ice cream.*
2. Use a colon after an independent clause to introduce a quotation.
   > *Emily explained her reason for leaving the magazine: "It's a dead-end job, no matter how hard I work."*
3. Use a colon between two independent clauses when you want to emphasize the second clause.
   > *The result of the poll was clear: Obama would probably win the election.*

Quotation Marks

Quotation marks are used around direct quotes—that is, the words a person or character says. For example:

> *Uncle John said, "It has been years since I have seen my sister's children."*
> *"I refuse to pay for this meal," Laura shouted, "because there is a bug in my salad!"*

Put punctuation marks before the first quotation mark and inside of the final quotation mark.

Quotation marks are also used around the names of poems, song titles, short stories, magazine or newspaper articles, essays, speeches, chapter titles, and other short works. (Titles of movies, books, TV series, etc. are usually set in italics.)

> *Her daughter would not stop singing "Row, Row, Row Your Boat" as they drove to the lake.*
> *My favorite poem is "Wild Geese," by Mary Oliver.*

Practice

Select the best revision of the following sentences.

15. Do you think Ted remembered his book, pen, and paper?
    a. Do you think Ted remembered his: book, pen, and paper?
    b. Do you think Ted remembered his book, pen and paper?
    c. Do you think Ted remembered his book; pen; and paper?
    d. The sentence is correct as is.

16. He was born in February 1994 at the main hospital in Duluth Minnesota.
    a. He was born in February 1994 at the main hospital in Duluth, Minnesota.
    b. He was born in February, 1994, at the main hospital in Duluth Minnesota.
    c. He was born in February, 1994 at the main hospital in Duluth, Minnesota.
    d. The sentence is correct as is.

17. My mother said, "I like vacationing in three states: Texas New Mexico and Arizona."
    a. My mother said, "I like vacationing in three states, Texas, New Mexico, and Arizona.
    b. My mother said, I like vacationing in three states: Texas, New Mexico, and Arizona.
    c. My mother said, "I like vacationing in three states: Texas, New Mexico, and Arizona."
    d. The sentence is correct as is.

Sentence Structure

Active and Passive Voice

Active and passive voice refers to the way you write about the subject and verb. If the subject is known and is doing the action, it's an active voice. If the subject is unknown or is not doing the action, it's a passive voice.

This concept is much easier to understand with an example. Look at the following sentence:

Barry hit the ball.

Barry is the subject and he's the one doing the action. That means the sentence is written in an active voice. What if we write the following:

The ball was hit by Barry.

Now *the ball* is the subject, but it's not doing anything; something is being done to it. The subject is no longer active, so the sentence is written in a passive voice.

Generally speaking, you should use the active voice, rather than the passive voice, when you write. The GED® test will likely include some questions that test your ability to identify the passive voice and to change it to an active voice.

Usage

Throughout the history of the English language, people have developed conventional ways of speaking that enable them to understand each other. These conventions are referred to as usage. On the GED® test, usage questions commonly test the following concepts:

- verb conjugation
- verb tense
- subject–verb agreement

Subject–Verb Agreement

As previously mentioned, a subject and verb are said to *agree* when they are either both plural or both singular. Usually, to make a noun plural you add an *-s*, and to make a verb plural you take an *-s* away. For example:

The dog growls.

or

The dogs growl.

On the GED® test, you're likely to see questions that will test common errors in subject–verb agreement. Here are a few common mistakes to watch out for:

- **doesn't/don't.** Incorrect: *He don't want to go.* Correct: *He doesn't want to go.*
- **wasn't/weren't.** Incorrect: *The pens wasn't in the drawer when I looked.* Correct: *The pens weren't in the drawer when I looked.*
- **there's/there are.** Incorrect: *There's a lot of people here.* Correct: *There are a lot of people here.*
- **here's/here are.** Incorrect: *Here's the instructions.* Correct: *Here are the instructions.*

Mechanics

In reference to writing, the term *mechanics* refers to the little things that make your writing look like it should: capitalization, spelling, and punctuation. Using correct mechanics may not change the substance of your writing; that is, a word may mean the same thing whether it's capitalized or not. Correct mechanics will change how your writing is perceived.

Organization

Organization refers to placing sentences and paragraphs in order so that the reader can best understand what you're trying to say in your writing. An organized paragraph typically includes one topic sentence, placed either at the beginning or at the end of the paragraph, and a few supporting sentences. An organized essay includes an introduction with a strong thesis statement, two or more body paragraphs, and a conclusion.

There are several common ways of organizing supporting sentences and paragraphs in an essay. Three of the most common are:

1. chronological order
2. order of importance
3. cause and effect

Chronological Order

Chronological order is the order in which things happen in time; in other words, what happens first, next, and last. If you were telling a story, giving instructions, or relating an event in your essay, you would probably do well to write in chronological order.

A common mistake made by beginning writers is to skip around in time. For example, when telling about a football game, one might write:

> *Our team got a touchdown! The running back got the ball at the 48 yard line and ran it all the way to the end zone. The coach told the quarterback to go long, but instead he handed it off to the running back.*

As you can see, this is not the order in which things actually happened; that is, it's not written in chronological order and may be confusing to some. A

more organized way to write the paragraph would be as follows:

> *The coach told the quarterback to go long, but instead he handed the ball off to the running back at the 48 yard line. Then the running back ran the ball all the way to the end zone. At last our team got a touchdown!*

Telling what happens first, next, and last—in that order—helps the reader keep track of what you're writing about.

TRANSITION WORDS

Transition words help readers know the direction you're going in your writing. Common transition words for chronological order include: *first, to begin, next, then, afterward, last,* and *finally.*

Order of Importance

To organize your writing based on order of importance means to put sentences or paragraphs in order from most to least important, or from least to most important. For example, let's say you're telling a coworker about your rotten weekend. Three terrible things happened to you: you lost your hat, you stubbed your toe, and you were very ill. Assuming that your illness is the most important event and losing your hat is the second most important event, you might tell the story like this:

> *This was a terrible weekend. I stubbed my toe so badly that now I can hardly walk. Even worse, on Saturday night I lost my hat. Worst of all, when I came home Saturday night I got violently ill!*

On the GED® test, you'll be expected to know when sentences or paragraphs are in the wrong order. Look for key words like *more/most*, *worse/worst*, and *better/best* to determine what order things should be in.

Cause and Effect

Cause and effect is an organizational style that either puts the entire cause of an event first, and then the effect, or vice versa. The key to this method is to be sure that the two are entirely separated and clear. For example, let's say you got in a car wreck because a deer ran out in front of you. You might write something like this:

> *(1) Last week, I had to get my front bumper replaced. (2) I also had to get my windshield replaced and the front tires realigned. (3) All this trouble came into my life because I ran into a deer last Monday.*

As you can see, the two sentences describing the effect are together at the beginning of the paragraph, while the sentence describing the cause is at the end. The paragraph would not be as well organized if you moved sentence (3) in front of sentence (2), thereby interrupting the organizational flow.

Quiz

Now that you've had a chance to review the writing skills needed to do well on the GED® test, give the following questions a try. Read each question, and then choose the one best answer for each.

18. Sentence (1): Every time my brother takes a shower, he leave a huge mess.
    Which revision should be made to sentence (1)?
    a. replace *Every* with *All*
    b. change *takes* to *take*
    c. change *leave* to *leaves*
    d. replace *mess* with *messy*

19. Sentence (1) I used to enjoy going out to dance. (2) When I was younger.
    Which revision should be made to sentence (2)?
    a. delete sentence (2) and add a sentence about dancing
    b. move sentence (2) in front of sentence (1) and add the word *However*
    c. add *for example* to the beginning of sentence (2) and *instead of* at the end of sentence (1)
    d. connect the sentences by removing the period at the end of sentence (1) and set *When* in lowercase

20. Sentence (1) She ate the cake. (2) Which the king had poisoned.
    Which revision should be made to sentence (2)?
    a. delete the word *which*
    b. change the word *Which* to *That*
    c. connect sentences with a comma instead of a period and set *Which* in lowercase
    d. add the word *And* to the beginning of the sentence

21. Sentence (1): Three of us began the race, however, only two of us finished it.

Which revision should be made to sentence (1)?

a. move *Three of us began the race* to the end of the sentence

b. change the first comma to a period and capitalize *however*

c. delete *however* and replace with *because*

d. change *however* to *nevertheless*

22. Sentence (1): The car was smashed by a cement mixer.

Which revision should be made to sentence (1)?

a. delete *was*

b. place a period after *smashed*

c. move *cement mixer* in front of *car*

d. change the order to *A cement mixer smashed the car*

23. Sentence (1): The last time I went to see my friend in Dallas, he's living on the south side.

Which of the following revisions should be made to sentence (1)?

a. delete *The*

b. change the comma to a period and capitalize *he's*

c. change *he's* to *he was*

d. move *he's living on the south side* to the beginning of the sentence

For questions 24 through 26, read the sentences and then choose the best answer.

(1) Last week I had too get my front bumper replaced. (2) I also has to get my windshield replaced and the front tires realigned. (3) All this trouble came into my life, because I ran into a deer last Monday.

24. Which of the following revisions should be made to sentence (1)?

a. move *Last week* to the end of the sentence

b. change *too* to *to*

c. delete the word *front*

d. change *has* to *had*

25. Sentence (2): I also has to get my windshield replaced and the front tires realigned.

Which of the following revisions should be made to sentence (2)?

a. delete *also*

b. change *has* to *had*

c. add a comma after *replaced*

d. add a semicolon after *and*

26. Sentence (3): All this trouble came into my life, because I ran into a deer last Monday.

Which of the following revisions should be made to sentence (3)?

a. delete the comma after *life*

b. move *because I ran into a deer last Monday* to the beginning of the sentence

c. add a comma after *deer*

d. change *Monday* to *monday*

27. Which of the following should a good introduction do?

a. summarize the essay

b. develop the argument

c. get the reader's attention

d. leave the reader with a sense of closure

Answers and Explanations

Chapter Practice

1. **Subject:** *the woman*; **Predicate:** *is waiting for Mr. Williams.* This is a complete sentence: it expresses a complete idea and includes a subject and a predicate. Note that the subject is *the woman*, not *the lobby*—the lobby isn't waiting for Mr. Williams.

2. **Subject:** *Mr. Williams*; **Predicate:** *went downstairs.* This is a complete sentence: It expresses a complete idea and includes a subject and a predicate.

3. **d.** This sentence uses a subordinating conjunction—*wherever*—but *wherever* doesn't make sense here. Here is a better use of *wherever* to combine two clauses: *Wherever I go with Andy, he always seems to know someone.*

4. **b.** This revision tries to blend the clauses together with a semicolon, but in the process it chops out some key words. By itself, *in the middle of nowhere* is not a clause and it doesn't make sense tacked on at the end with a semicolon.

5. **c.** The problem with the original sentence is that it contains a series (*apply to colleges, look for a better job, or staying in her current job*), but the series is not parallel. The third item (*staying in her current job*) doesn't fit with the first two, and it also doesn't make sense with the phrase that introduces the series (*she had to decide whether she was going to . . .*). This revision is correct because the third item has been fixed— it is now similar to the other two items (it starts off with the correct verb form, *stay*), and it makes sense logically in the sentence.

6. **c.** In this sentence, *They* identifies who or what is performing the action. It is therefore the subject of the sentence.

7. **a.** The first part of this sentence, *If you think it is a good team*, would be a fragment if it stood alone. It makes us wonder, okay, if we think the Heat is a good team, *then what?* It needs an additional thought to form a complete sentence.

8. **c.** *Not going to happen today* is a sentence fragment because it's missing a subject and a proper verb. If we add these elements, we can turn it into a complete sentence. For example: *The meeting is not going to happen today.*

9. **a.** This revision combines the first clause (*I'm going away on business*) and the third clause (*I'll be gone this weekend*) into one complete sentence. This is a good idea, because these clauses communicate related ideas—they provide the background information that the speaker wants the listener to know before he or she asks for a favor. This choice also turns *could you please watch the house* into its own sentence by capitalizing *could* and adding a question mark (all questions should end with a question mark). The last sentence is now its own sentence, too.

10. **d.** This sentence starts off with an independent clause and ends with a dependent clause. There is no reason for the comma.

11. **b.** Both *We're* (meaning *We are*) and the possessive *family's* are spelled correctly.

12. **c.** The possessives *Tom's* and the possessive *children's* are spelled correctly, as is *wasn't* (a contraction meaning *was not*).

13. **d.** The sentence should read: *You're not going to fix that car's problems without the proper tools.*

14. **c.** In this sentence, the phrase *my friend from high school* is a nonrestrictive appositive: it gives additional information about the subject, Larry, but is not essential to the meaning of the sentence (that he lives next door). Commas are always used to set off nonrestrictive appositives from the rest of the sentence.

15. **d.** The sentence is correctly punctuated as is.

16. a. There is no reason for commas in the date *February 1994* (a month and year), but there should be a comma between the city and state (*Duluth, Minnesota*).

17. c. This sentence requires a comma to set off the quote, quotation marks to surround the quote, a colon to introduce the list of three states (because it comes after an independent clause, *I like vacationing in three states*), and commas after the words *Texas* and *New Mexico*.

Quiz

18. c. The subject and verb must agree. The singular subject, *he*, requires a singular verb.

19. d. By itself, sentence (2) is a fragment. Connecting it to sentence (1) makes it a dependent clause of a complete sentence.

20. c. By itself, sentence (2) is a fragment. Connecting it to sentence (1) makes it part of a complete sentence.

21. b. When the word *however* is used between two clauses, you can place either a period or a semicolon at the end of the first clause.

22. d. It is preferable that sentences use an active voice rather than a passive voice. By changing the order of the words, you can have the subject be the thing doing the action.

23. c. The beginning of the sentence is written in the past tense, so the end of the sentence must also be in past tense. *He's*, which is a contraction for *he is*, is present tense.

24. b. *Too* and *to* are homonyms. *Too* means also, and is not the correct word in this sentence.

25. b. The verb *has* does not agree with the subject *I*, and also shifts the passage from past to present tense. Replacing *has* with *had* corrects these issues.

26. a. A comma is not needed in this sentence.

27. c. The purpose of an introduction is to introduce the topic and catch the reader's attention. This is your chance to make the reader want to continue reading your essay.

REVIEW

Sentence structure refers to the way words are put together to create sentences. It includes the following concepts:

- **Subjects and predicates.** A subject is who or what the sentence is about; a predicate is the verb and everything that comes after it. Every complete sentence has a subject and a predicate.
- **Independent and dependent clauses.** A clause is a group of words that includes a subject and a predicate. An independent clause is a complete sentence; a dependent clause is not complete on its own.
- **Fragments and run-ons.** A fragment is an incomplete sentence; a run-on is two complete sentences joined together with a comma or no punctuation at all.
- **Active and passive voice.** In an active voice, the subject of a sentence is doing the action. In a passive voice, the action is being done to the subject.

Usage refers to the rules that determine how words should be used in sentences. It includes the following concept:

- **Subject–verb agreement.** A verb should be made singular or plural to match its subject.

Mechanics are the nuts and bolts of writing, including punctuation, capitalization, and spelling. In regard to punctuation, one of the most important things to study is comma rules. In regard to spelling, you'll need to learn how to use homonyms correctly.

Organization refers to the way sentences and paragraphs are placed in order. There are three major types of organization:

- **Chronological order.** Events are written in the order in which they occurred in time.
- **Order of importance.** Sentences and paragraphs are written in order from least to most important, or vice versa.
- **Cause and effect.** Everything having to do with the cause is written separately from everything having to do with the effect.

On the GED® Test Reasoning through Language Arts (RLA) Review, you'll be expected to know when sentences or paragraphs are in the wrong order.

C H A P T E R

7 ▶ THE EXTENDED RESPONSE ESSAY: TIPS AND SCORING

CHAPTER SUMMARY
In this chapter, you'll learn how to recognize the parts of an effective essay. You'll also learn how to use the basic steps of the writing process to plan and draft an effective essay in response to a given prompt.

About the GED® Test Extended Response Question

The GED® Reasoning through Language Arts test features one extended response item that requires you to write a short essay in response to a reading passage or pair of passages. These reading passages are between 550 and 650 words, and will focus on presenting arguments or viewpoints along with supporting evidence. Your job will be to analyze these arguments and evidence, incorporating your own knowledge and views while still focusing mainly on the author and his or her intent. Your extended response should always include evidence presented within the passage itself as the main basis for your arguments. You should also analyze or evaluate the validity of the evidence presented in the passage. Note that this test item is not about choosing the "right" or "wrong" side of an issue. It is intended to test your ability to understand, analyze, and evaluate arguments.

Before you take the GED® RLA test, practice your typing skills. On exam day, you will have a lot to say, and you don't want to waste part of your 45 minutes hunting for letters on the keyboard. A good goal for taking the GED® RLA test is to be comfortable typing sentences on a computer. When you practice essay writing, set a timer for yourself so you can see what it feels like to type with the clock ticking.

Before You Write Your Essay

Producing a great essay for the GED® test requires a step-by-step process, and many of those steps take place *before* you write it. Take the time to work through this lesson, and you'll have a good foundation for writing your best essay on test day.

ERASABLE WHITEBOARDS

When you take the GED® test, you will be provided with an erasable whiteboard to jot down notes. These are especially useful during the extended response question, as you prepare to write your essay. If you need additional whiteboards during testing, you can request a fresh one and turn in the one that you've already used. You are allowed to have only one whiteboard at a time.

Understanding the Prompt

Writing an extended response essay requires you not only to analyze the passage(s) but also to respond to a specific prompt. Take a look at this sample prompt:

PROMPT

In the following article, the pros and cons of wearing school uniforms are discussed. In your response, analyze both positions to determine which view is better supported. Use relevant and specific evidence from the passage to support your response.

Type your response in the box; you will have approximately 45 minutes to complete it.

To understand exactly what you're being asked to write about, carefully read the prompt and identify:

- **The issue** (*pros and cons of wearing school uniforms*)
- **The description of what you are asked to do** (*analyze both positions; determine which view is better supported; use relevant and specific evidence from the passage to support your response*)
- **Instructions for completing the task** (*type your response in the box; you will have approximately 45 minutes to complete it*)

Reading the Passage(s)

There's a natural tendency to want to rush into writing the essay—that's what you are being tested on, after all—and to skimp on reading the passage(s). Avoid doing this. The only way to produce a good essay is to read the passage(s) carefully, understand it/them, and pull out what you will need when you write.

Follow these **five steps** as you read the passage(s). At the end of the process, you will have good information and ideas to use as you write your essay.

1. Before you start to read, **scan the passage(s)** to get a sense of what the passage(s) is/are about and note how the information is organized.
2. **Read the passage(s).** Because you know you will definitely have to respond, as you read try to relate the information in the passage(s) to your own life experiences.
3. As you read, use your whiteboard to **write down questions** that you have about the content.
4. **Determine the author's main argument**, and write that down. Then quickly outline the main points that the author makes to support that argument and restate them in your own words.
5. **Evaluate the author's argument.** Did he or she provide good support or enough evidence for it? Why or why not? Does the way the author writes affect you emotionally? Why or why not?

What's in an Essay

An **essay** is a short piece of nonfiction writing that presents the writer's point of view on a particular subject. Remember, *short* is a relative term; in this case, it basically means *shorter than a book*. An essay can actually be as short as a paragraph or two, or as long as 50 pages. On the GED® test, you'll want to shoot for a four or five paragraph essay.

Every essay has three main parts: an **introduction**, a **body**, and a **conclusion**, also known as a **beginning**, **middle**, and **end**. In a five-paragraph essay, the first paragraph is the introduction, the last paragraph is the conclusion, and the three paragraphs in the middle are the body.

The Introduction

The *introduction* is the first paragraph in an essay. In a five-paragraph essay such as the one you'll be writing for the GED® test, the introduction is usually about three or four sentences long. It has three main purposes:

- state the main idea of the essay
- catch the reader's attention
- set the tone for the rest of the essay

Stating the Main Idea

A **main idea** is the main thing the writer wants the reader to know. The main idea of a paragraph is stated in the **topic sentence**, and the topic sentence is often the first sentence of the paragraph. Like a paragraph, an essay has a main idea. It is stated in a single sentence called the **thesis statement**, which is generally the last sentence of the introduction.

On the GED® test, your thesis statement should be a clear, concise answer to the prompt. For example, a possible thesis sentence for a sample prompt asking what you would choose if you could relive one day of your life might be as follows:

> *If I could do one thing in my life again, I would relive my wedding day.*

This is a good thesis statement because it clearly answers the question in the prompt. It also presents the main idea of the essay without trying to tell the reader too much at once.

Catching the Reader's Attention

In addition to containing the thesis statement, a good introduction starts off with a couple of sentences that catch the reader's attention. Obviously, the content of these sentences will vary widely depending on your thesis statement. A possible introduction based on the sample thesis statement provided might look something like this:

> *What if you could live one day of your life over again? Some people might choose to relive a day in order to change something about their lives. Others might simply want a second chance to enjoy a great experience. If I could do one thing in my life again, I would relive my wedding day.*

As you can see, the three sentences at the beginning of the paragraph lead into the thesis statement in a relatively engaging way. It might not be *Harry Potter*, but it's definitely better than the following approach:

> *This is my paper about the thing I would like to do over again in my life. I would like to live my wedding day over again.*

The people who grade GED® test extended responses read dozens, perhaps even hundreds of essays written from the same prompt. An essay with a clear, creative introduction will almost certainly earn a higher score than an introduction that merely states what the essay is supposed to be about.

Setting the Tone for the Essay

Finally, a good introduction sets the tone for the rest of the essay. **Tone** refers to the attitude the writer takes toward the subject and the reader. For example, your tone might be formal, informal, humorous, ironic, aggressive, or apologetic. The tone you choose depends to some extent on your purpose for writing. For example, if your purpose is to amuse the reader, your tone will be humorous.

On the GED® test, it is a good idea to use a formal tone. That means using standard English vocabulary and grammar, rather than casual slang such as you might use with a friend. You should strive to use complete sentences with correct grammar and punctuation, and to keep contractions (words like *can't*, *don't*, and *won't*) to a minimum. Using a formal tone in your writing shows respect for your readers while proving that you are able to write correctly.

To better understand the difference between formal and informal tone, take a look at the following examples. The first example is written using an informal tone. The second uses a formal tone. In both examples the thesis statement is bold so that you can easily locate it.

Example 1: *You know, living your life over again would be like a dream. I guess some people would want to go back and try to change something they messed up the first time, and some people would probably just want to relive a day when they did something really cool.* **I would totally do my wedding day again.**

Example 2: *What if you could live one day of your life over again? Some people might choose to relive a day in order to change something about their lives. Others might simply want a second chance to enjoy a great experience.* **If I could do one thing in my life again, I would relive my wedding day.**

While the first example may be a more accurate representation of how people speak, it is not an acceptable way to write an academic essay. The second example uses a tone that is appropriate to academic writing. You will be expected to write using a similar tone on the GED® test.

Notice that in both introductions the thesis statement is the last sentence of the paragraph. You should strive to structure your introductions in the same way. Just as businesspeople generally chat for a few minutes before getting down to business, a good writer strives to get the reader's attention before stating the essay's main idea.

Now you try it. Using the space below, draft and write *an introduction only* in response to the following prompt:

What is your favorite thing? Whether it is a gift you were given during your childhood or something you saved up for years for and bought, you probably have something that is special to you. Write about this special object and why it is important to you.

Introduction:

_____

_____

_____

_____

_____

The Body

The *body* is the part of the essay where you develop and defend your argument. Like the essay itself, the body can range from a single paragraph to many pages in length. For the purposes of the GED® test, however, the body of your essay should be two or three paragraphs long.

You have learned that each paragraph must have a topic sentence stating the main idea of the paragraph. As previously mentioned, it's a good idea to make the topic sentence the first sentence of the paragraph so that your reader knows right away what the paragraph is going to be about.

The following paragraph is an example of a body paragraph that might follow the sample introduction on reliving one's wedding day:

> *Reliving my wedding day would give me the opportunity to see my family together again. It was the only day of my life when my mom's and my dad's families came together to celebrate in one place. Furthermore, my*

wedding day was the last time I saw my grandfather because he passed away a few weeks later.

The first sentence is the topic sentence and states the main idea of the paragraph—that reliving the wedding day would allow the writer to see his or her family together again. The other sentences support the main idea by providing examples of how the family was united that day. As a whole, the paragraph develops the main idea of the essay, which is that the writer would like to experience his or her wedding day again.

It's your turn. Using the space provided, write a thesis and body paragraph that explores the following prompt.

> *What is your favorite thing? Whether it is a gift you were given during your childhood or something you saved up for years for and bought, you probably have something that is special to you. Write about this special object and why it is important to you.*

Your thesis:

_____

_____

Body paragraph:

_____

_____

_____

_____

_____

THE EXTENDED RESPONSE ESSAY: TIPS AND SCORING

The Conclusion

The *conclusion* is the final paragraph of the essay. A good conclusion should accomplish the following things:

1. restate the main idea
2. give the reader a sense of closure

Restating the Main Idea

The purpose of restating the main idea in the conclusion is twofold; first, it reminds the reader of the most important thing you want him or her to remember. Second, it gives the essay a more unified feeling.

Restating the main idea, however, doesn't necessarily mean writing the exact same thing or simply switching the words around. You can be more creative this time around, including adding some extra information or restating your ideas in a new and interesting way. Here's one way to restate the thesis statement we've been working with throughout this chapter:

Original thesis:

If I could do one thing in my life again, I would relive my wedding day.

Restated:

Though I will never have the chance, I would love to be able to experience my wedding day again.

In this example, the main idea is given in both sentences, but in the second one it includes something more: the idea that reliving any moment of one's life is impossible. It adds a sense of regret to the essay that can leave the reader feeling pleasantly wistful.

Now it's your turn to write. Using the following lines, rewrite the thesis statement you wrote in the previous example as it would appear in the conclusion of your essay.

Original thesis:

_____

_____

Restated thesis:

_____

_____

Giving the Reader a Sense of Closure

To give readers a sense of closure means to make them feel satisfied with how the essay ends. It's difficult to say specifically what to do so that people come away with this feeling. It's fairly easy, however, to say what *not* to do. To ensure that readers feel a sense of closure at the end of your essay,

- don't introduce completely new ideas.
- don't only refer to narrow, specific examples.
- don't end your essay with a question.

An example of an effective conclusion for the topic of reliving some moment of your life would be:

Beautiful weather, a fairytale setting, my happy family; for one day of my life, everything was perfect. Although I know I will never have the chance, I would love to experience my wedding day again.

As you can see, the conclusion doesn't have to be long and involved. It just needs to be a long enough to tie the essay together and leave the reader feeling satisfied. Although conclusions can be difficult to write well, it becomes easier with practice.

Using the following space, write a conclusion for the essay you've been working on in the previous examples. Include the restated thesis you wrote in the last exercise.

Original thesis:

_____

_____

Restated thesis:

_____

_____

Conclusion:

_____

_____

_____

_____

How Your Essay Will Be Scored

Your extended response essay will be scored based on three traits, or elements:

- **Trait 1:** Creation of arguments and use of evidence
- **Trait 2:** Development of ideas and organizational structure
- **Trait 3:** Clarity and command of standard English conventions

Your essay will be scored on a scale where each trait is worth up to 2 points, for a possible total of 6 points. The total is then doubled, so the maximum number of possible points you can earn is 12.

Creation of Arguments and Use of Evidence

Trait 1 tests your ability to write an essay that takes a stance based on the information in the reading passage(s). To earn the highest score possible, you must carefully read the information and express a clear opinion about what you've read. You will be scored on how well you use the information from the passage(s) to support your argument.

NOTE

To earn the highest score possible, you must reference and restate information from the passage(s), not just mention information from your own personal experiences.

Your score will also be based on how well you analyze the author's argument in the passage(s), if he or she makes one. To earn the highest score possible, discuss whether you think the author is making a good argument, and why or why not.

For your reference, here is a table that the GED® test scorers will use when determining if your essay should get a score of 2, 1, or 0 for Trait 1.

TO ATTAIN A SCORE OF:	DESCRIPTION
2	■ Generates text-based argument(s) and establishes a purpose that is connected to the prompt ■ Cites relevant and specific evidence from the source text(s) to support argument(s) ■ Analyzes the issue and/or evaluates the validity of the argumentation within the source texts (e.g., distinguishes between supported and unsupported claims, makes reasonable inferences about underlying premises or assumptions, identifies fallacious reasoning, evaluates the credibility of sources, etc.)
1	■ Generates an argument and demonstrates some connection to the prompt ■ Cites some evidence from the source text(s) to support argument(s) (may include a mix of relevant and irrelevant citations or a mix of textual and non-textual references) ■ Partially analyzes the issue and/or evaluates the validity of the argumentation within the source texts; may be simplistic, limited, or inaccurate
0	■ May attempt to create an argument OR lacks purpose or connection to the prompt OR does neither ■ Cites minimal or no evidence from source text(s) (sections of text may be copied from source) ■ Minimally analyzes the issue and/or evaluates the validity of the argumentation within the source texts; may completely lack analysis or demonstrate minimal or no understanding of the given argument(s)

Development of Ideas and Organization Structure

Trait 2 tests whether you respond to the writing prompt with a well-structured essay. Support of your thesis must come from evidence in the passage(s), as well as personal opinions and experiences that build on your central idea. Your ideas must be fully explained and include specific details.

Your essay should use words and phrases that allow your details and ideas to flow naturally.

Here is a table that the GED® test scorers will use when determining if your essay should get a score of 2, 1, or 0 for Trait 2.

TO ATTAIN A SCORE OF:	DESCRIPTION
2	■ Contains ideas that are well developed and generally logical; most ideas are elaborated upon ■ Contains a sensible progression of ideas with clear connections between details and main points ■ Establishes an organizational structure that conveys the message and purpose of the response; applies transitional devices appropriately ■ Establishes and maintains a formal style and appropriate tone that demonstrate awareness of the audience and purpose of the task ■ Chooses specific words to express ideas clearly
1	■ Contains ideas that are inconsistently developed and/or may reflect simplistic or vague reasoning; some ideas are elaborated ■ Demonstrates some evidence of a progression of ideas but details may be disjointed or lacking connection to main idea ■ Establishes an organization structure that may inconsistently group ideas or is partially effective at conveying the message of the task; uses transitional devices inconsistently ■ May inconsistently maintain a formal style and appropriate tone to demonstrate an awareness of the audience and purpose of the task ■ May occasionally misuse words and/or choose words that express ideas in vague terms
0	■ Contains ideas that are insufficiently or illogically developed with minimal or no elaboration of main ideas ■ Contains an unclear or no progression of ideas; details may be absent or irrelevant to the main idea ■ Establishes an ineffective or no discernible organizational structure; does not apply transitional devices or does so inappropriately ■ Uses an informal style and/or inappropriate tone that demonstrates limited or no awareness of audience and purpose ■ May frequently misuse words, overuse slang, or express ideas in a vague or rapturous manner

Clarity and Command of Standard English Conventions

Trait 3 tests how well you create the sentences that make up your essay. To earn a high score, you will need to write sentences with variety—some short, some long, some simple, some complex. You will also need to prove that you have a good handle on standard English, including correct word choice, grammar, and sentence structure.

If you need to review any topics in grammar, usage, or mechanics, revisit Chapters 5 and 6 of this book.

Here is a table that the GED® test scorers will use when determining if your essay should get a score of 2, 1, or 0 for Trait 3.

TO ATTAIN A SCORE OF:	DESCRIPTION

2	■ Demonstrates largely correct sentence structure and a general fluency that enhances clarity with specific regard to the following skills:
	  ■ varied sentence structure within a paragraph or paragraphs
	  ■ correct subordination, coordination, and parallelism
	  ■ avoidance of wordiness and awkward sentence structures
	  ■ usage of transitional words, conjunctive adverbs, and other words that support logic and clarity
	  ■ avoidance of run-on sentences, fused sentences, or sentence fragments
	■ Demonstrates competent application of the conventions of English usage with specific regard to the following skills:
	  ■ frequently confused words and homonyms, including contractions
	  ■ subject–verb agreement
	  ■ pronoun usage, including pronoun antecedent agreement, unclear pronoun references, and pronoun case
	  ■ placement of modifiers and correct word order
	  ■ capitalization (e.g., proper nouns, titles, and beginnings of sentences)
	  ■ use of apostrophes, with possessive nouns
	  ■ use of punctuation (e.g., commas in a series or in appositives and other nonessential elements, end marks, and appropriate punctuation for clause separation)
	■ Response may contain some errors in mechanics and conventions but they do not interfere with comprehension; overall, standard usage is at a level appropriate for on-demand draft writing

1	■ Demonstrates inconsistent sentence structure; may contain some repetitive, choppy, rambling, or awkward sentences that may detract from clarity; demonstrates inconsistent control over skills listed in the first bullet under Trait 3, score of 2 ■ Demonstrates inconsistent control of basic conventions with specific regard to skills listed in the second bullet under Trait 3, score of 2 ■ May contain frequent errors in mechanics and conventions that occasionally interfere with comprehension; standard usage is at a minimally acceptable level of appropriateness for on-demand draft writing
0	■ Demonstrates consistently flawed sentence structure so that meaning may be obscured; demonstrates minimal control over skills listed in the first bullet of Trait 3, score of 2 ■ Demonstrates minimal control of basic conventions with specific regard to skills listed in the second bullet under Trait 3, score of 2 ■ Contains severe and frequent errors in mechanics and conventions that interfere with comprehension; overall standard usage is at an unacceptable level for appropriateness for on-demand draft writing OR ■ Response is insufficient to demonstrate level of mastery over conventions and usage

Avoid an Automatic Zero Score

If your essay has any of the following problems, it will *automatically* receive a score of 0:

- The entire essay is made up of text copied from the passage(s) or the prompt.
- The essay shows no evidence that the test taker has read the prompt.
- The essay is on the wrong topic.
- The essay is incomprehensible (cannot be understood).
- The essay is not in English.
- The essay section is blank.

Extended Response Practice

Use the following prompt to answer this sample extended response question. As you write your essay, be sure to:

- Decide which position presented in the passage(s) is better supported by evidence.
- Explain why your chosen position has better support.

- Recognize that the position with better support may not be the position you agree with.
- Present multiple pieces of evidence from the passage(s) to defend your assertions.
- Thoroughly construct your main points, organizing them logically, with strong supporting details.
- Connect your sentences, paragraphs, and ideas with transitional words and phrases.
- Express your ideas clearly and choose your words carefully.
- Use varied sentence structures to increase the clarity of your response.
- Reread and revise your response.

PROMPT

The following passage discusses the debate over violent video games and their effect on young people. Take no more than 45 minutes to read the passage, write your essay, and then revise it.

Violent Video Games—Are They Harmful to Young People?

The debate over the effects of video games on the behavior of youths continues today with reports of school shootings and violent acts in urban neighborhoods. Violent video games are often cited as the culprit for increased violent behavior in youths. Some people contend that these games desensitize players to violence and teach children that violence is an acceptable way to resolve conflicts. Video game supporters state that research on the topic is unsound and that no direct relationship has been found between video games and violent behavior. In fact, some argue that violent video games may reduce violence by providing a safe outlet for aggressive and angry feelings.

In testimony presented at a 2012 federal hearing addressing the regulation of the video game rating system, Cindy Marrix, a psychologist and researcher at the Media and Mind Institute at Wollash University, in Wollash, Idaho, stated there is overwhelming evidence that supports the link between violent video games and aggressive behavior in young people. Dr. Marrix stated that research shows that violent video games are more likely than other media to lead to aggressive behavior because of the repetitive nature of game activities and players' identification with violent characters.

Dr. Marrix also noted that the practice of being rewarded for many acts of violence may intensify a game player's learning of violent acts. She believes that electronic media play a significant role in the emotional and social development of youth. While there are many video games that promote learning and cooperative behavior, studies suggest that the video games that include aggression, violence, and sexualized violence may have a negative impact on children.

Research results reveal that violent video games do increase feelings of hostility and thoughts about aggression. Dr. Marrix contends that the entertainment industry must recognize the link between violent behaviors and violent video games, and that these games should depict the realistic consequences of violence to show children that violence is not an effective means of resolving conflict.

While the concerns about the effects of violent video games are understandable, there are also a number of experts who claim there is no link between video games and violence. After examination of the research evidence, several authorities have concluded that these studies do not scientifically validate the hypothesis that the games increase violence. In fact, millions of children and adults play these games without any ill effects.

Researchers Dr. Erica Trounce and Dr. Jacob Smith state that concerns about current video games are really no different than those of previous generations regarding the new media of earlier times. Drs. Trounce and Smith state that research findings that claim violent video games create violent behaviors come from poorly conducted studies and sensational news reports.

The findings of two recent studies were reported in 2014 in the scientific journal *Behind the Brain*. Participants of the first study were assigned to play either a violent or a nonviolent video game for two hours per day for 20 days. Although male participants were observed to have greater aggression during the time they played the violent game than female participants, the

(continues)

results of this study revealed no increase of real-life aggression in players of the violent games. Results of the second study indicated that a predisposition to respond to certain situations with acts of aggression, family violence, and male gender were predictive of violent crime, but exposure to violent video games was not. These results suggest that playing violent video games does not demonstrate a significant risk for future violent acts.

Worldwide video game sales are predicted to reach over $110 billion in 2016. As games get more complex and lifelike, the discussion over whether children should be allowed to be exposed to violent video games will continue.

Read the passage and construct an essay that addresses the following question: *Do violent video games promote violent behavior in youths?* In your response, analyze both positions to determine which is better supported. Use relevant and specific evidence to support your response.

_____

_____

_____

_____

_____

_____

_____

_____

_____

_____

THE EXTENDED RESPONSE ESSAY: TIPS AND SCORING

Extended Response Practice Sample Essays

Sample Score 2 Response

There is strong reason to believe that violent video games help create a culture of violence among America's youths. The playing of violent video games can cause players to blur the line between fantasy and reality and make them believe there are no consequences for violent actions. Evidence from a variety of sources such as psychologists and scientific researchers shows that we must take steps to curb children's exposure to violent video games.

As the testimony of Dr. Cindy Marrix makes clear, violent video games have a much greater impact on the behavior of players than other forms of media. Beyond the "repetitive nature of game activities and players' identification with violent characters" that she mentions, I would also argue that the interactive component of video games makes them more dangerous than violent movies or television. This is because players actively contribute to the games' violent story lines, whereas movies and television are passive viewing experiences. Additionally, as Dr. Marrix contends, the system of rewarding game players for violent actions both desensitizes players to violence and lends positive associations to violent acts.

While the passage contains evidence against the link between violent video games and violent behavior, I do not believe it is as strong as the argument represented by Dr. Marrix. Most significantly, the study published in *Behind the Brain* does not seem to take into consideration the long-term effects of playing violent video games over a sustained amount of time. Perhaps players' levels of aggression do not rise after a few days' or weeks' worth of play, but what about over the course of 10 or 15 years? Most game players I know, whether they play violent or nonviolent games, have been doing so since early childhood. Even if many years spent playing such games does not result in violent behavior, at the very least these games

remove the danger from violent behavior and make it appear almost normal. This can't be good for players' abilities to empathize with victims of violence or fully grasp the problem of violence in the world today.

Dr. Marrix is right to call for increased vigilance on the part of both the game makers and the general public when it comes to violence in video games. As the passage predicts, these games will only get more lifelike with time, raising further questions about the relationship between simulated and real violence. Factors such as a player's psychological health and family background definitely play a part in his or her tendencies toward violence, but the influence of interactive media on a child's emotional development cannot be ignored.

About This Essay

This extended response is a Score 2 because it contains an argument that is clearly connected to the prompt. The author does this by using evidence from the passage and attributing it correctly (this means that the writer explained who or what is the source of the evidence). The writer makes reasonable inferences, makes reasonable claims, and organizes his or her points in a logical way. He or she looks at both sides of the debate with fairness and objectivity, adding personal observations only when they are relevant to the response. The language, style, and tone of the essay remain formal throughout. Sentence structure is clear and precise, and the writer has a varied vocabulary. He or she follows basic grammar rules, including proper capitalization and punctuation.

Sample Score 1 Response

This essay discusses violence and video games. In my opinion violence is a problem today but video games don't make it any worse. Video games can even help with hand eye coordination and reflexes.

The first source, Dr. Marrix, discusses why she thinks that video games lead to violence. She says that people who play video games are more aggressive than people who don't and that they have a hard time telling the difference between what's real and what isn't. Maybe there is some truth to this but I know people who have played video games for years and they are not violent. I think it depends on people's families, if their families are good and teach them not to be aggressive and violent then they should be able to play video games without resulting in social violence. Dr. Marrix believes that players "identify" with violent characters and that this makes them want to act like the characters in real life, but I think it's more like the second source, Doctor Trounce, says: "violent behaviors come from poorly conducted studies and sensational news reports." What she means is that the news media is responsible for blowing up the problem of violent video games to sensationalize a story. It really has no grounding in reality. I also agree with the study in Behind the Brain magazine, that states that there is no increase in real-life aggression when people play video games. This refutes Dr. Marrix's point that there is a link between the two. The study also backs up what I said about the importance of family in raising nonviolent children.

The article states that people are going to spend "73.5 billion" dollars on games by the end of 2013. This alone is enough to show that games are not going away and that they are very difficult to regulate because they take up such a large part of the economy. Dr. Marrix suggests they change the content of the games, but that will be difficult because so many people buy them. Instead they should let the consumers decide if they can handle the content of the games. Games like Grand theft Auto can even help people's driving abilities and even pilots sometimes train on simulators so it is proven that simulated electronic media can have positive value in society. Plus the magazine study shows that it is usually only males that have the problem with violence and video games, not the entire population. In conclusion I do not see an established link between violence and video games, at least not enough so that we have to change

our national policy toward games, like Dr. Marrix suggests.

About This Essay

This extended response is a Score 1 because the argument has some connection to the prompt, but the author wanders in making his or her point. He or she does not follow a logical progression to explain his or her argument. The writer does not analyze the evidence from the text in depth, and little is done to show how it connects to the author's thesis. The essay writer makes similar points repeatedly, using a tone that wavers between formal and casual. There are run-on sentences, some errors in punctuation and capitalization, inaccurate quotes, and awkward transitions between parts of the essay.

Sample Score 0 Response

The article says video games lead to violence I agree cuz video games r violent & lotsa people play em that r violent. i'd say ban all the video games cuz they lead to violence! The game Call of Duty's very violent, I know ppl who play it n the graffix r super real looking. Not good for society to have ppl playin these games. in the article it sez ppl get aggressive when they play too many games. I would agree wit this, they have trouble telling whats real and whats fake. The dr. in the article sez these games have "negative impact" which is true if you've ever seen how violent the games can b. other parts in the article talk bout how the games arent that violent that ppl can play them w/o being violent but I dont know, I think they raise aggression in players. games once were simpler, not so violent, but now theyre super violent, the doctors in the article even think so. ppl are gonna spend "7.53 billion" on games the article states, so its a bigger problem then really anyone can handle at this point . . . its one of the biggest parts of the media and ppl will find ways to get their games. its to bad b/c I think its bad for society to have all these people playing so many games not thinking about real problems in society like war etc. but I dunno I dont think theres a solution rite now . . . sad that ppl become so violent with games.

About This Essay

This extended response is a Score 0 because it has little or no connection to the prompt, follows no logical progression, and includes little evidence from the passage. There is very little analysis of the issue or of the studies mentioned in the passage; while there is a very general thesis, it is not fully explained. The author uses slang and shorthand spellings (for instance, "sez" and "dunno") and writes in a tone that is too casual. There are many errors in spelling, capitalization, punctuation, and basic grammar rules, and the dollar amount is quoted inaccurately. These prevent the reader from fully understanding what the writer is trying to say.

8 ▶ THE EXTENDED RESPONSE ESSAY: PLANNING AND REVISING

CHAPTER SUMMARY
This chapter helps you prepare to manage your writing time on exam day, practice pre-writing skills, and revise your initial draft on the spot. These skills can also transfer to writing tasks above and beyond the GED® Reasoning through Language Arts test.

How to Write a Powerful Essay

An *effective* essay is one that clearly and completely accomplishes its purpose. There are many possible purposes for an essay: to inform, to persuade, to entertain, to compare, to prove, or to disprove. The purpose of your essay on the GED® test will most likely be either to inform the reader regarding your opinion of an issue or to persuade the reader to agree with your point of view on an issue.

Planning
Writing an effective essay requires planning, something that new writers are often reluctant to do. Why? Many students are impatient and just want to get the job over with. Others worry that taking the time to plan out their essay will cause them to run out of time to write.

However, planning what you are going to write beforehand should make the writing process much smoother and easier. It will also help you come up with ideas for what to write, organize your ideas effectively, and express your ideas clearly once you start writing. Most of the writing you did in the preceding chapter was much like planning; in this chapter, you will learn how to plan more.

Prewriting Strategies

We have all been there: at that first moment before you begin to write. You open your exam book, double check your scratch paper and pencil, sigh a huge sigh, whisper to yourself, "Okay, here goes," and then . . . nothing. Blank. Nada. It happens to the best of us. And it is the hardest part about writing. But, here's the good news: Once you have gotten past those first few agonizing moments, and you begin to put your thoughts in motion, the hardest part is over! You remember that you are a person with a purpose, and you are ready to embark on your GED® extended response essay.

Organizing your thoughts before writing is absolutely critical. It is probably the most important step in the entire writing process. Before you even put fingers on keys, you have to start thinking. So, do whatever you can to put yourself in a mental state of free-flowing thought. You need to allow yourself the ability to really focus.

This chapter will include the following aspects of organizing your writing:

- Thinking styles
- Outlining
- Order of importance

Thinking Styles

This might sound more like a lesson in Zen Buddhism, but clear thinking makes all the difference in your writing performance. You can start by first figuring out what type of thinker you are. This seems funny, but isn't it obvious in everyday life how differently people think? Just try getting three small children and their grandmother to agree on what to have for dinner, and you will see what I mean. You could conceivably have ten people in a room with each person looking at the same issue in a diametrically different way. So, you have to understand what kind of thinker you are. There are two basic thinking styles that can be associated with writing: *linear thinking* and *free association*.

Linear Thinker

You are a **linear thinker** if you organize your ideas in chronological or sequential order. If you are working with a time line, you simply list events chronologically, starting with the first event:

Example
The school library needs to be reorganized. Given its enormous size, several student volunteers will be involved in the reorganization. As a result, you need to make a chronological list—bulleted or numerical, from beginning to present—of the steps that must be taken in order to get the job done.

Sample notes: **Linear thinker** (using chronology):

- Reorganization agreed upon March 23, 2014; project to be completed May 23, 2014.
- Step 1 (March 26–April 9): Remove all books from shelves.
- Step 2 (April 16–22): Clean shelves, removing all shelf labels and notations from the old organization system.
- Step 3 (April 23, 11 A.M.): Meeting to approve new reorganization system.
- Step 4 (April 25–May 9): Donate unneeded books, order new books, and label book spines with new organization system notation.
- Step 5 (May 10–May 17): Place all books on shelves, leaving ample room for future book acquisitions.
- Step 6 (May 18–May 22): Test out new organization system, receive feedback from employees, and make necessary changes.
- Step 7 (May 23): Project completion.

If you are thinking *sequentially*, you make an outline or a list that begins with your most important ideas.

You then move down your list of thoughts in descending order of importance:

Example

You need to write an essay comparing the effectiveness of two different pieces of writing. So, you sketch a quick outline that covers what you need to say in order of importance.

Sample notes: **Linear thinker** (using sequence):

1. Introduce topic and first essay author (remembering our minimum wage essay, that would be President Roosevelt).
2. List points of support:
   a. We must "reduce the lag in the purchasing power of industrial workers and . . . strengthen and stabilize the markets for the farmers' products."
   b. Our nation has resources and a hardworking population, and we should treat people fairly, if we consider ourselves a "self-supporting and self-respecting democracy."
   c. Child labor and worker exploitation are unforgivable.
   d. "Enlightened business" means knowing that competition is not more important than the humans doing the work to earn the profits.
3. Introduce second author:
   a. Ralph Phillips, asking for "informed alternative views."
   b. Increasing minimum wage will harm the economy—government doesn't belong in the workplace.
   c. Employers will have to pay workers more, which means firing workers, raising prices, and making less profit.
   d. Phillips worked in a very low-paying job and still achieved professional stability. Why can't everyone do that?
4. Analyze the support each author provides for his argument, using specific evidence.

Free Association Thinker

You are a **free association thinker** if you use no particular sequence in your initial thinking.

You have a thought, jot it down as it comes to you, and then provide supporting details last. You might write down key words that you know will trigger your memory later. You will eventually do an outline, but you need to see all your ideas laid out on paper first.

You can refer to this type of thinking as bubble thinking. Thoughts may come to you at lightning speed, so you should write down notes as quickly as you think of them. You can then circle each separate idea in its own bubble so you can categorize them logically later. When you're done taking notes, rearrange each bubble until the essay flows sensibly.

The thinking style notes in this section are obviously very brief, but they address the important points. Of course, the length of your outline will vary depending on the level of detail you have time for, and how much you know about the essays you're responding to. The important thing to determine is what kind of thinker you are. Once you have done that, you can apply yourself to your next step: organizing your notes logically.

There are three main steps to successfully planning an essay:

1. come up with a thesis statement
2. brainstorm ideas related to your thesis statement
3. organize your ideas into an outline

The following subsections describe each step in detail.

Coming Up with a Thesis Statement

Many students find it difficult to come up with an effective thesis statement. Often, writing a thesis statement for the GED® test is as simple as answering a question about yourself, a question that may appear in the prompt. Then all you have to do is answer it. For example:

What is your favorite thing? Whether it is a gift you were given during your childhood or something you saved up for years to buy, you probably have something that is special to you. Write about this special object and why it is important to you.

The question here is *What is your favorite thing?* Your thesis statement should answer that question in a complete sentence.

Sometimes, the prompt provided is in the form of a statement. In this case, there will be a sentence that gives you instructions to *tell*, *describe*, or *explain* some-thing. Simply take the sentence that instructs you to do something and turn it into a question. For example:

Many people believe that humans' spirits remain on earth after they die, in the form of ghosts. Explain why you do or do not believe that ghosts exist.

Notice that the second sentence of the prompt gives you instructions: *Explain why*. Drop the word *explain* and turn the statement into a question: *Do you or do you not believe that ghosts exist?* Again, your thesis statement should answer that question.

Let's practice what you've learned so far. Write a thesis statement in response to the following prompt:

Embarrassing moments often remain clear in our memories, despite the fact that we would like to forget them. Tell about one of your most embarrassing experiences.

Thesis statement:

_____

_____

Brainstorming Your Ideas

Brainstorm is simply another way of saying *write down anything you can think of as fast as you possibly can*. The purpose of brainstorming is to help you get all your ideas down on paper so that you can figure out how to organize them later.

So let's say you've come up with the following thesis statement: *If I could do one thing in my life again, I would relive my wedding day*. To brainstorm ideas related to this thesis, you would take out a blank sheet of paper, write your thesis at the top, and then spend about three or four minutes writing down whatever related thoughts come to you, in no particular order. Here is a sample brainstorm on this thesis statement:

- *flowers*
- *beautiful day*
- *perfect temperature*
- *no rain*
- *family together*
- *husband handsome*
- *felt like a princess*
- *beautiful hair*
- *grandmother's dress*
- *mom and dad happy*
- *mom's family and dad's family*
- *no fighting*
- *laughter*
- *great music*

At this point, the brainstorm doesn't look anything like an essay; it just looks like a bunch of ideas. The next thing to do is to sort through the mess by going over each thing you wrote down, circling related ideas, and connecting them by drawing a line between them. This leaves you with a brainstorm that looks like this:

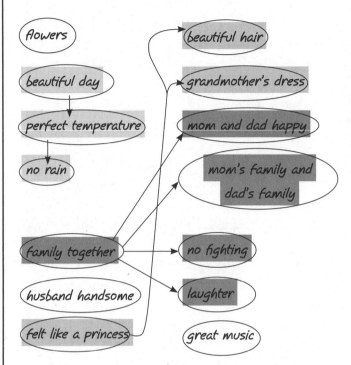

The largest groups in the brainstorm should tell you what the main ideas will be for the body of your essay. In this brainstorm, there are three ideas related to the weather (beautiful day, perfect temperature, no rain), three related to the bride's appearance (felt like a princess, beautiful hair, grandmother's dress), and five ideas related to the family (family together, mom and dad happy, mom's family and dad's family, no fighting, and laughter). That means the three body paragraphs in the essay should have to do with weather, the bride's appearance, and the family.

Collecting Details from Passages

To support your thesis, gather information from the passage(s) that will allow you to express a strong opinion. A good essay will include specific details that will help the reader understand your position.

TAKE NOTE

On the GED® test, you must include evidence from the passage(s) that supports your thesis statement and must also analyze evidence in the passage(s) that *does not* support your position.

As you jot down details from the passage(s) to use in your essay, ask the following questions:

1. Does this information support my thesis statement?
2. Does this evidence persuade the reader to believe or agree with my position?

The following is an example of a passage that presents an issue (the pros and cons of school uniforms). We will analyze this passage in the next section. Write down notes, important details, and a thesis statement as you read.

The Pros and Cons of School Uniforms for Your Child

Although uniforms have been a mainstay of private schools, public schools jumped on the bandwagon in 1994, when the California school district of Long Beach implemented school uniforms. According to the Long Beach school district, within one year after the implementation of uniforms, the fights and muggings at school decreased by 50%, while committed sexual offenses were reduced by 74%. Across the country, similar statistics abound; for example, at Ruffner Middle School in Norfolk, Virginia, the number of discipline referrals decreased by 42% once uniforms were enforced. Subsequently, fueled by these statistics, more schools across the country are implementing uniforms in public schools. Nonetheless, there are other statistics that argue that uniforms are not as beneficial as school administrators believe. Thus, the question still remains: Are public school uniforms good for your child?

There are fundamentally two benefits associated with school uniforms: a focus on learning, as well as a reduction of violence on campus. Many school administrators and parents believe that uniforms create a better learning environment at school. First and foremost, students are not distracted by how they look and therefore pay more attention to learning at school. The peer pressures of stylish dressing with the best brands are alleviated, and students can focus more on their schoolwork, rather than on social appearances. In fact, the socioeconomic differences present among students are equalized with school uniforms, minimizing the pressure to fit in with the right clothing choices.

According to the publication *School Administrator*, the mandate of uniforms on campuses has reduced tardiness, skipped classes, suspensions, and discipline referrals. In addition, with the visual uniformity present across all students, school pride has increased. Similar to athletic team uniforms, dressing cohesively increases pride, unity, and a renewed commitment to the school. With uniforms, a more professional tone is set in school, encouraging students to take their studies more seriously. Uniforms are more expensive up front, as the parent must invest in all of the staples; however, as the school year progresses, there are fewer purchases that need to be made. Last, uniforms at school reduce the prevalence of violence, which is a major concern for many public schools. Outsiders who do not belong on campus are easily identified and thus do not pose a great threat to the students. Uniforms also reduce the cliques and gangs on school campuses. When it is not easy to identify members of gangs, the fights and violence decrease. Students can no longer be distracted by who is wearing which gang color, and therefore, the campus is kept safer with less incidence of fighting.

The opponents of public school uniforms, as outlined by the ACLU's argument for the First Amendment, argue that uniforms stifle a student's need for self-expression. Students need to be encouraged to embrace their individualism, and uniforms deny that self-expression. According to opponents of uniforms, even preschoolers should have input into their wardrobes, and the need to encourage personality, confidence, and independence grows more important as the student becomes older. Without the outlet of expression in their clothing choices, students may turn to inappropriate hairstyles, jewelry, or makeup. Denying students their ability to express individualism and belief in a subculture, whether preppy, hip-hop, punk, or jock, could stymie their transition from childhood into adulthood. Controlling the socialization process could harm them as

(continues)

adults; they may not be prepared for the real world, where people are indeed judged by their appearances. In addition, others argue that uniforms may not be comfortable for all students. As it is important to ensure that the student is comfortable in order to maximize learning outcomes, uniforms may stymie academic focus. Students cannot wear their uniforms outside of school, and thus, there is the double cost of both uniforms and a casual wardrobe.

—Adapted from "Public School Uniforms: The Pros and Cons for Your Child," by Grace Chen, April 23, 2008, publicschoolreview.com.

Organization of Your Essay

A good GED® test essay starts with an introductory paragraph that presents the main idea, follows with body paragraphs that contain support for the main idea, and closes with a concluding paragraph.

Writing Your Introduction

Keep in mind these two goals as you write your introduction:

1. **Clearly state your main point or thesis statement.**
   As you write the body paragraphs, you can refer to your introduction to make sure your evidence supports the thesis.
2. **Present your plan to support your main point.**
   For example, if you are going to refer to three points of evidence from the passage(s), briefly mention them in the introduction. This will give your essay some structure—helpful for your readers, because they will know what to expect, and helpful for you, because you will have a built-in guide as you write the rest of the piece.

   It's also a good way to make sure up front that you will be able to defend your argument with evidence. If you can't find evidence to

support your claim, then you need to rethink your thesis statement.

Problems to Avoid in Introductions

1. **Don't mention how you plan to write your essay.** Your position and supporting evidence should speak for themselves.
   Incorrect: *I am going to tell you why students in public schools should wear uniforms. I will present the best argument for this position that shows why this is a good thing to do. I will also explain why the information against school uniforms does not present a good argument.*
   Correct: *There are many benefits that result from mandating student uniforms in public schools. These benefits include an overall lower cost, the sense of school harmony they promote, and the respect that is associated with them. Evidence from school administrators, students, and parents supports these advantages, which outweigh the negatives of mandating school uniforms.*
2. **Don't use meaningless or empty words to sound clever or repeat the same point using synonyms.** Consider the following example:
   School uniforms are critical to student success. They are essential for helping students accomplish their best in school. Uniforms play a significant role in helping students have a positive experience in school.
   These three sentences all say the same thing!

3. **Don't make excuses for your writing.** You want to convey a clear, confident position to the reader. Don't start your essay with something like the following:

Although I'm not familiar with the debate over school uniforms, I think I would probably say that it's a good idea for students to wear them.

Building Your Argument

To write the body of your essay, you will need to provide support for your claim or thesis statement. Return to your notes to see what evidence you highlighted as you read the passage(s). On the extended response, it is okay to use evidence from your personal experiences, but much of the essay should be based on evidence found in the reading passage(s) and on your analysis of this evidence.

If the writer of the passage makes his or her own argument, you should also include an analysis of the author's argument, or arguments, in your essay. To earn the highest score possible, you should discuss whether you think the writer is making a good case, and why or why not.

NOTE

Don't try to argue a claim if you can't fully support it. If you cannot find enough evidence from the passage(s) to back up your thesis, then you will have to develop a new one.

A good way to arrange your evidence is in the order of strength: start with the weakest evidence and end with the strongest. In addition to listing details that support your thesis, you should also list details that go *against* your thesis and then talk about why you disagree with them. Arguments like this help strengthen your point.

After you have grouped your supporting evidence using the erasable whiteboard, you will be ready to construct a simple outline to draft your essay.

Constructing a Draft

One method of constructing a draft, or the first version of your essay, is to create a simple outline. You can do this on the computer in the space provided for the essay and then erase it after you finish writing the essay. You might also want to create the outline on your personal whiteboard, which has the advantage of saving space on the computer screen.

Begin by thinking about your thesis. Decide the stance you want to take, and write your thoughts into one complete sentence. For example, what thesis statement would you make for an essay about the school uniform passage?

Every extended response essay should follow this basic structure:

1. **Introduction** (states thesis)
2. **Body** (explains and supports thesis with evidence from the passage and your insights)
3. **Conclusion** (brings closure and restates thesis)

Here is an example, using the passage about school uniforms:

Thesis statement: *There are many benefits that result from mandating student uniforms in public schools.*

Body paragraph(s): Make sure these include evidence from the text, not only your opinion:

1. *Decrease in negative behavior*
   Evidence from the passage: *School administrators report a reduction in fighting, tardiness, and other discipline problems.*

2. *Increase in learning*

    Evidence from the passage: *School administrators and parents report a better focus on learning because students are not distracted by the pressure to fit in.*

3. *Professional, respectful atmosphere at school*

    Evidence from the passage: *Schools report an increase in school pride and commitment to school.*

Conclusion: *Evidence from school administrators and other experts supports these advantages, which outweigh the negatives of mandating school uniforms.*

Sometimes three paragraphs—an introductory paragraph, a body paragraph, and a concluding paragraph—are enough to make your point, but you may need more (usually extra body paragraphs).

NOTE

For an essay to be effective, each paragraph must be effective, too. This means that each paragraph must be well developed. Each paragraph should have a minimum of three sentences, but it's usually necessary to write five to eight sentences to explain your thoughts adequately.

Once you have a clear, detailed outline, you can begin to write your essay. As noted earlier, your introduction should include your claim or thesis statement. Here is an example of an introductory paragraph:

There are many benefits that result from mandating student uniforms in public schools. These benefits include an overall lower cost, the sense of school harmony they promote, and the respect that is associated with them. Evidence from school administrators, students, and parents

supports these advantages, which outweigh the negatives of mandating school uniforms.

After you have composed your introduction, write the body of the essay to support your claim, and then add a conclusion paragraph that makes a final comment and restates your thesis.

WARNING!

You *cannot* copy and paste exact text from the passage(s) into the body of your essay without using quotation marks. If you do make this mistake, your essay will receive a score of 0! You are required either to include quotation marks or to paraphrase the points (put what the author says into your own words).

Example of an Extended Response Essay

Now take a look at this great example of a high-scoring essay, which follows the structure we've discussed. The writer is responding to the prompt for the school uniform passage.

PROMPT

In the following article, the pros and cons of wearing school uniforms are discussed. In your response, analyze both positions to determine which view is better supported. Use relevant and specific evidence from the passage to support your response.

    Type your response in the box; you will have approimately 45 minutes to complete it.

Pros and Cons of School Uniforms

There are many benefits that result from mandating student uniforms in public schools. These benefits include an overall lower cost, the sense of harmony they promote, and the respect that is associated with them. Evidence from school administrators, students, and parents supports these advantages, which outweigh the negatives of mandating school uniforms.

As noted in the article by Grace Chen, evidence from schools in California and elsewhere revealed that when students were required to wear uniforms, there was a significant drop in negative behaviors on campus. For example, one school district reported that after one year of students wearing uniforms, the number of fights and muggings went down by 50%. The publication *School Administrator* had similar findings: when students wore uniforms, there was a decrease in tardiness, skipping school, and even suspensions.

School administrators and parents also report that when students are not focused on how they look or succumbing to pressure from their classmates to dress in a certain way, more attention can be paid to the task of learning in the school environment. While Chen cites the opinion that uniforms repress individual style, students have opportunities to express their style outside the school setting. Opponents also claim that there could be a greater financial cost to families if uniforms are required; however, in my experience, this is a weak argument. For example, in my school district, there is financial aid available to every family in need to help with the cost of uniforms, and in some schools, uniforms are free to qualifying families.

In addition, Chen notes that uniforms create "a more professional tone . . . in school," saying that this practice encourages students to take pride in their school and creates a sense of community. These are skills that young people need in adulthood whether they go on to college or enter the workforce. If wearing school uniforms helps students at a young age to increase their awareness of some of the things that are important for college and career readiness, then this is something school districts need to consider. A young person's ability to transition successfully to adulthood requires far more than attentiveness to his or her individual style. Many workplaces have employee dress codes, and those who do not follow the company policy for appropriate dress may face termination. Therefore, school uniforms may actually help young people develop the mind-set they need to be effective team players in the workplace.

Although some students may complain about the requirement of school uniforms, the evidence presented in this article strongly suggests that the benefits outweigh the disadvantages. Chen notes that school officials have data that prove the positive effects of uniforms: fewer behavior problems, an increase in school pride, and greater attention to learning. Based on this evidence, more districts should consider implementing uniforms in their schools.

Notice that the fourth paragraph includes a phrase from the passage, and it's correctly enclosed by quotation marks. What are the three dots in the quote? They are an ellipsis, which indicates that the essay writer removed one or more words from the original phrase. The original line in the passage is *a more professional tone is set in school*. This doesn't work grammatically in the sentence in the essay, so the essay writer removed *is set* and replaced those two words with an ellipsis.

Essay Outline

A complete essay outline will look something like this:

Introduction:
What if you could live one day of your life over again? Some people might choose to relive a day to change something about their lives. Others might simply want a second chance to enjoy a great experience.

Thesis statement:
As for me, if I could do one thing in my life again, I would relive my wedding day.

Body Paragraph #1 (Topic Sentence):
The weather was perfect on my wedding day.

Support #1:
perfect temperature

Support #2:
no rain

Body Paragraph #2 (Topic Sentence):
I felt like a princess that day.

Support #1:
beautiful hair

Support #2:
holding flowers

Support #3:
wearing my grandmother's dress

Body Paragraph #3 (Topic Sentence):
The best thing about my wedding day was seeing my family happy together.

Support #1:
mom's and dad's family there

Support #2:
no fighting

Support #3:
everyone laughing

Conclusion:
Beautiful weather, a fairytale setting, my happy family; for one day of my life, everything was perfect. Though I know I will never have the chance, I would love to experience my wedding day again.

That's it for planning. Now you know what your essay is going to be about, what the topic sentences of your body paragraphs are going to be, and what support you're going to use to back them up. You're now ready to move on to the next step: writing the essay.

Using the following outline form as a guide, create an outline for the essay topic you've been working on about your favorite object.

Introduction:

_____

_____

_____

_____

Thesis Statement:

_____

_____

Body Paragraph #1—Topic Sentence:

_____

_____

_____

_____

Support #1:

_____

_____

Support #2:

_____

_____

Support #3:

_____

_____

Body Paragraph #2—Topic Sentence:

_____

_____

_____

_____

Support #1:

_____

_____

Support #2:

_____

_____

Support #3:

_____

_____

Body Paragraph #3—Topic Sentence:

_____

_____

_____

_____

Support #1:

_____

_____

Support #2:

_____

_____

Support #3:

_____

_____

Conclusion:

_____

_____

_____

_____

Writing

Once you've thoroughly planned your essay, writing it should be a relatively simple process of expanding on what you've already written in your outline. As mentioned in previous sections, you'll want to begin your introduction with a few sentences to catch the reader's attention and lead into the thesis statement. Each body paragraph will start with the topic sentence you've already written and continue with the support you've noted to explain and develop the main idea. Finally, the conclusion will bring the essay to an end, restating the thesis and giving the reader a sense of closure.

A sample essay based on the outline in the previous section might look like this:

What if you could live one day of your life over again? Some people might choose to relive a day to change something about their lives. Others might simply want a second chance to enjoy a great experience. As for me, if I could do one thing in my life again, I would relive my wedding day.

The weather was perfect on my wedding day. Although it was supposed to rain that day, it didn't. The sun was shining, and the temperature was perfect. I could tell from the start that it was going to be a great day.

I felt like a princess that day. My hair was styled beautifully. As I walked down the aisle, _I carried a bouquet of daisies, just as I had always imagined princesses doing as a little girl. I was even wearing my grandmother's wedding dress, which had a long, old-fashioned train, just as I imagine royalty must wear._

The best thing about my wedding day was seeing my family happy together. My parents are divorced, but both my mom's and my dad's families came to the wedding. For the first time in my life, they didn't fight. They were all laughing together and having a good time.

Beautiful weather, a fairytale setting, my happy family; for one day of my life, everything was perfect. Though I know I will never have the chance, I would love to experience my wedding day again.

Now it's your turn. Write an essay on your favorite object, using all the tools and strategies covered thus far. The prompt is reprinted below for your convenience.

What is your favorite thing? Whether it is a gift you were given during your childhood or something you saved up for years to buy, you probably have something that is special to you. Write about this special object and why it is important to you.

Revising an Essay

Good planning can save you a lot of time, both in writing and in revising your essay. Ideally, you should not have to make any major revisions like adding sentences or moving paragraphs around. However, it is a good idea to take the last few minutes before your time is up to read over your essay and check for proper grammar, punctuation, and word choice. Here are a few things to look out for:

- **Capitalization.** Make sure the first word of every sentence and all proper nouns are capitalized.
- **Punctuation.** Make sure you've ended each sentence with a period or a question mark, as appropriate. Also check to see that you haven't thrown in any unnecessary punctuation, like commas or apostrophes.
- **Spelling.** Double-check homonyms like *to/too*, *its/it's*, *your/you're*, and *there/their/they're*. It's easy to make mistakes with them when you're in a hurry.
- **Repetition.** If you see a word, a phrase, or an idea that has been repeated, draw a single line through the second usage.
- **Unrelated information.** If you come across a sentence that has nothing to do with the rest of your essay, draw a line through it.
- **Clarity.** If something in your essay doesn't make sense to you, it probably won't make sense to anyone else, either. Take a moment to figure out what you were trying to say and rewrite it.

   If you've spent enough time in the planning phase and followed your outline well, you should need no more than five minutes to complete your revisions. When time is up, you should feel confident that you are handing in a complete and well-written essay.

Sample Extended Response Question

Read the following pair of speech excerpts, consider the prompt, and take a look at the sample essay provided.

Excerpt from President George W. Bush's Speech on Global Climate Change, June 11, 2001

Our country, the United States, is the world's largest emitter of man-made greenhouse gases. We account for almost 20 percent of the world's man-made greenhouse emissions. We also account for about one-quarter of the world's economic output. We recognize the responsibility to reduce our emissions. We also recognize the other part of the story—that the rest of the world emits 80 percent of all greenhouse gases. And many of those emissions come from developing countries.

This is a challenge that requires a 100 percent effort; ours, and the rest of the world's. The world's second-largest emitter of greenhouse gases is China. Yet, China was entirely exempted from the requirements of the Kyoto Protocol.

India and Germany are among the top emitters. Yet, India was also exempt from Kyoto. These and other developing countries that are experiencing rapid growth face challenges in reducing their emissions without harming their economies. We want to work cooperatively with these countries in their efforts to reduce greenhouse emissions and maintain economic growth.

Kyoto also failed to address two major pollutants that have an impact on warming: black soot and tropospheric ozone. Both are proven health hazards. Reducing both would not only address climate change, but also dramatically improve people's health.

Kyoto is, in many ways, unrealistic. Many countries cannot meet their Kyoto targets. The targets themselves were arbitrary and not based upon science. For America, complying with those mandates would have a negative economic impact, with layoffs of workers and price increases for consumers. And when you evaluate all these flaws, most reasonable people will understand that it's not sound public policy.

Excerpt from President Barack Obama's speech on climate change at Georgetown University, June 25, 2013

In my State of the Union address, I urged Congress to come up with a bipartisan, market-based solution to climate change, like the one that Republican and Democratic senators worked on together a few years ago. And I still want to see that happen. I'm willing to work with anyone to make that happen.

But this is a challenge that does not pause for partisan gridlock. It demands our attention now. And this is my plan to meet it—a plan to cut carbon pollution; a plan to protect our country from the impacts of climate change; and a plan to lead the world in a coordinated assault on a changing climate. . . .

Now, what you'll hear from the special interests and their allies in Congress is that this will kill jobs and crush the economy, and basically end American free enterprise as we know it. And the reason I know you'll hear those things is because that's what they said every time America sets clear rules and better standards for our air and our water and our children's health. And every time, they've been wrong.

For example, in 1970, when we decided through the Clean Air Act to do something about the smog that was choking our cities— and, by the way, most young people here aren't old enough to remember what it was like, but when I was going to school in 1979–1980 in Los Angeles, there were days where folks couldn't go outside. And the sunsets were spectacular because of all the pollution in the air.

But at the time when we passed the Clean Air Act to try to get rid of some of this smog, some of the same doomsayers were saying new pollution standards will decimate the auto industry. Guess what—it didn't happen. Our air got cleaner.

In 1990, when we decided to do something about acid rain, they said our electricity bills would go up, the lights would go off, businesses around the country would suffer—I quote—"a quiet death." None of it happened, except we cut acid rain dramatically.

See, the problem with all these tired excuses for inaction is that it suggests a fundamental lack of faith in American business and American ingenuity. These critics seem to think that when we ask our businesses to innovate and reduce pollution and lead, they can't or they won't do it. They'll just kind of give up and quit. But in America, we know that's not true. Look at our history.

Prompt

These two passages present different arguments regarding the issue of reducing greenhouse gas emissions. In your response, analyze both positions to determine which one is better supported. Use relevant and specific evidence from the passages to support your response.

Sample Response

These passages offer two significantly different views on how the United States should address its problem of greenhouse gas emissions. Both speakers concede that the United States is responsible for significant greenhouse gas emissions, and both speakers acknowledge the need for reducing these emissions. However, each speaker adopts a different attitude regarding implementation of such policies.

In this excerpt from President Bush's speech, he emphasizes the importance of an international, cooperative effort to deal with the problem. He does state that the United States generates one-fifth of the world's greenhouse gases. However, he quickly follows this information by stating that the United States is responsible for one-quarter of all economic activity, and then points out that four-fifths of the world's greenhouse gases are generated by other nations. By doing so, he attempts to explain the reason for high U.S. greenhouse emissions while also shifting the focus to other nations. Indeed, he goes on to point out how China and India are exempt from restricting greenhouse gas emissions, even though they are among the top greenhouse gas emitters.

Another key argument in Bush's speech emphasizes the economic perils of forcing drastic reductions in greenhouse gas emissions. Bush argues that to do so would devastate the U.S. economy, causing massive job layoffs and raising the cost of consumer goods. This argument also serves as the focal point in the excerpt from President Obama's speech. However, Obama refutes the claim that greenhouse gas restrictions will harm the economy. To support his position, Obama offers several historical examples where similar claims were made when businesses faced government-imposed restrictions. In each of those cases, the dire predictions of economic harm proved to be unfounded.

In essence, Bush's speech emphasizes fair play among all nations to ensure that the United States is not being held responsible for more than its share of the problem. Obama's speech emphasizes leadership by example, noting that the United States has successfully dealt with similar issues in the past. Of the two, I find Obama's position to be better supported through his use of historical examples. I also find his statement of leadership through action more compelling than Bush's call for fairness and cooperation.

Also note that the writing style is formal and that the word choice is precise in order to convey specific ideas.

Practice Essay

This practice allows you to compose your response to the given task and then compare it with examples of responses at the different score levels. You will also get a scoring guide that includes a detailed explanation of how official GED® test graders will score your response. You may use this scoring guide to score your own response.

Before you begin, it is important to note that on the official test this task must be completed in no more than 45 minutes. But don't rush to complete your response; take time to carefully read the passage(s) and the question prompt. Then think about how you would like to respond.

As you write your essay, be sure to:

- Decide which position presented in the passages is better supported by evidence.
- Explain why your chosen position has better support.
- Recognize that the position with better support may not be the position you agree with.
- Present multiple pieces of evidence from the passage to defend your assertions.

- Thoroughly construct your main points, organizing them logically, with strong supporting details.
- Connect your sentences, paragraphs, and ideas with transitional words and phrases.
- Express your ideas clearly and choose your words carefully.

- Use varied sentence structures to increase the clarity of your response.
- Reread and revise your response.

Good luck!

Please use the following to answer the essay question.

An Analysis of Nuclear Energy

1   America runs on energy. As a matter of fact, the United States is the second largest energy consumer in the world, behind China. In recent years, it can be argued that we need to ease our dependence on foreign countries that supply us with oil and develop energy at home. But where can we get the energy we need?

Benefits of Nuclear Energy

2   The U.S. Department of Energy (DOE) promotes the development of safe, domestic nuclear power, and there are many who support the idea that nuclear power is the answer. Compared to fossil fuels such as gas, coal, and oil, nuclear energy is the most efficient way to make electricity. For example, the Idaho National Laboratory reports that "one uranium fuel pellet—roughly the size of the tip of an adult's little finger—contains the same amount of energy as 17,000 cubic feet of natural gas, 1,780 pounds of coal, or 149 gallons of oil."

3   Supporters of nuclear energy cite that nuclear generators don't create great amounts of poisonous carbon dioxide, nitrogen oxides, and sulfur dioxide like the burning of fossil fuels does. The DOE reports that a nuclear generator produces 30 tons of spent fuel a year compared to the 300,000 tons of coal ash produced by a coal-powered electrical plant.

4   In terms of safety, the Nuclear Regulatory Commission ensures that each and every nuclear reactor maintains strict safety standards. Radioactive waste is contained deep underground behind steel-reinforced, 1.2-meter-thick concrete walls. The DOE also points out that "ash from burning coal at a power plant emits 100 times more radiation into the surrounding environment than a nuclear power plant."

(continues)

Arguments against Nuclear Energy

5   Opponents of nuclear energy argue that nuclear reactors endanger all life on Earth for three basic reasons. First, nuclear radioactivity is deadly and must be contained for thousands of years. Second, no matter how many safety measures are in place, accidents happen, and nuclear meltdowns are global environmental catastrophes. Finally, nuclear fuel used to generate electricity can also be used to build atomic bombs.

6   Nuclear generators use radioactive plutonium and uranium for fuel. Scientists say that exposure to a millionth of an ounce of plutonium causes cancer. Even nuclear energy proponents agree that life-threatening nuclear waste must be contained for half a million years before it becomes safe to be around. Radioactive dumps last generations.

7   Opponents of nuclear energy also cite the ever-present threat of meltdowns. Widespread radioactive contamination and death caused by the nuclear accidents at Three Mile Island, Chernobyl, and Fukushima are cautionary lessons. Researchers disagree on how possible it is to safely contain radioactivity, but it's undeniable that nuclear meltdown causes widespread contamination of the air, water, and land with deadly radioactivity. It is also verifiable that nuclear accidents have caused environmental catastrophes that continue to this day.

8   Perhaps even more disturbing than the threat of toxic waste and meltdown is the use of uranium for sinister purposes. On December 7, 2013, Reuters reported that ". . . in news that may concern world powers . . . Iran is moving ahead with testing more efficient uranium enrichment technology. . . ." Indeed, the United Nations and the entire world are worried about Iran's enhancement of uranium for use in nuclear power plants because the same enhanced uranium can be used to build atomic weaponry.

9   Opponents argue that in the same way we learned that fossil fuels are limited and destroy the environment, so must we learn from nuclear disasters. Opponents say the answer is to develop safe, clean, and renewable sources of alternative energy, such as solar, wind, tidal, and geothermal power. Why gamble? The future of the world is at stake.

PROMPT:

Nuclear energy proponents argue that it is safe and efficient, while opponents make the case for alternative energy sources, citing the deadly consequences of nuclear disaster.

In your response, analyze both positions presented in the article to determine which one is better supported. Use relevant and specific evidence from both articles to support your response.

You should expect to spend up to 45 minutes planning, drafting, and editing your response.

_____

_____

_____

_____

_____

_____

_____

_____

_____

_____

_____

_____

_____

_____

_____

_____

_____

The Final Steps

The sample essay you just read is the final, submitted version of the essay. When you write *your* essay, you will probably need to revise your first draft before you get to this stage. You'll want to read it over carefully and make changes to improve it. Focus on improving the text (what you say) and style (how you say it), as well as fixing grammar and language errors that you may not have noticed when you were writing.

Evaluating Your Work

Use this checklist to help you evaluate your first draft to make revisions. Your response should:

- Introduce a clear point of view, distinguishing it from an opposing point of view as necessary.
- Develop the point of view and an opposing point of view fairly, give evidence for each, and point out the strengths and weaknesses of both.
- Provide a conclusion that supports the argument presented.
- Follow the rules of standard written English.

Managing Your Time

You will have 45 minutes to complete your extended response for the GED® RLA test. This requires careful planning and time management to read the passage(s) and then write your essay.

In general, you should organize your time by spending:

10–12 **minutes** reading the passage(s) and establishing your thesis

20–25 **minutes** creating a quick outline and writing your response

10–15 **minutes** reviewing and revising your response

When you respond to a practice essay prompt, set a timer to make sure that you are on track.

Quiz

Now that you know what's involved in writing an effective essay, use what you've learned to answer the following questions.

1. What is the purpose of a prompt?
   a. to help the student start writing about the topic
   b. to state the main idea of the essay
   c. to provide support for the main idea
   d. to suggest a possible conclusion

2. Which of the following states the main idea of an essay?
   a. thesis statement
   b. transition
   c. topic sentence
   d. introduction

3. Which of the following sentences would be a good thesis statement?
   a. My favorite object is my grandfather's old leather bag.
   b. This is an essay about my favorite object.
   c. The bag is made of leather.
   d. My grandfather's leather bag

4. Why is it helpful to brainstorm when writing?
   a. It helps give you ideas of what to write about.
   b. It takes up time.
   c. It helps you write the thesis statement.
   d. It puts your ideas in order.

5. What is the purpose of creating an outline?
   a. to organize your ideas
   b. to take up time
   c. to practice your spelling
   d. to make revision unnecessary

6. Which of the following should always state the main idea of a paragraph?
   a. topic sentence
   b. transition
   c. thesis statement
   d. introduction

7. How many main ideas should a paragraph have?
   a. one
   b. two
   c. three
   d. no fewer than two

8. Which of the following is a purpose of supporting sentences?
   a. to provide examples
   b. to state the main idea
   c. to restate the thesis
   d. to give the reader a sense of closure

9. Which of the following should a good conclusion do?
   a. state a new idea
   b. end with a question
   c. use specific examples
   d. leave the reader with a sense of closure

10. What is the purpose of revising when writing?
   a. to move paragraphs
   b. to rewrite the essay
   c. to restate the thesis
   d. to correct minor errors

11. *Practice proofreading this paragraph:*
   My best friend Janet and me decide that we would bake brownis to take to the picnic that our Algebra Club was planning for Friday afternoon. We look up a recipe online, and we checked to see if either of us had all the ingredients we needed. Sure enough, everything was their and ready at Janet's house. Then we stopped by the store at lunch to get extra cute paper napkins and plates, and then we got distract looking at magazines and nail polish in the drug store next door. Suddenly the time was late, the cookies never got made we were in a hurry to get back to work. I guess cookies were just not meant to be.

Practice Essay Prompts

12. *Read the following writing prompt and write an essay that appropriately addresses it. Be sure to review and edit your work.*
   Many parents give children a weekly or monthly allowance regardless of their behavior because they believe an allowance teaches children to be financially responsible. Other parents only give children an allowance as a reward for completing chores or when they have behaved properly. Explain what you think parents should do and why.

13. *Read the following writing prompt and write an essay that appropriately addresses it. Be sure to review and edit your work.*
   More and more farmers and food manufacturers are genetically modifying their crops to reduce susceptibility to disease, improve flavor, and reduce costs. Do you think genetically modifying foods is a good idea? Why or why not? Use specific reasons and examples to support your position.

14. *Read the following writing prompt and write an essay that appropriately addresses it. Be sure to review and edit your work.*

   Good habits improve our physical, emotional, and/or financial health. Select one of your good habits and write an essay persuading readers to make that habit a part of their lives.

15. *Read the following writing prompt and write an essay that appropriately addresses it. Be sure to review and edit your work.*

   Some people think of the United States as a nation of "couch potatoes." Write an essay persuading readers to be more physically active.

16. *Read the following writing prompt and write an essay that appropriately addresses it. Be sure to review and edit your work.*

   Today's top professional athletes often have salaries and bonuses in the tens of millions of dollars. Do you think these athletes deserve such high compensation? Why or why not? Explain your position and use specific reasons and examples.

17. *Read the following writing prompt and write an essay that appropriately addresses it. Be sure to review and edit your work.*

   Is reading fiction a waste of time? Why or why not? Explain your answer using specific reasons and examples to support your position.

18. *Read the following writing prompt and write an essay that appropriately addresses it. Be sure to review and edit your work.*

   Many people feel that the use of surveillance cameras in public places, such as parking lots, is a good idea that can help ensure our safety. Others worry that too many cameras violate our right to privacy and give law enforcement officials too much power. In your opinion, should we install more surveillance cameras in public places? Why or why not? Support your position with specific reasons and examples.

19. *Read the following writing prompt and write an essay that appropriately addresses it. Be sure to review and edit your work.*

   Alexander Smith said, "The great man is the man who does a thing for the first time." Do you agree with this definition of greatness? Why or why not? Support your position with specific reasons and examples.

20. *Read the following writing prompt and write an essay that appropriately addresses it. Be sure to review and edit your work.*

   Should people lease or buy new cars? Make a case for the option that you think is better. Use specific reasons and examples to support your position.

21. *Read the following writing prompt and write an essay that appropriately addresses it. Be sure to review and edit your work.*

   The inventor and statesman Benjamin Franklin said, "Money never made a man happy yet, nor will it. There is nothing in its nature to produce happiness." Do you agree with this statement? Why or why not? Use specific reasons and examples to support your position.

Answers and Explanations

1. a. The prompt is meant to get you started thinking about the topic of your writing. As you write, your essay will address the prompt using details and support.

2. a. The thesis statement tells the main idea of the entire essay. Each paragraph contains a topic sentence that states the main idea of that paragraph.

3. a. The thesis statement should be a complete sentence that answers the question stated in the prompt.

4. a. Brainstorming helps you get all your ideas down on paper. After you brainstorm, you can choose which ideas to include and put these ideas in proper order.

5. a. An outline helps you organize your ideas and decide which will be the main ideas and which will be supporting details.

6. a. The topic sentence tells what the paragraph will be about. The rest of the sentences support the topic sentence.

7. a. Each paragraph should have one main idea. All of the sentences in the paragraph should explain or support that idea.

8. a. Supporting sentences help explain the main idea by providing examples and additional information.

9. d. The conclusion restates the main idea, wraps up the essay, and provides a sense of closure for the reader.

10. d. Revising is the step in which you correct errors in spelling, capitalization, and grammar. This is also the time to remove unrelated or unnecessary information, and clarify ideas as needed.

11. *Corrected version:*
Some errors were technical, like replacing "me" with "I" and making sure the tense of each verb matched ("decided," "stopped," "looked,"). Others were errors of consistency or clarity.

My best friend Janet and ~~me~~ **I** decide**d** that we would bake ~~brownis~~ **brownies** to take to the picnic that our Algebra Club was planning for Friday afternoon. We look**ed** up a recipe online, and we checked to see if either of us had all the ingredients we needed. Sure enough, everything was ~~their~~ **there** and ready at Janet's house. ~~Then~~ **W**e stopped by the store at lunch to get extra cute paper napkins and plates, ~~and~~ **but** then we got distract**ed** looking at magazines and nail polish in the drug store next door. Suddenly the time was late, the ~~cookies~~ **brownies** never got made**, and** we were in a hurry to get back to ~~work~~ **school**. I guess ~~cookies~~ **brownies** were just not meant to be.

12. Sample Response

Starting when I was about eight years old, my parents gave me a list of chores that had to be completed each week. If I did my chores, I got an allowance, a bit of change that I could use as I pleased. If I didn't do my chores, I didn't get my allowance. There was no other punishment, but no other punishment was necessary. That dollar or two a week was all the incentive I needed to help out around the house. Whether it was the latest Barbie or a six-pack of Hubba Bubba chewing gum, there was always something I wanted to buy. My parents could always count on me doing my chores.

I think that giving children an allowance for doing chores is a smart parenting move, for it accomplishes four important goals: It helps ensure that important work gets done around the house; it teaches children that they need to do their part to make things run smoothly for the whole family; it rewards children in a realistic, practical way for good behavior; and it helps teach children how to handle money.

I know that some people consider money for chores a form of bribery, and others feel that children should just do their chores anyway, without the incentive of an allowance. They argue that giving kids money for doing chores undermines the lesson that they need to help the family and do their part. I can understand that point of view, and when parents give their children too much money, it does undermine those lessons. But when the allowance is small, it is simply a modern version of the age-old practice of rewarding good behavior. Once children reach a certain age, money is an appropriate and effective reward that helps them learn how to be responsible and how to manage money. They get a sense of what things are worth and how much they have to save and spend to get what they want. And learning to save in order to purchase a desired item teaches them patience and helps children better understand the value of hard work.

Giving children money for doing chores is also a good introduction to the reality of the workplace. If they do the work, they get paid; if they don't do the work, they don't. Extra work can be rewarded with bonuses and extra praise; poor work may result in a pay cut or demotion.

It's important for parents to find the right amount to give. Too much money may make a child feel like hired help and will undermine the goal of teaching children to help simply because they are part of a family that must work together. On the other hand, too little money may make a child feel resentful, as if his or her work isn't worth anything to the household. What's an appropriate amount? It depends upon the amount of chores the child is expected to do and the child's age. If your nine-year-old is only expected to clean his or her room, a dollar a week is probably plenty. If your

14-year-old is expected to keep his room clean, take out the trash, water the plants, and vacuum the house, then ten dollars a week is more appropriate. Being paid for my chores helped me have a good attitude about housework, taught me how to save money and spend it wisely, and enabled me to appreciate the hard work my parents did around the house. I'm really grateful that this was the way my parents chose to handle chores in our household.

13. Sample Response

A few decades ago, manipulating genes in people, plants, and animals was just science fiction. Today, it's a reality, and genetic modification may have many positive applications in the future, including the eradication of many hereditary diseases. But like most scientific and technological advances, the genetic modification of organisms for our food supply can be as dangerous as it is beneficial. Because of the potential dangers of this technology, I think genetically altering plants and animals in the food supply is a practice that should be very tightly controlled and carefully studied before it is an accepted and common practice. Unfortunately, it may already be too late for that.

Many people don't even realize that many of their foods are genetically modified organisms (GMOs). GMOs are already prevalent in supermarkets and grocery stores across the country, but manufacturers are not required to label foods as having been made from GMOs. As a result, millions of Americans purchase and eat GMOs every day without even knowing it. Yet we don't even know if GMOs are harmful to our health. We don't really know how GMOs may affect our bodies or our ecosystem. When we mess with DNA, we may be making changes that have all sorts of dangerous repercussions, including some that we may not even realize for several generations.

One of the main concerns about GMOs is the unpredictability of the behavior of altered genes and of the bacteria, plants, and animals that interact with the altered organism. For example, a crop of corn genetically modified to be less susceptible to a particular insect may take on other unwanted characteristics due to the change. It may, for example, become *more* susceptible to another disease, or it could develop a tougher skin on its kernels, or it could decrease the crop's ability to produce vitamin E.

More frightening is the domino effect of genetically modifying foods. Any change in an organism's DNA has the potential to affect not only the organism but also anything that feeds off of it, *including us.* How do we know how GMOs might affect us on a microscopic, genetic level? We don't know, and can't know, without years of studies that track all sorts of potential outcomes over several generations.

Another fear is that transferred genes may escape from one organism into another. For example, imagine that Strain A of sweet peas was altered by adding a gene that would increase its sugar production. Through cross-pollination, this altered genetic code could enter other strains and slowly (or quickly) infect the entire subspecies. If the alteration was beneficial, this could be a good thing. But the altered gene might not act the same way in all varieties, and the change may not be a good thing in the first place, and/or it may have unintended consequences.

Genetically modifying foods is a practice that has been driven by the desire to make more food available more quickly and more cheaply than ever before. This attitude puts profit first and consumers and the environment last, and that is simply dangerous. The agribusiness needs to slow down and stop selling us GMOs until their safety is certain.

14. Sample Response

When I was 15, I wanted to get a job so I could buy a car when I turned 16. My father sat me down at the kitchen table and said, "Excellent. But only on one condition: 10% of every paycheck must go into a savings account. And you cannot touch that money except in an emergency."

"But Dad," I argued, "if I have to put 10% away, how will I ever save enough money to buy a car?"

"You'll have enough," he replied. "And you'll soon see how important it is to set money aside for savings."

I didn't believe him at the time, and in fact I often resented having to put that 10% into a separate account. But two years later when the transmission on my car blew, I didn't have to fret about coming up with the money for repairs. I was able to cover the cost easily and was back on the road in no time. It was then that I began to see the wisdom of my father's rule, which I adopted as my own. This habit has helped to give me a secure financial life, and I urge you to make this practice part of your life.

Ten percent of each paycheck may sound like a lot, and if you're on a tight budget to begin with, you might be thinking, "I just can't afford to do it." In truth, you can't afford not to do it. You never know when you are going to need an extra $100 or $1,000; life is full of surprises, and lots of them are expensive.

As tight as your budget may be, it's important to get started right away. If you are absolutely scraping by with every last penny going to bills, then start with just 5%, but move up to 10% as soon as you can. If you earn $500 a week, for example, put $25–$50 in your savings account each week. At first, this may mean clipping coupons, renting a movie instead of going to the theater, or pressing your own shirts instead of taking them to the cleaner. Think carefully about ways you can save just a few dollars—because just a few dollars from each paycheck is all it takes to build up a solid savings account.

The money you save will add up quickly. For example, if your annual salary is $40,000, each year you would put $4,000 into your savings account. That still leaves you with $36,000 to cover all your expenses. After ten years, you will have saved $40,000, plus interest. And the more money in your account, the more interest you earn, the larger your emergency fund, the more you can afford to relax later in your life.

Once you get in the habit of putting 10% of your money into savings, it won't feel like a sacrifice. The 90% that's left will be your working budget, and you won't even miss that 10% because you won't be used to spending it. Yet you will know that it is there, ready for an emergency, helping to keep you financially secure. So take my father's advice, and mine: Put a piece of each paycheck into your savings. It's a habit that's worth every penny.

15. Sample Response

Is your favorite place in the home sitting on the couch in front of the television? Do you spend hours and hours there each day, surrounded by bags of chips and cans of soda? Do you panic when you can't find the remote control and think that you might actually have to get up off the sofa to change the channel?

If you answered "yes" to any of these questions, you are not alone. In fact, you are one of the millions of Americans who are "couch potatoes": people who spend their days and nights "vegging out" in front of the "tube."

Well, spud, it's time to get up out of that armchair and get some exercise!

I know how seductive television can be. I know how easy it is to plop onto the sofa and lose yourself in the world of sports, reality shows, and good old make-believe. I know how mesmerizing MTV and other channels can be and how hard it can be to pull yourself away. But all that television spells disaster for your body because it needs to be active to be healthy. And it's no good for your mental health or social life, either.

Think about what all that time in front of the television is doing to your body. Think about what all that sagging muscle and growing belly is doing to your life. Think about how your lack of energy affects you at work.

Now think about how different things would be if you spent some of that TV time getting exercise instead: You would feel better during the day. You would sleep better at night. You would have more energy. You would look better. You would have more confidence. You would be more creative. You would be healthier and happier. And you would not even miss the television.

What sort of exercise can you do? Anything! Go for a walk. Ride a bike. Jog. Lift weights. Take an aerobics class. Do yoga. Join a basketball or hockey league. Swim. Rollerblade. Grab a friend, a fellow couch potato, and exercise together.

You can start with just 15 minutes a day, two or three days a week, and build up slowly. Before you know it, your couch potato days will be over, and you will wonder how on earth you ever spent so much time in front of the TV.

16. Sample Response

Why do top athletes earn such inflated salaries? Because they bring big bucks into their cities and franchises. But what sort of service do they provide to society? Do they save lives? No. Do they improve the standard of living or promote positive social change? No. Do they help keep our streets safe or educate our kids? No. True, many of the top athletes are good role models for our children. But seven-figure salaries don't always mean model behavior.

It is true that professional athletes work hard, and many have spent their lives pursuing their goals. It is also true that most professional athletes have a relatively short career span—a decade perhaps at the top of their game.

Limited as their professional sporting career may be, they don't deserve such high salaries. After their professional sports careers are over, they can certainly pursue other careers and work "regular" jobs like the rest of us.

Ending their stint as professional athletes doesn't mean they have to stop earning incomes. They just have to earn incomes in a different way. Why should they be any different from the rest of us who may need to switch careers?

It is also true that professional athletes may be injured while on the job; their work is indeed physical, and especially in contact sports like football, injuries are bound to happen. But, like the rest of us, they have insurance, and in nearly all cases, their exorbitant salaries more than cover their medical costs. And theirs is not the only high-risk job. What about miners, construction workers, or firefighters? They are at risk for physical injury every day, too—injuries that could likewise end their careers. But they sure aren't earning millions of dollars a year.

It is also true that professional athletes may spend years and years practicing with farm teams for a fraction of the salary they receive once they make it to the top. But in every career path, we start off with lower wages and must pay our dues and work our way up. Besides, farm team salaries are not always so low.

We're a sports-crazy country, a nation of fanatic sports fans and celebrity worshippers. We're awed and entertained by the best of them, but as much as they may inspire and amuse us, professional athletes do not deserve such high salaries. Those millions could be much more wisely spent.

17. Sample Response

Remember the last book that captured your imagination, that transported you to another place and time? Remember a book that made you fall in love with its characters, made you feel their pain and joy? Remember a story that taught you an important lesson, that helped you better understand others and make sense of the human condition? If so, then you can understand why the question "Is reading fiction a waste of time?" is such a silly question.

Fiction, unlike a user manual, a magazine article, or a newspaper editorial, probably won't offer you any practical knowledge that you can put to immediate use. It won't inform you of current events or give you advice on how to cultivate a better garden. It probably won't help you decide which candidate to vote for or which product to buy. But that certainly doesn't mean it's useless or impractical. Indeed, fiction serves three important functions for human beings: It helps us be more compassionate to others, it helps us better understand ourselves, and it cultivates our imaginations. It can also teach us about history, psychology, even biology and other sciences.

Compassion for others is rooted in understanding and acceptance, and a good story brings us into the inner world of its characters so that we can understand them. In Toni Morrison's novel *The Bluest Eye*, for example,

Morrison peels away the layers of her characters' histories piece by piece like an onion until we see into their core and understand what drives them.

They may still do awful things to each other, but she shows us *why* they do the things that they do, and we learn that we shouldn't judge others until we understand their pasts. Their stories are sad and painful, and we learn to love even the outcast Pecola. In fact, we learn that those outcasts are the ones who need our love the most.

Many stories and novels also help us better understand ourselves. Joseph Conrad's dark and powerful novel *Heart of Darkness* helps us see that all of us have a dark side and that we need to acknowledge this dark side in order to control it. It makes us question just how civilized we are and indeed what it means to be civilized in the first place.

Good fiction also cultivates our imagination, which is more important to us than some might think. Without imagination, we live a sad, empty life. Imagination is central to our emotional health and is a key factor in our level of intelligence. Facts are one thing, but facts can be of no real use unless coupled with imagination. Fiction can help us by keeping our imagination fresh and active. In a story like Franz Kafka's "Metamorphosis," for example, we are asked to imagine that Gregor, the main character, wakes up one morning and has turned into a giant bug. Crazy? Perhaps. But once we accept this premise and imagine Gregor as a five-foot-long cockroach, we can feel his family's horror and imagine his agony as he finds himself trapped in his room and abandoned by those he loves.

Is reading fiction a waste of time? That's like asking if laughing is a waste of time. We don't need fiction to survive, but we do need it to be kinder, more understanding, and more creative human beings.

18. Sample Response

Not long ago, the nation was gripped by the horrifying news that a baby had been stolen from a car in a parking lot while her mother, who was returning a shopping cart, was just a few feet away. Thanks to the description of the kidnapper captured by surveillance cameras in the parking lot and broadcast over radios, television, and highway overpass signs, the kidnapper was quickly caught and the baby returned, unharmed, to her mother.

Had it not been for those surveillance cameras, that mother would probably never have seen her baby girl again.

I can't think of a much better argument for the use of surveillance cameras in public places. That baby's life was saved by those parking lot cameras. Many people worry about the use of surveillance cameras in public places such as parking lots, stores, parks, and roadways. They don't like the idea that they are being watched. They worry that the information captured on the surveillance tapes can somehow be used against them. But how? It seems to me that the only reason we should worry about being caught on surveillance cameras is if we are doing something wrong. If we are behaving lawfully in a public place, then why worry if it is captured on film?

Surveillance cameras can provide two immensely important services. One, they can help us find those who commit crimes, including thieves, kidnappers, vandals, and even murderers. Two, they can serve as a powerful deterrent to crime. A thief who plans to steal a car may think twice if he knows he will be caught on video. A woman who hopes to kidnap a child may abandon her plans if she knows she will be captured on film.

Surveillance cameras can also help us in less critical but nonetheless practical ways. In some towns in England, for example, radio dee-jays use information from surveillance cameras to announce the availability of parking spaces in crowded public parking lots. Problems of all shapes and sizes can also be noted and addressed through video surveillance. For example, imagine a video camera installed in a local town square. Reviewing the films, officials might realize that people who meet in the square move quickly into the shade of the one tree in the center of the square. This could move officials to plant more trees or provide tables with umbrellas so that people could meet and relax in the shade. Similarly, a video camera in a grocery store might reveal that aisle 7 is always overcrowded, prompting the manager to rearrange items to more evenly distribute shoppers.

Of course it's possible to have too much of a good thing, and if surveillance cameras cross the line and start being installed on private property—that is, in our offices and homes—then we will have the "Big Brother is watching" scenario opponents fear. If that were the case, I would be against surveillance cameras, too. But as long as surveillance cameras are limited to public places, they can help ensure our safety.

19. Sample Response

Just as there are many definitions of success, there are also many definitions of greatness. Alexander Smith said that a great person is someone who does a thing for the first time. He's right, and the list of those great people is long and includes the likes of Neil Armstrong, Jackie Robinson, and Thomas Edison. But Smith's definition isn't broad enough to include many other people who I believe are also great. In my opinion, greatness can also be attained by doing something to improve the lives of others.

Mother Teresa is the first person to come to mind under this broadened definition. Mother Teresa, who received the Nobel Peace Prize in 1979, dedicated her life to helping the poor, the sick, and the hungry. She left her homeland of Yugoslavia to work with the impoverished people of India, where she self-lessly served others for almost 70 years. She became a nun and founded the Missionaries of Charity sisterhood and the House for the Dying. She embraced those whom many in society chose to disdain and ignore: the crip-pled and diseased, the homeless and helpless. She gave them food, shelter, medical care, and the compassion that so many others denied them. She was certainly not the first to dedicate her life to the care of others, but she was cer-tainly a great woman.

Another great person who also won a Nobel Peace Prize was Dr. Albert Schweitzer, a German doctor who, like Mother Teresa, also selflessly served the poor and sick. Schweitzer dedicated himself to the people of Africa. There, he built a hospital and a leper colony, a refuge for those who had been rejected by society. Again, he was not the first to offer care and comfort for the sick and suffering. But he cer-tainly was great.

Harriet Tubman is also clearly a great woman. She led hundreds of American slaves to freedom along the Underground Railroad, risk-ing her life over and over again to bring her fel-low slaves to freedom. She gave them the greatest gift one can offer: freedom to live a bet-ter way of life. She wasn't the first to escape, and she wasn't the first to go back for others. But she was the one who kept going back. She knew that each time she returned for another, she was risking her life. But like Mother Teresa and Dr. Schweitzer, Harriet Tubman was utterly dedi-cated to improving the lives of others.

Greatness comes in many forms, and we are lucky to have many examples of greatness upon which to model our lives. Some great people are those who were able to be the first to accomplish something marvelous.

Others, like Mother Teresa, Albert Schweitzer, and Harriet Tubman, are great because they worked tirelessly to ease the suffering of their fellow human beings.

20. Sample Response

Planning to lease a car because you don't think you can afford to buy? Think again. Leasing can end up being just as expensive as buying—and you don't even get to keep the car. Even if you decide to buy the car at the end of your lease, you may end up paying considerably more money than if you'd decided to buy from the beginning.

Most people who are thinking about leasing are attracted to this option because they believe it will cost them less money. And they're right—it is cheaper, but only in the short term. For example, if you were to lease a 2002 Subaru Forester, with $2,500 down, you might pay $250 per month for the car. If you were to buy the same car, with $2,500 down, you would pay closer to $350 per month. Over a three-year lease, that's $3,600—a big savings. But after your lease is over, you have to give the car back. If you want to keep driving it, either you'll have to put another down payment on another lease, or, if you have the option to buy the car, you'll have to pay thousands of dollars to purchase the vehicle—dollars that won't be spread out in more manageable monthly payments.

Many people want to lease because they can then drive a nicer car than they might otherwise be able to afford. For example, if your monthly budget allowed you to spend $250 on your car, you might be able to lease a brand-new Ford Explorer. For the same price, you might have to buy an Explorer that was two or three years old with 50,000 miles, or buy a new but considerably less expensive make and model. A lease therefore allows you to drive the latest models of more expensive cars. But when your lease is over, you will have to return that Explorer. Whatever car you can afford to buy, you get to keep it, and it will always have a resale or trade-in value if you wanted to later upgrade to a newer car.

Furthermore, people who lease cars are often shocked by how much they must pay when the lease is over. Most leases limit you to a certain number of miles, and if you go over that allotment, you must pay for each mile. As a result, at the end of your lease, you may end up paying thousands of dollars in mileage fees. For example, if your lease covers you for 25,000 miles over three years, but you drive 40,000, that's an extra 15,000 miles. At $.11 per mile, that's $1,650 you'll have to pay. And you still won't have a car.

In addition, when you lease, you still have to pay for regular maintenance and repairs to the vehicle. Since you must return the car when your lease expires, you are paying to repair *someone else's car*. If you own the car, however, you know that every dollar you spend maintaining or repairing the car is an investment in a real piece of property—your property, not someone else's.

By now, the benefits of buying over leasing should be clear. But if you're still not convinced, remember this fundamental fact: If you lease, when your lease is up, after you've made all of your monthly payments, paid for extra mileage, and paid for repairs, *you must give the car back*. It isn't yours to keep, no matter how much the lease cost you. Whatever make or model you can afford to buy is yours to keep after you make your payments. There's no giving it back, and that makes all the difference.

21. Sample Response

Benjamin Franklin is one of the greatest figures in American history, and I have a great deal of respect for this incredible inventor, politician, and writer. But I must respectfully disagree with his claim that "Money never made a man happy yet, nor will it. There is nothing in its nature to produce happiness." I agree that money in and of itself does not make a person happy; but I believe that money can help provide one thing that is essential to happiness: good health.

While money can do nothing to change our genetic makeup and our physiological predisposition to illness and disease, it can give us access to better healthcare throughout our lives. This begins with prenatal care and childhood vaccinations. In impoverished third-world countries, infant mortality rates are three, four, even ten times higher than in the United States, and as many as one in four women still die in childbirth because they do not have access to modern medical care. Sadly, people who are too poor to afford vaccinations and routine health-care for their children watch helplessly as many of those children succumb to illnesses and diseases that are rarely fatal here in the United States.

Money also enables us to afford better doctors and see specialists throughout our lives. If your child has difficulty hearing, for example, and you have insurance (which costs money) or cash, you can see a hearing specialist and pay for therapy. If you have migraines that make you miserable, you can see a headache specialist and afford medication and treatment. Having money also means being able to afford preventive measures, such as taking vitamins and getting regular checkups. It means being able to afford products and services that can enhance our health, such as gym memberships, organic foods, and acupuncture.

Another important thing money can do is enable us to live in a healthy environment. Many of the world's poorest people live in dirty, dangerous places—unsanitary slums crawling with diseases and health hazards of all sorts. In a particularly poor area of the Bronx, for example, children had an abnormally high rate of asthma because their families couldn't afford to move away from the medical waste treatment plant that was poisoning the air.

Money can also help us be healthy by enabling us to afford proper heating and cooling measures. This includes being able to afford a warm winter coat and the opportunity to cool off at a pool or in the ocean. On a more basic level, it means being able to afford heat in the winter and air-conditioning in the summer. During heat waves, victims of heat stroke are often those who are too poor to afford air-conditioning in their apartments. In extreme cold, the same is true: People who freeze to death or become gravely ill from the cold are often those who are unable to afford high heating bills.

Having money may not make people happy, but it sure goes a long way toward keeping them healthy. And as they say, if you haven't got your health, you haven't got anything.

A Final Word

Whew! Throughout this book, you've reviewed a number of reading comprehension strategies that will help you do your best on the GED® Reasoning through Language Arts test. In this chapter, you've learned some tips that will help you do your best as you put the writing strategies into practice. You are on your way to earning an outstanding score on the test and bringing home the ultimate prize—your GED® test credential!

Certainly, remembering all this information and facing the GED® test can be intimidating, but you are taking all the right steps toward doing your best. Review these strategies until you are comfortable and confident in your abilities with each. Take the practice tests in this book and monitor your own learning. If there are skills you need to brush up on, go back to that section of the book and review the information. When you find skills that you have mastered, give yourself a pat on the back. You've earned it!

Keep the test-taking, prewriting, draft, and revision tips in this book in mind any time you take a test, not just the GED® test! Read passages and answer choices carefully, pay attention to details, take time to plan out your writing, proofread thoroughly, and select the best answer choice for multiple-choice questions. These are all great ways to succeed in test taking.

And don't sweat it when you come across a question that seems tough or a prompt you have no idea how to answer. It happens to everyone, no matter how you prepare. Remember to map out your short answers and essay responses, to brainstorm or outline, and to revise thoughtfully. Don't waste your time trying to fill up the space with meaningless or nonsensical words. Take a deep breath, choose your strongest idea as a topic sentence, and, if nothing else, make a brief outline. Move on if you need to—you can always come back at the end if time allows, and having the extra time to think may be all the help you need.

Remember, you're on the right track. Taking charge of your own learning and being prepared are great first steps toward a successful GED® test experience. Good luck!

REVIEW

In this chapter, you have reviewed strategies for writing an effective essay.

1. An **essay** has three main parts:
   - an introduction
   - a body
   - a conclusion

   You can think of these three parts as the beginning, middle, and end.

2. The **introduction** catches the reader's attention and introduces the main idea of the essay in the form of a thesis statement. The **body** develops the thesis statement in two or three paragraphs. The **conclusion** restates the thesis statement and brings the essay to a close.

3. The **writing** process has three main steps:
   - planning
   - writing
   - revising

4. **Planning** is an important step in the writing process. It helps you decide what you want to write about and organize your ideas effectively. Planning includes writing a thesis statement, brainstorming ideas, and then organizing them into an outline. Once you've completed these three steps, writing your essay should go more smoothly.

5. **Revising** gives you one last chance to make sure your essay is as good as it can be. If you have planned well, you should not have to make any major changes during the revision process. Some things to check for include capitalization, punctuation, repetition, and clarity.

9 ▶ GED® RLA PRACTICE TEST 1

This practice test is modeled on the format, content, and timing of the official GED® Reasoning through Language Arts test.

Part I

Like the official exam, this section presents a series of questions that assess your ability to read, write, edit, and understand standard written English. You'll be asked to answer questions based on informational and literary reading passages. Refer to the passages as often as necessary when answering the questions.

Work carefully, but do not spend too much time on any one question. Be sure you answer every question.

Set a timer for 95 minutes (1 hour and 35 minutes), and try to take this test uninterrupted, under quiet conditions.

Part II

The official GED® Reasoning through Language Arts test also includes an essay question, called the Extended Response. Set a timer for 45 minutes, and try to read the given passage and then brainstorm, write, and proofread your essay without interruption, under quiet conditions.

Complete answer explanations for every test question and sample essays at different scoring levels follow the exam. Good luck!

Part I

48 total questions
95 minutes to complete

Please use the following to answer questions 1–6.

Remarks by the First Lady on a Visit to Thank USDA Employees

May 3, 2013

1   Thank you for supporting our farmers and our ranchers and working tirelessly to market their products across the globe, which, by the way, helps to create jobs right here at home. Thank you for protecting our environment by promoting renewable energy sources that will power our country for generations to come. So that's an impact on not just us but our children and our grandchildren and their children. Thank you for that work. Thank you for lifting up rural communities. And thank you for keeping our food safe. And I think this is something most of the country doesn't realize—the work that you do here to protect the environment, you keep our food safe, working to end hunger, improve nutrition for families across this country.

2   And the nutrition issue, as Tom mentioned, as you all know, is something near and dear to my heart, not just as First Lady but as a mother. In fact, one of the first things that I did as, you know, as First Lady, was to plant the garden at the White House. And it's really pretty. [*Laughter.*] I hope you guys get a chance to see it—it's beautiful now. It rained a couple of days. Thank you. [*Laughter.*] And the idea with planting the garden wasn't just to encourage kids to eat more vegetables. I also wanted to teach them about where their food comes from.

3   I think you've known this—we see this as we traveled around the country—some kids have never seen what a real tomato looks like off the vine. They don't know where a cucumber comes from. And that really affects the way they view food. So a garden helps them really get their hands dirty, literally, and understand the whole process of where their food comes from. And I wanted them to see just how challenging and rewarding it is to grow your own food, so that they would better understand what our farmers are doing every single day across this country and have an appreciation for that work, that tradition—that American tradition of growing our own food and feeding ourselves.

4   And the garden helped spark a conversation in this country about healthy eating that led us to create Let's Move. As you know, it's a nationwide initiative to end childhood obesity in this country in a generation, so that all of our kids can grow up healthy. And all of you all at USDA, let me just tell you, have been such a critical part of this effort right from the very start. This would not happen—all the conversation, all the movement around health—that's all because of so many of you right here in this room and throughout this building, and in agencies and facilities all over this country. You helped to launch our new MyPlate icon, which is changing the way families serve their meals and gives them a really easy way to understand what a healthy plate looks like.

1. What is the likely overall purpose or intent of the passage?
   a. to discuss the programs Mrs. Obama began with the goal of inspiring kids to eat healthier
   b. to thank farmers for their work
   c. to introduce Mrs. Obama's nutrition initiative
   d. to emphasize the important role of USDA employees in creating good nutrition in the United States

2. Write your response in the box below.

   According to Mrs. Obama, ⬚ mentioned that the nutrition issue is something near and dear to her heart.

3. Based on the passage, Mrs. Obama would most likely
   a. take her children to watch a professional basketball game.
   b. spend an evening teaching her children how to cook dinner.
   c. organize a family game night.
   d. spend an afternoon playing soccer with her husband, the president.

4. Which statement is NOT supporting evidence that the health of United States citizens is important to the First Lady?
   a. "Thank you for protecting our environment by promoting renewable energy sources that will power our country for generations to come."
   b. "And thank you for keeping our food safe."
   c. "And the nutrition issue, as Tom mentioned, as you all know, is something near and dear to my heart, not just as a First Lady but as a mother."
   d. "You helped to launch our new MyPlate icon, which is changing the way families serve their meals and gives them a really easy way to understand what a healthy plate looks like."

5. Which of the following is a synonym of the word **initiative** as it's used in this sentence: "[I]t's a nationwide initiative to end childhood obesity in this country in a generation, so that all of our kids can grow up healthy"?
   a. program
   b. enthusiasm
   c. disinterest
   d. involvement

6. How does the inclusion of paragraph 3 affect the overall theme of the passage?
   a. It damages Mrs. Obama's claim.
   b. It strengthens Mrs. Obama's position.
   c. It has no effect on the overall theme.
   d. It intentionally confuses the reader.

Please use the following to answer questions 7–11.

Excerpt from "The Cask of Amontillado," by Edgar Allan Poe

1 He had a weak point—this Fortunato—although in other regards he was a man to be respected and even feared. He prided himself on his connoisseurship in wine. Few Italians have the true virtuoso spirit. For the most part their enthusiasm is adopted to suit the time and opportunity, to practice imposture upon the British and Austrian millionaires. In painting and gemmary, Fortunato, like his countrymen, was a quack, but in the matter of old wines he was sincere. In this respect I did not differ from him materially—I was skillful in the Italian vintages myself, and bought largely whenever I could.

2 It was about dusk, one evening during the supreme madness of the carnival season, that I encountered my friend. He accosted me with excessive warmth, for he had been drinking much. The man wore motley. He had on a tight-fitting parti-striped dress, and his head was surmounted by the conical cap and bells. I was so pleased to see him that I thought I should never have done wringing his hand.

3 I said to him—"My dear Fortunato, you are luckily met. How remarkably well you are looking to-day. But I have received a pipe of what passes for Amontillado, and I have my doubts."

4 "How?" said he. "Amontillado, a pipe? Impossible! And in the middle of the carnival!"

5 "I have my doubts," I replied, "and I was silly enough to pay the full Amontillado price without consulting you in the matter. You were not to be found, and I was fearful of losing a bargain."

6 "Amontillado!"

7 "I have my doubts."

8 "Amontillado!"

9 "And I must satisfy them."

10 "Amontillado!"

11 "As you are engaged, I am on my way to Luchresi. If anyone has a critical turn it is he. He will tell me—"

12 "Luchresi cannot tell Amontillado from Sherry."

13 "And yet some fools will have it that his taste is a match for your own."

14 "Come, let us go."

15 "Whither?"

16 "To your vaults."

17 "My friend, no; I will not impose upon your good nature. I perceive you have an engagement. Luchresi—"

18 "I have no engagement—come."

19 "My friend, no. It is not the engagement but the severe cold with which I perceive you are afflicted. The vaults are insufferably damp. They are encrusted with nitre."

20 "Let us go, nevertheless. The cold is merely nothing. Amontillado! You have been imposed upon. And as for Luchresi, he cannot distinguish Sherry from Amontillado."

21 Thus speaking, Fortunato possessed himself of my arm; and putting on a mask of black silk and drawing a roquelaire closely about my person, I suffered him to hurry me to my palazzo.

7. Who are Fortunato's "countrymen"?
- **a.** Italians
- **b.** Britons
- **c.** Austrians
- **d.** Spaniards

8. What do Fortunato and the narrator have in common?
- **a.** an interest in Italian history
- **b.** they are wearing the same clothing
- **c.** a passion for wine
- **d.** a love of the carnival season

9. Which statement, in context, is NOT supporting evidence that Fortunato has a passion for wine?
- **a.** "[B]ut in the matter of old wines he was sincere."
- **b.** "I was so pleased to see him that I thought I should never have done wringing his hand."
- **c.** "Luchresi cannot tell Amontillado from Sherry."
- **d.** "The cold is merely nothing. Amontillado!"

10. In the context of the story, which of the following is an example of irony?
- **a.** "He prided himself on his connoisseurship in wine."
- **b.** "For most part their enthusiasm is adopted to suit the time and opportunity . . ."
- **c.** "My dear Fortunato, you are luckily met."
- **d.** "The vaults are insufferably damp."

11. Why does the narrator first insist that he will ask Luchresi's opinion of the Amontillado?
- **a.** because Luchresi has more expertise in wine than Fortunato does
- **b.** because Fortunato and the narrator are known enemies
- **c.** to gain the trust of Fortunato
- **d.** to prey on Fortunato's pride

Please use the following to answer questions 12–16.

Excerpt from "My First Lie, and How I Got Out of It," by Mark Twain

1   I do not remember my first lie, it is too far back; but I remember my second one very well. I was nine days old at the time, and had noticed that if a pin was sticking in me and I advertised it in the usual fashion, I was lovingly petted and coddled and pitied in a most agreeable way and got a ration between meals besides.

2   It was human nature to want to get these riches, and I fell. I lied about the pin—advertising one when there wasn't any. You would have done it; George Washington did it, anybody would have done it. During the first half of my life I never knew a child that was able to raise above that temptation and keep from telling that lie. Up to 1867 all the civilized children that were ever born into the world were liars—including George. Then the safety pin came in and blocked the game. But is that reform worth anything? No; for it is reform by force and has no virtue in it; it merely stops that form of lying, it doesn't impair the disposition to lie, by a shade. It is the cradle application of conversion by fire and sword, or of the temperance principle through prohibition.

3   To return to that early lie. They found no pin and they realized that another liar had been added to the world's supply. For by grace of a rare inspiration a quite commonplace but seldom noticed

(continues)

fact was borne in upon their understandings—that almost all lies are acts, and speech has no part in them. Then, if they examined a little further they recognized that all people are liars from the cradle onward, without exception, and that they begin to lie as soon as they wake in the morning, and keep it up without rest or refreshment until they go to sleep at night. If they arrived at that truth it probably grieved them—did, if they had been heedlessly and ignorantly educated by their books and teachers; for why should a person grieve over a thing which by the eternal law of his make he cannot help? He didn't invent the law; it is merely his business to obey it and keep it still; join the universal conspiracy and keep so still that he shall deceive his fellow-conspirators into imagining that he doesn't know that the law exists. It is what we all do—we that know. I am speaking of *the lie of silent assertion*; we can tell it without saying a word, and we all do it—we that know. In the magnitude of its territorial spread it is one of the most majestic lies that the civilizations make it their sacred and anxious care to guard and watch and propagate.

4   For instance. It would not be possible for a humane and intelligent person to invent a rational excuse for slavery; yet you will remember that in the early days of the emancipation agitation in the North the agitators got but small help or countenance from anyone. Argue and plead and pray as they might, they could not break the universal stillness that reigned, from pulpit and press all the way down to the bottom of society—the clammy stillness created and maintained by the lie of silent assertion—the silent assertion that there wasn't anything going on in which humane and intelligent people were interested.

12. Which of the following can be inferred from the first two paragraphs?
a. The author grew up in the same state as George Washington.
b. Before 1867, parents punished infants by poking them with pins.
c. Before 1867, infants wore diapers fastened with straight pins.
d. Safety pins were critical to eliminating a child's disposition to lie.

13. In the first two paragraphs, which of the following does the author present as evidence that humans are born liars?
a. scientific data
b. personal experience
c. physical evidence
d. historical documentation

14. Which of the following best expresses the author's position on lying?
a. It should be forbidden.
b. It should be forgiven, but only for children.
c. It should be studied so that its cause can be found and eliminated.
d. It should be accepted as a fundamental part of human nature.

15. Based on the fourth paragraph, why does the author think that slavery was allowed to continue for so long?
a. because people acted as though it was not an important issue
b. because people understood the economic importance of slaves to the South
c. because slave owners lied to everyone else about how they treated their slaves
d. because agitators in the North didn't state their case

16. Which of the following details does NOT support the main idea of the passage?
  a. Even babies have a disposition to lie.
  b. The introduction of the safety pin occurred in 1867.
  c. People often lie through acts rather than words.
  d. Early opponents of slavery faced indifference from society.

Please use the following to answer questions 17–20.

Rebecca Dyer, Executive Director
Abacus Childcare
2404 Bellevue Ave
Baton Rouge, LA 70810

(1) I would like to submit an application for the childcare position that was recently posted on your website. I have (2) with children in varying capacities for almost four years, and absolutely love kids of all ages. I have a high energy level and infinite amount of patience that blends well with successfully managing a group of children.

(3), I nannied two preschool-aged twins before they entered kindergarten. During that time, I learned to effectively develop entertaining and educational activities, manage disputes and disruptive behavior in a caring yet firm manner, and maintain a safe environment in the home. I also helped teach the children proper manners, personal cleanliness, and appropriate social skills. I believe the time I spent working with the family allowed me to develop excellent communication skills and management capabilities.

Outside of my work experience, I'm detail-oriented and very organized. I pride myself in (4) problem-solving abilities and love working hard to provide value to my work environment. I am dependable, always on time, and keep the promises that I make.

I would love to speak with you regarding the position if you feel like I would be a good fit on your team. I have attached my resume with contact information and have three references available upon request.

Thank you for your time,

Mallory Holloway

17. Which is the correct choice for (1)?
  a. Dear Ms. Dyer,
  b. dear ms. dyer,
  c. dear ms. Dyer,
  d. Dear ms. dyer,

18. What is the correct form of the verb "to work" in (2)?
  a. to work
  b. works
  c. worked
  d. work

19. Which transitional word fits best in the beginning of (3)?
  a. Recently
  b. Currently
  c. However
  d. In addition

20. Which of the following is a correct fit for (4)?
  a. your
  b. me
  c. my
  d. mine

Please use the following to answer questions 21–24.

John F. Kennedy's Inaugural Address, 1961

1 Vice President Johnson, Mr. Speaker, Mr. Chief Justice, President Eisenhower, Vice President Nixon, President Truman, Reverend Clergy, fellow citizens:

2 We observe today not a victory of party but a celebration of freedom—symbolizing an end as well as a beginning—signifying renewal as well as change. For I have sworn before you the same solemn oath our forebears prescribed nearly a century and three quarters ago.

3 The world is very different now. For man holds in his mortal hands the power to abolish all forms of human poverty and all forms of human life. And yet the same revolutionary beliefs for which our forebears fought are still at issue around the globe.

4 We dare not forget today that we are the heirs of that first revolution. Let the word go forth from this time and place, to friend and foe alike, that the torch has been passed to a new generation of Americans—born in this century, tempered by war, disciplined by a hard and bitter peace, proud of our ancient heritage—and unwilling to witness or permit the slow undoing of those human rights to which this nation has always been committed, and to which we are committed today at home and around the world.

5 Let every nation know, whether it wishes us well or ill, that we shall pay any price, bear any burden, meet any hardship, support any friend, oppose any foe, to assure the survival and the success of liberty.

6 This much we pledge—and more.

7 To those old allies whose cultural and spiritual origins we share, we pledge the loyalty of faithful friends. United, there is little we cannot do in a host of cooperative ventures. Divided, there is little we can do—for we dare not meet a powerful challenge at odds and split asunder.

(continues)

8 To those new states whom we welcome to the ranks of the free, we pledge our word that one form of colonial control shall not have passed away merely to be replaced by a far more iron tyranny. We shall not always expect to find them supporting our view. But we shall always hope to find them strongly supporting their own freedom—and to remember that, in the past, those who foolishly sought power by riding the back of the tiger ended up inside.

9 To those peoples in the villages of half the globe struggling to break the bonds of mass misery, we pledge our best efforts to help them help themselves, for whatever period is required—not because the communists may be doing it, not because we seek their votes, but because it is right. If a free society cannot help the many who are poor, it cannot save the few who are rich.

10 To our sister republics south of our border, we offer a special pledge—to convert our good words into good deeds—in a new alliance for progress—to assist free men and free governments in casting off the chains of poverty. But this peaceful revolution of hope cannot become the prey of hostile powers. Let all our neighbors know that we shall join with them to oppose aggression or subversion anywhere in the Americas. And let every other power know that this hemisphere intends to remain the master of its own house.

11 To that world assembly of sovereign states, the United Nations, our last best hope in an age where the instruments of war have far outpaced the instruments of peace, we renew our pledge of support—to prevent it from becoming merely a forum for invective—to strengthen its shield of the new and the weak—and to enlarge the area in which its writ may run.

12 Finally, to those nations who would make themselves our adversary, we offer not a pledge but a request: that both sides begin anew the quest for peace, before the dark powers of destruction unleashed by science engulf all humanity in planned or accidental self-destruction.

21. Which sentence best represents the theme of the speech?
   a. "We observe today not a victory of party but a celebration of freedom—symbolizing an end as well as a beginning—signifying renewal as well as change."
   b. "We dare not forget today that we are the heirs of that first revolution."
   c. "But this peaceful revolution of hope cannot become the prey of hostile powers."
   d. "Let all our neighbors know that we shall join with them to oppose aggression or subversion anywhere in the Americas."

22. What word or phrase signifies to the reader the meaning of the word **tyranny** in the following sentence? "To those new states whom we welcome to the ranks of the free, we pledge our word that one form of colonial control shall not have passed away merely to be replaced by a far more iron tyranny."
   a. new states
   b. ranks of the free
   c. colonial control
   d. iron

23. What is the purpose of repeating "little we cannot do" and "little we can do" in the following sentence? "United, there is little we cannot do in a host of cooperative ventures. Divided, there is little we can do—for we dare not meet a powerful challenge at odds and split asunder."

    a. to contrast the difference between being united and being divided

    b. to highlight the similarity of being united and being divided

    c. to stress the United States' role in foreign politics

    d. to promise what Kennedy wants to accomplish during his presidency

24. From the list of five choices below, circle *all* of the characteristics that Kennedy displays in this speech.

    1. fear

    2. a strong will

    3. compassion

    4. morality

    5. aggression

Please use the following to answer questions 25–30.

Franklin Delano Roosevelt's Pearl Harbor Address to the Nation, 1941

1 Mr. Vice President, Mr. Speaker, Members of the Senate, and of the House of Representatives:

2 Yesterday, December 7, 1941—a date which will live in infamy—the United States of America was suddenly and deliberately attacked by naval and air forces of the Empire of Japan.

3 The United States was at peace with that nation and, at the solicitation of Japan, was still in conversation with its government and its emperor looking toward the maintenance of peace in the Pacific.

4 Indeed, one hour after Japanese air squadrons had commenced bombing in the American island of Oahu, the Japanese ambassador to the United States and his colleague delivered to our Secretary of State a formal reply to a recent American message. And while this reply stated that it seemed useless to continue the existing diplomatic negotiations, it contained no threat or hint of war or of armed attack.

5 It will be recorded that the distance of Hawaii from Japan makes it obvious that the attack was deliberately planned many days or even weeks ago. During the intervening time, the Japanese government has deliberately sought to deceive the United States by false statements and expressions of hope for continued peace.

6 The attack yesterday on the Hawaiian Islands has caused severe damage to American naval and military forces. I regret to tell you that very many American lives have been lost. In addition, American ships have been reported torpedoed on the high seas between San Francisco and Honolulu.

7 Yesterday, the Japanese government also launched an attack against Malaya.

(continues)

8 Last night, Japanese forces attacked Hong Kong.

9 Last night, Japanese forces attacked Guam.

10 Last night, Japanese forces attacked the Philippine Islands.

11 Last night, the Japanese attacked Wake Island.

12 And this morning, the Japanese attacked Midway Island.

13 Japan has, therefore, undertaken a surprise offensive extending throughout the Pacific area. The facts of yesterday and today speak for themselves. The people of the United States have already formed their opinions and well understand the implications to the very life and safety of our nation.

14 As Commander in Chief of the Army and Navy, I have directed that all measures be taken for our defense. But always will our whole nation remember the character of the onslaught against us.

15 No matter how long it may take us to overcome this premeditated invasion, the American people in their righteous might will win through to absolute victory.

16 I believe that I interpret the will of the Congress and of the people when I assert that we will not only defend ourselves to the uttermost but will make it very certain that this form of treachery shall never again endanger us.

17 Hostilities exist. There is no blinking at the fact that our people, our territory, and our interests are in grave danger.

18 With confidence in our armed forces, with the unbounding determination of our people, we will gain the inevitable triumph.

19 I ask that the Congress declare that since the unprovoked and dastardly attack by Japan on Sunday, December 7, 1941, a state of war has existed between the United States and the Japanese empire.

25. What is the tone of the address?
a. shocked but assertive
b. timid and fearful
c. surprised and scared
d. insecure yet aggressive

26. What purpose does the word **indeed** serve in the fourth paragraph?
a. to conclude his former idea
b. to alert the audience of a new premise
c. to emphasize the surprise of the attack
d. to introduce a new theme in the speech

27. What can be inferred from the first sentence in paragraph 5?
a. Japan is close to Hawaii.
b. Japan and Hawaii are a significant distance apart.
c. The United States mainland is as close to Hawaii as Japan is.
d. Japan announced that it was going to attack.

28. What is the purpose of repeating the phrase "Last night, Japanese forces attacked"?
   a. to show that Japanese forces were disorganized
   b. to emphasize that it is cowardly to attack at night
   c. to show how other countries are united against Japan
   d. to emphasize the extent of Japan's attack

29. Which of the following describes "the character of the onslaught against us"?
   a. expected
   b. aggressive
   c. regretful
   d. unintentional

30. Which of the following is NOT evidence that the attack came as a surprise?
   a. "The United States was at peace with that nation."
   b. "[O]ne hour after Japanese air squadrons had commenced bombing in the American island of Oahu, the Japanese ambassador to the United States and his colleague delivered to our Secretary of State a formal reply to a recent American message."
   c. "During the intervening time, the Japanese government has deliberately sought to deceive the United States by false statements and expressions of hope for continued peace."
   d. "Hostilities exist."

Please use the following to answer questions 31–34.

Memo to: All Employees
From: Alexandra Chandler
Subject: Work Hours

Hello all!

(1) Beginning next week, we will poll the office in order to receive everyone's input as we modify work hours.

The company (2) they want to change the schedule in order to better fit the needs of the employees. We will have three options to choose from. The first option is to keep the work schedule as it is currently: 9 to 5, Monday through Friday. The second option is to work one more hour per day on Monday through Thursday, but work only half a day on Friday. The third option is to work two extra hours on Monday through Thursday, and have Fridays off.

Although (3) completely open to all three options, the members of the executive board feel that the second option may fit the goals of the company and employees the best. Many of us already stay to work late at the beginning of the week, and the extra hour would not feel unnatural. We have also noticed that on (4). We understand this to be normal behavior and want to alter hours so that we can better serve you.

We think that the second option would fit well with the patterns we have already observed; however, we still want your opinions. We will be sending questionnaires via e-mail for you to fill out within the week. Please take some time to think about your responses before completing the survey as we want the possible change to best reflect the needs of the office.

Please keep a lookout for the questionnaire and return it to us by the end of next week.

Thank you for your time,

Alexandra Chandler

31. Which choice fits correctly in (1)?

   a. We are announcing some really big changes that might really affect us in the next few months.

   b. We would like to announce some potential changes affecting our team in the next few months.

   c. FYI, stuff might be different soon.

   d. PS: Thank you for your cooperation.

32. Choose the correct form of **decide** for (2).

   a. will decide

   b. has decided

   c. decides

   d. decide

33. Which choice fits correctly in (3)?

   a. there

   b. their

   c. they is

   d. they are

34. Which choice fits correctly in (4)?

   a. Friday, afternoons employee activity drops

   b. Friday afternoons employee, activity drops

   c. Friday afternoons, employee activity drops

   d. Friday afternoons employee activity, drops

Please use the following to answer questions 35–42.

Excerpt from Barack Obama's First Inaugural Address, January 20, 2009

1 In reaffirming the greatness of our nation we understand that greatness is never a given. It must be earned. Our journey has never been one of short-cuts or settling for less. It has not been the path for the faint-hearted, for those that prefer leisure over work, or seek only the pleasures of riches and fame. Rather, it has been the risk-takers, the doers, the makers of things—some celebrated, but more often men and women obscure in their labor—who have carried us up the long rugged path towards prosperity and freedom.

2 For us, they packed up their few worldly possessions and traveled across oceans in search of a new life. For us, they toiled in sweatshops, and settled the West, endured the lash of the whip, and plowed the hard earth. For us, they fought and died in places like Concord and Gettysburg, Normandy and Khe Sahn.

3 Time and again these men and women struggled and sacrificed and worked till their hands were raw so that we might live a better life. They saw America as bigger than the sum of our individual ambitions, greater than all the differences of birth or wealth or faction.

4 This is the journey we continue today. We remain the most prosperous, powerful nation on Earth. Our workers are no less productive than when this crisis began. Our minds are no less inventive, our goods and services no less needed than they were last week, or last month, or last year. Our capacity remains undiminished. But our time of standing pat, of protecting narrow interests and putting off unpleasant decisions—that time has surely passed. Starting today, we must pick ourselves up, dust ourselves off, and begin again the work of remaking America.

5 For everywhere we look, there is work to be done. The state of our economy calls for action, bold and swift. And we will act, not only to create new jobs but to lay a new foundation for growth. We

(continues)

will build the roads and bridges, the electric grids and digital lines that feed our commerce and bind us together. We'll restore science to its rightful place and wield technology's wonders to raise health care's quality and lower its cost. We will harness the sun and the winds and the soil to fuel our cars and run our factories. And we will transform our schools and colleges and universities to meet the demands of a new age. All this we can do. All this we will do.

6   Now, there are some who question the scale of our ambitions, who suggest that our system cannot tolerate too many big plans. Their memories are short, for they have forgotten what this country has already done, what free men and women can achieve when imagination is joined to common purpose and necessity to courage. What the cynics fail to understand is that the ground has shifted beneath them, that the stale political arguments that have consumed us for so long no longer apply.

7   The question we ask today is not whether our government is too big or too small, but whether it works—whether it helps families find jobs at a decent wage, care they can afford, a retirement that is dignified. Where the answer is yes, we intend to move forward. Where the answer is no, programs will end. And those of us who manage the public's dollars will be held to account, to spend wisely, reform bad habits, and do our business in the light of day, because only then can we restore the vital trust between a people and their government.

Excerpt from Barack Obama's Second Inaugural Address, January 21, 2013

1   We, the people, still believe that every citizen deserves a basic measure of security and dignity. We must make the hard choices to reduce the cost of health care and the size of our deficit. But we reject the belief that America must choose between caring for the generation that built this country and investing in the generation that will build its future. For we remember the lessons of our past, when twilight years were spent in poverty, and parents of a child with a disability had nowhere to turn. We do not believe that in this country, freedom is reserved for the lucky, or happiness for the few. We recognize that no matter how responsibly we live our lives, any one of us, at any time, may face a job loss, or a sudden illness, or a home swept away in a terrible storm. The commitments we make to each other—through Medicare, and Medicaid, and Social Security—these things do not sap our initiative; they strengthen us. They do not make us a nation of takers; they free us to take the risks that make this country great.

2   We, the people, still believe that our obligations as Americans are not just to ourselves, but to all posterity. We will respond to the threat of climate change, knowing that the failure to do so would betray our children and future generations. Some may still deny the overwhelming judgment of science, but none can avoid the devastating impact of raging fires, and crippling drought, and more powerful storms. The path towards sustainable energy sources will be long and sometimes difficult. But America cannot resist this transition; we must lead it. We cannot cede to other nations the technology that will power new jobs and new industries—we must claim its promise.

(continues)

That's how we will maintain our economic vitality and our national treasure—our forests and waterways; our croplands and snowcapped peaks. That is how we will preserve our planet, commanded to our care by God. That's what will lend meaning to the creed our fathers once declared.

3 We, the people, still believe that enduring security and lasting peace do not require perpetual war. Our brave men and women in uniform, tempered by the flames of battle, are unmatched in skill and courage. Our citizens, seared by the memory of those we have lost, know too well the price that is paid for liberty. The knowledge of their sacrifice will keep us forever vigilant against those who would do us harm. But we are also heirs to those who won the peace and not just the war, who turned sworn enemies into the surest of friends, and we must carry those lessons into this time as well.

4 We will defend our people and uphold our values through strength of arms and rule of law. We will show the courage to try and resolve our differences with other nations peacefully—not because we are naïve about the dangers we face, but because engagement can more durably lift suspicion and fear. America will remain the anchor of strong alliances in every corner of the globe; and we will renew those institutions that extend our capacity to manage crisis abroad, for no one has a greater stake in a peaceful world than its most powerful nation. We will support democracy from Asia to Africa, from the Americas to the Middle East, because our interests and our conscience compel us to act on behalf of those who long for freedom. And we must be a source of hope to the poor, the sick, the marginalized, the victims of prejudice—not out of mere charity, but because peace in our time requires the constant advance of those principles that our common creed describes: tolerance and opportunity; human dignity and justice.

35. Which best summarizes the main idea expressed in the first paragraph of Obama's First Inaugural Address?
  a. Luck made the United States a successful and great nation.
  b. Those who worked hard and took risks shaped America.
  c. The United States is a great nation and hard work will keep it so.
  d. Obama feels very fortunate to have been elected president.

36. Which sentence's meaning is strengthened by the "men and women [who] sacrificed and struggled" mentioned in the first three paragraphs in Obama's First Inaugural Address?
  a. "Our capacity remains undiminished."
  b. "For everywhere we look, there is work to be done."
  c. "We'll restore science to its rightful place and wield technology's wonders to raise health care's quality and lower its cost."
  d. "Their memories are short, for they have forgotten what this country has already done, what free men and women can achieve when imagination is joined to common purpose and necessity to courage."

37. From the list of five choices below, circle *all* of the phrases that support the main idea of Obama's First Inaugural Address.

1. "Our journey has never been one of short-cuts or settling for less."
2. "This is the journey we continue today."
3. "All this we can do. All this we will do."
4. "We will harness the sun and the winds and the soil to fuel our cars and run our factories."
5. "What the cynics fail to understand is that the ground has shifted beneath them, that the stale political arguments that have consumed us for so long no longer apply."

38. What is Obama's purpose in beginning each of three paragraphs of his Second Inaugural Address with "We, the people"?
   a. to show American pride
   b. to stress past successes in order to prove the country does not need to change
   c. to quote the Preamble
   d. to emphasize the theme of betterment in the United States of America

39. What is the effect of repeating the words **generation** and **build** to compare "the generation that built this country" with the "generation that will build its future"?
   a. because Obama is talking about the same people
   b. to create a connection between the past and the future
   c. because he thinks the next generation will be better than the last
   d. to emphasize that both generations still have work to do

40. Which of the following does NOT support Obama's claim in his Second Inaugural Address that Americans feel an obligation to future generations?
   a. "For we remember the lessons of our past, when twilight years were spent in poverty, and parents of a child with a disability had nowhere to turn."
   b. "We will respond to the threat of climate change, knowing that the failure to do so would betray our children and future generations."
   c. "Time and again these men and women struggled and sacrificed and worked till their hands were raw so that we might live a better life."
   d. "We will defend our people and uphold our values through strength of arms and rule of law."

41. Where will Obama support democracy, according to his Second Inaugural Address?
   a. in the Americas
   b. worldwide
   c. in Europe
   d. in the Middle East

42. Which of the following sentences from the Second Inaugural Address best fits into the theme of the First Inaugural Address?
   a. "They do not make us a nation of takers; they free us to take the risks that make this country great."
   b. "That's what will lend meaning to the creed our fathers once declared."
   c. "We, the people, still believe that enduring security and a lasting peace do not require perpetual war."
   d. "We must make the hard choices to reduce the cost of health care and the size of our deficit."

Please use the following to answer questions 43–48.

Remarks upon Signing the Civil Rights Bill (July 2, 1964), Lyndon Baines Johnson

1 My fellow Americans:

2 I am about to sign into law the Civil Rights Act of 1964. I want to take this occasion to talk to you about what that law means to every American.

3 One hundred and eighty-eight years ago this week a small band of valiant men began a long struggle for freedom. They pledged their lives, their fortunes, and their sacred honor not only to found a nation, but to forge an ideal of freedom—not only for political independence, but for personal liberty—not only to eliminate foreign rule, but to establish the rule of justice in the affairs of men.

4 That struggle was a turning point in our history. Today in far corners of distant continents, the ideals of those American patriots still shape the struggles of men who hunger for freedom.

5 This is a proud triumph. Yet those who founded our country knew that freedom would be secure only if each generation fought to renew and enlarge its meaning. From the minutemen at Concord to the soldiers in Viet-Nam, each generation has been equal to that trust.

6 Americans of every race and color have died in battle to protect our freedom. Americans of every race and color have worked to build a nation of widening opportunities. Now our generation of Americans has been called on to continue the unending search for justice within our own borders.

7 We believe that all men are created equal. Yet many are denied equal treatment.

8 We believe that all men have certain unalienable rights. Yet many Americans do not enjoy those rights.

9 We believe that all men are entitled to the blessings of liberty. Yet millions are being deprived of those blessings—not because of their own failures, but because of the color of their skin.

10 The reasons are deeply imbedded in history and tradition and the nature of man. We can understand—without rancor or hatred—how this all happened.

11 But it cannot continue. Our Constitution, the foundation of our Republic, forbids it. The principles of our freedom forbid it. Morality forbids it. And the law I will sign tonight forbids it.

43. Which sentence is NOT an example of an American ideal?

  a. "We believe that all men are created equal."

  b. "The principles of our freedom forbid it."

  c. "Not only for political independence, but for personal liberty."

  d. "Yet many are denied equal treatment."

44. Which sentence expresses the same idea as "Yet many are denied equal treatment"?

  a. "Yet many Americans do not enjoy those rights."

  b. "We believe that all men are entitled to the blessings of liberty."

  c. "We can understand—without rancor or hatred—how this all happened."

  d. "Americans of every race and color have died in battle to protect our freedom."

45. Based on Johnson's remarks, which is the best example of the United States' "unending search for justice within our own borders"?

  a. Civil War

  b. The Grand Canyon

  c. Civil Rights Act of 1964

  d. Vietnam War

46. Which answer best summarizes the main idea expressed in the paragraph that begins "One hundred and eighty-eight years ago"?

  a. The United States was formed a long time ago.

  b. The founding fathers worked hard to create a just nation.

  c. The country has always treated everyone fairly.

  d. Men of all races fought for freedom 188 years ago.

47. Which sentence best expresses the theme of President Johnson's remarks?

  a. American ideals include fair treatment for everyone.

  b. The United States is a great country.

  c. Everyone is treated the same in the United States.

  d. Lyndon B. Johnson was one of the best presidents.

48. Which of the following does NOT support Lyndon B. Johnson's stance that the Civil Rights Bill is in line with American values?

  a. "They pledged their lives, their fortunes, and their sacred honor not only to found a nation, but to forge an ideal of freedom."

  b. "Today in far corners of distant continents, the ideals of those American patriots still shape the struggles of men who hunger for freedom."

  c. "Americans of every race and color have died in battle to protect our freedom."

  d. "The reasons are deeply imbedded in history and tradition and the nature of man."

Part II

1 question
45 minutes to complete

This practice allows you to compose your response to the given task and then compare it with examples of responses at the different score levels. You will also get a scoring guide that includes a detailed explanation of how official GED® test graders will score your response. You may use this scoring guide to score your own response.

It is important to note that on the official test this task must be completed in no more than 45 minutes. Before you begin planning and writing, read the two texts:

Page 227: excerpt from George W. Bush's First Inaugural Address

Page 228: excerpt from Barack Obama's First Inaugural Address

As you read the texts, think about the details from both texts that you might use in your argumentative essay. After reading the texts, plan your essay. Think about the ideas, facts, definitions, details, and other information and examples that you will want to use. Think about how you will introduce your topic and what the main topic will be for each paragraph.

As you write your argumentative essay, be sure to do the following:

- Introduce your claim.
- Support your claim with logical reasoning and relevant evidence from the texts.
- Acknowledge and address an alternative or opposing claim.
- Organize the reasons and evidence logically.
- Use words, phrases, and clauses to connect your ideas and to clarify the relationships among claims, counterclaims, reasons, and evidence.
- Establish and maintain a formal style.
- Provide a concluding statement or section that follows from and supports the argument presented.

Good luck!

Please use the following to answer the essay question.

George W. Bush's First Inaugural Address
January 20, 2001

1   We have a place, all of us, in a long story—a story we continue, but whose end we will not see. It is the story of a new world that became a friend and liberator of the old, a story of a slave-holding society that became a servant of freedom, the story of a power that went into the world to protect but not possess, to defend but not to conquer.

2   It is the American story—a story of flawed and fallible people, united across the generations by grand and enduring ideals.

3   The grandest of these ideals is an unfolding American promise that everyone belongs, that everyone deserves a chance, that no insignificant person was ever born.

4   Americans are called to enact this promise in our lives and in our laws. And though our nation has sometimes halted, and sometimes delayed, we must follow no other course.

5   Through much of the last century, America's faith in freedom and democracy was a rock in a raging sea. Now it is a seed upon the wind, taking root in many nations.

6   Our democratic faith is more than the creed of our country, it is the inborn hope of our humanity, an ideal we carry but do not own, a trust we bear and pass along. And even after nearly 225 years, we have a long way yet to travel.

7   While many of our citizens prosper, others doubt the promise, even the justice, of our own country. The ambitions of some Americans are limited by failing schools and hidden prejudice and the circumstances of their birth. And sometimes our differences run so deep, it seems we share a continent, but not a country.

(continues)

8   We do not accept this, and we will not allow it. Our unity, our union, is the serious work of leaders and citizens in every generation. And this is my solemn pledge: I will work to build a single nation of justice and opportunity.

9   And we are confident in principles that unite and lead us onward.

10 America has never been united by blood or birth or soil. We are bound by ideals that move us beyond our backgrounds, lift us above our interests and teach us what it means to be citizens. Every child must be taught these principles. Every citizen must uphold them. And every immigrant, by embracing these ideals, makes our country more, not less, American.

11 Today, we affirm a new commitment to live out our nation's promise through civility, courage, compassion and character.

12 America, at its best, matches a commitment to principle with a concern for civility. A civil society demands from each of us good will and respect, fair dealing and forgiveness.

Excerpt from Barack Obama's First Inaugural Address
January 20, 2009

1   In reaffirming the greatness of our nation we understand that greatness is never a given. It must be earned. Our journey has never been one of short-cuts or settling for less. It has not been the path for the faint-hearted, for those that prefer leisure over work, or seek only the pleasures of riches and fame. Rather, it has been the risk-takers, the doers, the makers of things—some celebrated, but more often men and women obscure in their labor—who have carried us up the long rugged path towards prosperity and freedom.

2   For us, they packed up their few worldly possessions and traveled across oceans in search of a new life. For us, they toiled in sweatshops, and settled the West, endured the lash of the whip, and plowed the hard earth. For us, they fought and died in places like Concord and Gettysburg, Normandy and Khe Sahn.

3   Time and again these men and women struggled and sacrificed and worked till their hands were raw so that we might live a better life. They saw America as bigger than the sum of our individual ambitions, greater than all the differences of birth or wealth or faction. This is the journey we continue today. We remain the most prosperous, powerful nation on Earth. Our workers are no less productive than when this crisis began. Our minds are no less inventive, our goods and services no less needed than they were last week, or last month, or last year. Our capacity remains undiminished. But our time of standing pat, of protecting narrow interests and putting off unpleasant decisions—that time has surely passed. Starting today, we must pick ourselves up, dust ourselves off, and begin again the work of remaking America.

(continues)

4   For everywhere we look, there is work to be done. The state of our economy calls for action, bold and swift. And we will act, not only to create new jobs, but to lay a new foundation for growth. We will build the roads and bridges, the electric grids and digital lines that feed our commerce and bind us together. We'll restore science to its rightful place, and wield technology's wonders to raise health care's quality and lower its cost. We will harness the sun and the winds and the soil to fuel our cars and run our factories. And we will transform our schools and colleges and universities to meet the demands of a new age. All this we can do. All this we will do.

5   Now, there are some who question the scale of our ambitions, who suggest that our system cannot tolerate too many big plans. Their memories are short, for they have forgotten what this country has already done, what free men and women can achieve when imagination is joined to common purpose, and necessity to courage. What the cynics fail to understand is that the ground has shifted beneath them, that the stale political arguments that have consumed us for so long no longer apply.

6   The question we ask today is not whether our government is too big or too small, but whether it works—whether it helps families find jobs at a decent wage, care they can afford, a retirement that is dignified. Where the answer is yes, we intend to move forward. Where the answer is no, programs will end. And those of us who manage the public's dollars will be held to account, to spend wisely, reform bad habits, and do our business in the light of day, because only then can we restore the vital trust between a people and their government.

PROMPT: There is ongoing debate in the political arena about what it means to be an American and what goals society should set.

Weigh the opinions and vision of two United States Presidents and then write an argumentative essay supporting either vision. Be sure to use relevant and specific evidence from both texts in your argumentative essay. Remember to take only 45 minutes to plan, draft, and edit your response.

_____

_____

_____

_____

_____

_____

_____

Answers and Explanations

Part I

1. **Choice d is correct.** This is the only answer that encompasses everything Mrs. Obama speaks on, from thanking the USDA employees to explaining how the healthy initiatives could not succeed without them.
   Choice **a** is incorrect. Although Mrs. Obama discusses different programs she has created with that goal, she uses those examples to demonstrate the greater theme.
   Choice **b** is incorrect. Mrs. Obama shows her appreciation for farmers, but this answer ignores many other ideas and information brought up throughout the passage.
   Choice **c** is incorrect. Mrs. Obama mentions the Let's Move initiative, but it is clear from her comments that the initiative is already underway; therefore, the purpose of Mrs. Obama's remarks is not to introduce Let's Move.

2. According to Mrs. Obama, a man named **Tom** mentioned that the nutrition issue is something near and dear to her heart. In the second paragraph, Mrs. Obama states: ". . . the nutrition issue, as Tom mentioned, as you all know, is something near and dear to my heart . . ."

3. **Choice b is correct.** Selecting this answer choice shows that the reader comprehends the importance Mrs. Obama places on family and healthy habits.
   Choice **a** is incorrect. This answer ignores the main topics of the passage, which include an emphasis on participating in an active lifestyle, not watching one.
   Choice **c** is incorrect. This answer choice only identifies one theme and ignores the focus on nutrition.
   Choice **d** is incorrect. Although this answer incorporates both the themes of family and having healthy habits, it disregards Mrs. Obama's emphasis on teaching children healthy habits.

4. **Choice a is correct.** Even though Mrs. Obama is stating another of the USDA's contributions, this answer does not focus on health or food, but rather renewable resources. Also, the other three answer choices clearly support the question's conclusion.
   Choice **b** is incorrect. This sentence demonstrates Mrs. Obama's concern through her gratitude.
   Choice **c** is incorrect. This statement explicitly states Mrs. Obama's personal interest in health in the United States.
   Choice **d** is incorrect. In this sentence, Mrs. Obama gives a specific example of the ways in which she, along with the USDA, has worked to teach citizens healthy habits.

5. **Choice a is correct.** If you replace the word "initiative" with the word "program," the sentence would retain its meaning.
   Choice **b** is incorrect. The word "enthusiasm" does not fit the context.
   Choice **c** is incorrect. "Disinterest" is an antonym of "initiative."
   Choice **d** is incorrect. Replacing "initiative" with "involvement" loses the meaning of the sentence.

6. **Choice b is correct.** It demonstrates the necessity of garden programs by highlighting the fact that some children don't know how food is grown or where their food comes from. Choice **a** is incorrect. This response neglects Mrs. Obama's emphasis on why nutritional programs are important. Choice **c** is incorrect. The paragraph supports the theme of the speech by providing information about why the programs and worker involvement are necessary. Choice **d** is incorrect. Mrs. Obama is very clear and explicitly states that children not only do not know about nutrition, but do not know where their food comes from. This ties into the overall theme of health and demonstrates why Mrs. Obama believes these programs are needed.

7. **Choice a is correct.** Two sentences before "countrymen," the narrator says, "Few Italians have the true virtuoso spirit." The next few sentences, including the one that uses "countrymen," are descriptions of traits that Italians do or do not have, according to the narrator. Choice **b** is incorrect. Two sentences before "countrymen," the narrator says "Few Italians have the true virtuoso spirit." The next few sentences discuss how the enthusiasm of many Italians is often a deception to take advantage of the British or Austrians, according to the narrator. Choice **c** is incorrect. Two sentences before "countrymen," the narrator says "Few Italians have the true virtuoso spirit." The next few sentences discuss how the enthusiasm of many Italians is often a deception to take advantage of the British or Austrians, according to the narrator. Choice **d** is incorrect. There is no mention or indication in the passage that Fortunato is a Spaniard.

8. **Choice c is correct.** The narrator states that Fortunato is "sincere" in his knowledge of "old wines," and "In this respect I did not differ from him materially." Choice **a** is incorrect. At no point does the narrator say anything about Italian history. Choice **b** is incorrect. The narrator describes Fortunato's "parti-striped dress," but does not describe his own clothing. Choice **d** is incorrect. The narrator states the events happened "one evening during the supreme madness of the carnival season," but makes no declarations about his feelings at the time.

9. **Choice b is correct.** This describes the narrator's reaction to finding Fortunato, not Fortunato's feelings about wine. Choice **a** is incorrect. The narrator is clearly stating Fortunato knows wine. Choice **c** is incorrect. Fortunato is attempting to prove that he knows wines and convince the narrator to take him to the cask of Amontillado instead of consulting their friend Luchresi. Choice **d** is incorrect. After the narrator warns Fortunato that his health would be in danger if they went to find the vault because of the cold, Fortunato dismisses the concern in favor of the wine.

10. **Choice c is correct.** Fortunato is actually quite unlucky as he has just stumbled across a man who wants to, and later does, kill him. Choice **a** is incorrect. The narrator is being sincere. Choice **b** is incorrect. This is a follow-up statement used to explain the narrator's claim that "[f]ew Italians have the true virtuoso spirit." Choice **d** is incorrect. Although the narrator does not actually mean to deter Fortunato from the journey to his death, there is no text-based reason to believe that the vaults are not cold and wet.

11. Choice d is correct. Early in the text, the narrator states that Fortunato "had a weak point—this Fortunato—although in other regards he was a man to be respected and even feared. He prided himself on his connoisseurship in wine."

Choice **a** is incorrect. There is nothing in the text that indicates Luchresi has more expertise in wine than Fortunato. As a matter of fact, the narrator himself states that "in the matter of old wines [Fortunato] was sincere."

Choice **b** is incorrect. On the contrary, if the narrator and Fortunato were known enemies, Fortunato would not trust him and follow him down to the vault.

Choice **c** is incorrect. The two men already know and trust each other, which is evidenced in their interactions and dialogue.

12. Choice c is correct. The author suggests that before 1867 many babies were poked by pins, and then the safety pin came along and eliminated the problem. It can be inferred that the reason the earlier babies were being poked was because their diapers were fastened with straight pins.

Choice **a** is incorrect. The only connection the author makes between himself and George Washington is that he, like Washington, was born into the world a liar.

Choice **b** is incorrect. Although the author suggests that before 1867 infants were often poked by pins, he does not imply that pin-poking was a form of parental punishment.

Choice **d** is incorrect. Although the author states that safety pins made children unable to "lie" by crying as if they had been poked by a pin, the author also states that this "doesn't impair the disposition to lie."

13. Choice b is correct. The author states, "During the first half of my life I never knew a child that was able to raise above that temptation and keep from telling that lie."

Choice **a** is incorrect. The author offers no scientific data to support his claim.

Choice **c** is incorrect. The author does not present any physical evidence to support his claim.

Choice **d** is incorrect. Although the author states that George Washington lied as a child, he offers no historical documentation to support this statement.

14. Choice d is correct. The author states that "all people are liars from the cradle onward" and also asks, "[W]hy should a person grieve over a thing which by the eternal law of his make he cannot help?"

Choice **a** is incorrect. The author does not suggest that lying should be forbidden and, in fact, argues that stopping a person from lying does not remove a person's disposition to lie.

Choice **b** is incorrect. The author does not suggest that different rules should be applied to adults and children.

Choice **c** is incorrect. The author does not suggest that eliminating lying is a goal toward which people should strive.

15. Choice a is correct. The author argues that those who didn't speak up about slavery implied "that there wasn't anything going on in which humane and intelligent people were interested," which was a quiet way of countering antislavery activists.

Choice **b** is incorrect. The author does not mention economics as an issue related to slavery.

Choice **c** is incorrect. The author does not suggest that slave owners lied to others; the main idea of the paragraph is that people lied to themselves about slavery.

Choice **d** is incorrect. The author says that antislavery agitators in the North would "[a]rgue and plead and pray," but they didn't get enough support in response.

16. Choice b is correct. While this detail is mentioned in the passage, it does not reflect the main idea of the passage, which is that lying is a part of human nature.

Choices **a**, **c**, and **d** are incorrect. These details support the main idea of the passage, which is that lying is a part of human nature.

17. Choice a is correct. All three words need to be capitalized. Beginning letters of sentences are always capitalized, and people's names and titles are capitalized.

Choice **b** is incorrect. This answer lacks all necessary capitalization. All three words need to be capitalized. Beginning letters of sentences are always capitalized, and people's names and titles are capitalized.

Choices **c** and **d** are incorrect. All three words must be capitalized.

18. Choice c is correct. This is the correct past tense for a singular subject.

Choice **a** is incorrect. "I have to work with children" does not make sense within the context. The author is explaining what she has done in the past.

Choices **b** and **d** are incorrect. These answer choices do not make sense in context.

19. Choice a is correct. This word correctly matches the past-tense verb "nannied."

Choice **b** is incorrect. This does not fit in context with the past-tense verb "nannied."

Choice **c** is incorrect. The word "however" indicates contrast with a previous statement. The ideas in the sentence complement previous sentences, and do not offer contrast.

Choice **d** is incorrect. This answer choice does not make sense in context. In order to keep with form, "recently" is a better answer.

20. Choice c is correct. "My" is the correct possessive pronoun.

Choice **a** is incorrect. This is not the correct possessive pronoun. The speaker is talking about her abilities.

Choice **b** is incorrect. "Me" is not a possessive pronoun. It is clear that the abilities belong to someone.

Choice **d** is incorrect. Although "mine" is possessive, one uses it to indicate objects that belong to them, and it would be awkward to say "mine abilities."

21. Choice a is correct. This choice summarizes the passage in totality, identifying Kennedy's emphasis on the past and the present as he accepts the presidency.

Choice **b** is incorrect. This choice neglects Kennedy's focus on the future of the nation and the world.

Choice **c** is incorrect. Kennedy stresses hope and good things to come throughout the text; however, this is just a small slice of everything he says and is not the main theme.

Choice **d** is incorrect. Although Kennedy speaks about the United States' and its allies' role in furthering peace and democracy, this choice ignores the weight Kennedy puts on how the past shaped the country.

22. Choice c is correct. The use of "replaced" and "more" signifies that "colonial control" and "tyranny" mean similar things.

Choice **a** is incorrect. The sentence is addressed to the "new states" to whom the promise of a guard against more tyranny is made.

Choice **b** is incorrect. This phrase represents the opposite of tyranny, the state to which the countries have been "welcomed." The second half of the sentence is a promise to protect them and guard against tyranny.

Choice **d** is incorrect. "Iron" is an adjective used to describe tyranny.

23. Choice a is correct. Kennedy is contrasting being united with being divided in order to make a point about why countries should cooperate (because they can accomplish anything "in a host of cooperative ventures").

Choice **b** is incorrect. This is the opposite of Kennedy's intention.

Choice **c** is incorrect. Kennedy is focusing on everyone working together and not on foreign policy.

Choice **d** is incorrect. Although Kennedy says that he is committed to peace and cooperation, this speech focuses on discussing the perils of not working together.

24. Choice 1 is incorrect. Kennedy makes a point of saying that the United States will "pay any price, bear any burden, meet any hardship, support any friend, oppose any foe, in order to assure the survival and the success of liberty." This does not show fear.

Choice 2 is correct. Many times Kennedy emphasizes doing what is necessary to help those in need and that the United States will "pay any price."

Choice 3 is correct. Kennedy stresses that he is committed to showing people who are "struggling" how to "help themselves," and wants to "assist free men and free governments in casting off the chains of poverty."

Choice 4 is correct. Kennedy states he pledges the United States' "best efforts" not for political reasons, "but because it is right." He also says he wants to "convert our good words into good deeds."

Choice 5 is incorrect. In the last paragraph, Kennedy explicitly asks "that both sides begin anew the quest for peace." He does not threaten his opponents but rather warns against the consequences of not working together.

25. Choice a is correct. Roosevelt emphasizes that the attack was a complete surprise because the two nations were not warring, yet states that he has "directed that all measures be taken for our defense." Even though he was not expecting the event, he knows that "hostilities exist" and has handled the situation.

Choice **b** is incorrect. Roosevelt says the United States has "confidence in our armed forces" and "determination of our people" and will "gain the inevitable triumph." These are not words of a timid or fearful person.

Choice **c** is incorrect. Although he asserts many times that the attack came as a surprise, he does not show fear through his words. Rather, he shows confidence in the country.

Choice **d** is incorrect. Some of what Roosevelt says is aggressive, like asking Congress to declare war, but he seems confident in the abilities of the nation rather than insecure.

26. Choice c is correct. Roosevelt is effectively stressing how "[t]he United States was at peace with that nation" by emphatically pointing out that the Japanese ambassador responded to the American message.

Choice **a** is incorrect. The fourth paragraph says that there were "existing diplomatic negotiations," an example of how Japan was "still in conversation," as stated in the previous paragraph.

Choice **b** is incorrect. The fourth paragraph supports the premise of the third paragraph.

Choice **d** is incorrect. The fourth paragraph supports the theme of the previous paragraphs.

27. Choice b is correct. Roosevelt is implying that the two islands are far enough apart that the attack had to have been "deliberately planned."

Choice **a** is incorrect. The attack wouldn't have had to have been planned "days or even weeks ago" if the island was close and easy for the Japanese to attack.

Choice **c** is incorrect. The United States mainland is not mentioned and is irrelevant in this context.

Choice **d** is incorrect. There is no evidence in the speech to support this answer choice. The opposite is true.

28. Choice d is correct. The drumbeat rhythm of repetition emphasizes the great number of attacks on one country after another.

Choice **a** is incorrect. There is no evidence in the speech that Japan was disorganized. In fact, evidence in the speech supports the conclusion that the opposite was true.

Choice **b** is incorrect. There is no evidence in the speech to support this conclusion.

Choice **c** is incorrect. There is no mention of how the other countries handled or will handle the attack.

29. Choice b is correct. Roosevelt states many times the attack was an intentional move that put "our interests . . . in grave danger."

Choice **a** is incorrect. Contrary to this answer choice, evidence in the speech supports the conclusion that Japan launched a surprise attack on the United States.

Choice **c** is incorrect. There is no evidence in the speech to support this conclusion.

Choice **d** is incorrect. It is clear from the speech that the attack was planned.

30. Choice d is correct. This sentence comes after describing how the surprise attack was carried out, acknowledging resulting clear and present danger.

Choice **a** is incorrect. An attack is not expected from a nation in peaceful accord with the United States.

Choice **b** is incorrect. This sentence shows that the nations were working together to find a solution prior to the attack.

Choice **c** is incorrect. This sentence describes how Japan worked to make sure the attack was a surprise by deceiving the United States.

31. Choice b is correct. The tone is appropriate for a work e-mail.

Choice **a** is incorrect. The phrases "some really big" and "that might really affect" are informal and awkward.

Choice **c** is incorrect. The tone is too informal for a work e-mail.

Choice **d** is incorrect. A postscript (PS) comes at the end of a letter, not at the beginning.

32. Choice b is correct. This is the past participle verb. The decision "has" already been made.

Choice **a** is incorrect. This is the future tense, and the decision has already been made.

Choice **c** is incorrect. This is the present tense, and the action is not happening now.

Choice **d** is incorrect. This is the present tense of the verb.

33. Choice d is correct. The plural pronoun matches the plural form of the verb. The contraction of these two words is "they're" and is a homophone of "there" and "their."

Choice **a** is incorrect. The word "there" refers to location.

Choice **b** is incorrect. "Their" is a possessive pronoun.

Choice **c** is incorrect. Although this has the correct plural pronoun, "is" is for singular subjects.

34. Choice c is correct. This answer correctly closes off the thought from the first part of the sentence before introducing the second part of the sentence. It shows a natural pause.

Choice **a** is incorrect. "Friday" modifies "afternoons," so they cannot be broken up by a comma.

Choice **b** is incorrect. "Employee" serves as an adjective for "activity." They cannot be separated.

Choice **d** is incorrect. "Activity" is the noun and "drops" is the verb. They should not be separated.

35. Choice b is correct. Obama remarks that greatness is not a given and must be earned, implying that the United States is not great by luck, but by work and determination.

Choice **a** is incorrect. Luck is not mentioned as making a great nation.

Choice **c** is incorrect. The future is not mentioned in the first paragraph.

Choice **d** is incorrect. Obama does not discuss his personal feelings about being president in the address.

36. Choice d is correct. The sentence later in the passage recalls the men and women mentioned earlier to stress that the cynics are wrong in thinking great things cannot be accomplished.

Choice **a** is incorrect. Although this answer recognizes the theme of the sentence, that the United States has a large and historical "capacity" for greatness, it does not explicitly call on the image of the people working or modify that idea.

Choice **b** is incorrect. This choice neglects the connection Obama makes between the people who worked hard to shape America and the cynics who are ignoring their struggles by doubting change.

Choice **c** is incorrect. This phrase in the question has nothing to do with the cost of healthcare or technology.

37. Choice 1 is correct. The main idea in the address is that America was formed by hard work, and that attitude needs to and will be continued throughout this presidency. This phrase supports that by firmly stating that taking the easy way out is not what "our journey" has been about.

Choice 2 is correct. This phrase supports the theme of the future of the United States.

Choice 3 is correct. This phrase supports the idea that citizens and the government must work hard and will work hard.

Choice **4** is incorrect. This phrase is about renewable energy, which is used as a detail of what Obama wants to focus on and is not the main focus.

Choice **5** is incorrect. This phrase stresses the negative and opposition to progress; it does not support the idea of ambition.

38. Choice d is correct. Obama draws on the history of the United States, like "the creed our fathers once declared," to stress that citizens have an "obligation" to help "all posterity."

Choice **a** is incorrect. Although Obama does carefully praise the country throughout, the point of the passage is to discuss the future challenges and how past successes enable us to face those challenges.

Choice **b** is incorrect. Choosing this answer shows the reader clearly does not comprehend that the main focus of the text is what Obama believes needs to change.

Choice **c** is incorrect. This is the tool Obama is utilizing, not the effect of utilizing that tool.

39. Choice b is correct. Obama uses words, or rhetoric, to show that he thinks the two are connected and that their interests both matter.

Choice **a** is incorrect. This choice neglects the verb tense change of "built" to "will build." This shows he is talking about past people/actions and future people/actions.

Choice **c** is incorrect. This sentence makes no value judgment on either party, and does not state one is better than the other.

Choice **d** is incorrect. One generation's actions are in the past, as "built" is the past tense verb; their work is done.

40. Choice d is correct. Obama is stressing American might and willingness to use its power, not speaking of obligations to future generations.

Choice **a** is incorrect. In this sentence, Obama looks to the past for solutions to today's problems.

Choice **b** is incorrect. Obama is looking to the future, arguing that failure to act to halt climate change would "betray our children and future generations."

Choice **c** is incorrect. Here, Obama draws on the past as a reason United States citizens must fight for the future.

41. Choice b is correct. Specifically, Obama says, "We will support democracy from Asia to Africa; from the Americas to the Middle East . . ."

Choices **a**, **b**, and **c** are incorrect. Obama says, "We will support democracy from Asia to Africa; from the Americas to the Middle East . . ."

42. Choice b is correct. This sentence supports the first inaugural's theme of continuing the hard work of the past in order to secure prosperity and freedom for tomorrow.
Choice **a** is incorrect. This sentence refers to healthcare and taking care of the country's citizens; this is mentioned in the first address, but it is not the theme.
Choice **c** is incorrect. Obama's First Inaugural Address did not focus on war.
Choice **d** is incorrect. These details are not the theme of the first address.

43. Choice d is correct. It is not an American ideal to deny freedom. The opposite is true. Freedom is the theme of American ideals.
Choice **a** is incorrect. This American ideal is cited in paragraph 7.
Choice **b** is incorrect. This American ideal is cited in the last paragraph.
Choice **c** is incorrect. This American ideal is cited in paragraph 3.

44. Choice a is correct. People not having the same rights as others means roughly the same thing as the denial of equal treatment.
Choice **b** is incorrect. This means the opposite of the quotation in question.
Choice **c** is incorrect. In this sentence, Johnson is explaining that there were reasons for what happened rather than restating the problem of people being treated differently.
Choice **d** is incorrect. Johnson is affirming that Americans of all races have contributed to their country.

45. Choice c is correct. This is the best answer because one of the main points of the remarks is to explain that the Civil Rights Act will bring the United States closer to achieving its goals and values.
Choice **a** is incorrect. Johnson does not mention the Civil War in the passage.
Choice **b** is incorrect. The Grand Canyon is one of America's natural wonders, unrelated to America's unending search for justice domestically.
Choice **d** is incorrect. Johnson alludes to the Vietnam War in the text and uses it as an example of how American values are spanning the globe, but this is a small detail in the passage rather than a main idea. As well, Vietnam is outside of "our own borders."

46. Choice b is correct. Johnson talks about the values that the forefathers focused on when forming the nation in this paragraph.
Choice **a** is incorrect. This is a detail of the passage, but not the main theme.
Choice **c** is incorrect. This idea is not stated in the paragraph, and it also runs counter to the entire point of the speech.
Choice **d** is incorrect. There is no evidence to support this conclusion in the remarks.

47. Choice a is correct. Johnson expresses many times and in a variety of ways that equality is one of the cornerstones of American values.
Choice **b** is incorrect. Johnson talks about how he believes America is a great country, but this is not the main idea of his remarks.
Choice **c** is incorrect. Johnson's remarks are about America's ideal of ensuring equality, yet to be achieved.
Choice **d** is incorrect. Johnson makes no value judgment about himself.

48. Choice d is correct. This is Johnson's brief explanation of how inequality happened, rather than an explanation of how the law aligns with American values.

Choice **a** is incorrect. Johnson uses history and the vision of the forefathers to illustrate that freedom is a core American value and that freedom includes equality.

Choice **b** is incorrect. Johnson says that because American values are shaping foreign struggles, the United States must continue to make sure that it upholds its own values.

Choice **c** is incorrect. Johnson uses this sentence to say that all kinds of people, regardless of race, have fought for the country.

Part II

Your extended response will be scored based on three traits, or elements:

- **Trait 1:** Creation of arguments and use of evidence
- **Trait 2:** Development of ideas and organizational structure
- **Trait 3:** Clarity and command of standard English conventions

Your essay will be scored on a 6-point scale—each trait is worth up to 2 points. The final score is counted twice, so the maximum number of points you can earn is 12.

Trait 1 tests your ability to write an essay that takes a stance based on the information in the reading passages. To earn the highest score possible, you must carefully read the information and express a clear opinion on what you have read. You will be scored on how well you use the information from the passages to support your argument.

Your response will also be scored on how well you analyze the author's arguments in the passages. To earn the highest score possible, you should discuss whether you think the author is making a good argument, and why or why not.

For your reference, here is a table that readers will use when scoring your essay with a 2, 1, or 0.

TRAIT 1: CREATION OF ARGUMENTS AND USE OF EVIDENCE	
2	• Makes text-based argument(s) and establishes an intent connected to the prompt • Presents specific and related evidence from source text(s) to support argument (may include a few unrelated pieces of evidence or unsupported claims) • Analyzes the topic and/or the strength of the argument within the source text(s) (e.g., distinguishes between supported and unsupported claims, makes valid inferences about underlying assumptions, identifies false reasoning, evaluates the credibility of sources)
1	• Makes an argument with some connection to the prompt • Presents some evidence from source text(s) to support argument (may include a mix of related and unrelated evidence that may or may not cite the text) • Partly analyzes the topic and/or the strength of the argument within the source text(s); may be limited, oversimplified, or inaccurate
0	• May attempt to make an argument OR lacks an intent or connection to the prompt OR attempts neither • Presents little or no evidence from source text(s) (sections of text may be copied from source directly) • Minimally analyzes the topic and/or the strength of the argument within the source text(s); may present no analysis, or little or no understanding of the given argument
Non-scorable	• Response consists only of text copied from the prompt or source text(s) • Response shows that test-taker has not read the prompt or is entirely off-topic • Response is incomprehensible • Response is not in English • No response has been attempted (has been left blank)

Trait 2 tests whether you respond to the writing prompt with a well-structured essay. Support of your thesis must come from evidence in the passages, as well as personal opinions and experiences that build on your central idea. Your ideas must be fully explained and include specific details. Your essay should use words and phrases that allow your details and ideas to flow naturally. Here is a table that outlines what is involved in earning a score of 2, 1, or 0.

TRAIT 2: DEVELOPMENT OF IDEAS AND ORGANIZATIONAL STRUCTURE	
2	• Contains ideas that are generally logical and well-developed; most ideas are expanded upon • Contains a logical sequence of ideas with clear connections between specific details and main ideas • Develops an organizational structure that conveys the message and goal of the response; appropriately uses transitional devices • Develops and maintains an appropriate style and tone that signal awareness of the audience and purpose of the task • Uses appropriate words to express ideas clearly
1	• Contains ideas that are partially developed and/or may demonstrate vague or simplistic logic; only some ideas are expanded upon • Contains some evidence of a sequence of ideas, but specific details may be unconnected to main ideas • Develops an organizational structure that may partially group ideas or is partially effective at conveying the message of the response; inconsistently uses transitional devices • May inconsistently maintain an appropriate style and tone to signal an awareness of the audience and purpose of the task • May contain misused words and/or words that do not express ideas clearly
0	• Contains ideas that are ineffectively or illogically developed, with little or no elaboration of main ideas • Contains an unclear or no sequence of ideas; specific details may be absent or unrelated to main ideas • Develops an ineffective or no organizational structure; inappropriately uses transitional devices, or does not use them at all • Uses an inappropriate style and tone that signals limited or no awareness of audience and purpose • May contain many misused words, overuse of slang, and/or express ideas in an unclear or repetitious manner
Non-scorable	• Response consists only of text copied from the prompt or source text(s) • Response shows that test-taker has not read the prompt or is entirely off-topic • Response is incomprehensible • Response is not in English • No response has been attempted (has been left blank)

Trait 3 tests how you create the sentences that make up your essay. To earn a high score, you will need to write sentences with variety—some short, some long, some simple, some complex. You will also need to prove that you have a good handle on standard English, including correct word choice, grammar, and sentence structure.

Here is a table that outlines what is involved in attaining a score of 2, 1, or 0.

TRAIT 3: CLARITY AND COMMAND OF STANDARD ENGLISH CONVENTIONS	
2	• Demonstrates generally correct sentence structure and an overall fluency that enhances clarity with regard to the following skills: 1) Diverse sentence structure within a paragraph or paragraphs 2) Correct use of subordination, coordination, and parallelism 3) Avoidance of awkward sentence structures and wordiness 4) Use of transitional words, conjunctive adverbs, and other words that enhance clarity and logic 5) Avoidance of run-on sentences, sentence fragments, and fused sentences • Demonstrates proficient use of conventions with regard to the following skills: 1) Subject–verb agreement 2) Placement of modifiers and correct word order 3) Pronoun usage, including pronoun antecedent agreement, unclear pronoun references, and pronoun case 4) Frequently confused words and homonyms, including contractions 5) Use of apostrophes with possessive nouns 6) Use of punctuation (e.g., commas in a series or in appositives and other non-essential elements, end marks, and punctuation for clause separation) 7) Capitalization (e.g., beginnings of sentences, proper nouns, and titles) • May contain some errors in mechanics and conventions that do not impede comprehension; overall usage is at a level suitable for on-demand draft writing
1	• Demonstrates inconsistent sentence structure; may contain some choppy, repetitive, awkward, or run-on sentences that may limit clarity; demonstrates inconsistent use of skills 1–5 as listed under Trait 3, Score Point 2 • Demonstrates inconsistent use of basic conventions with regard to skills 1–7 as listed under Trait 3, Score Point 2 • May contain many errors in mechanics and conventions that occasionally impede comprehension; overall usage is at the minimum level acceptable for on-demand draft writing
0	• Demonstrates improper sentence structure to the extent that meaning may be unclear; demonstrates minimal use of skills 1–5 as listed under Trait 3, Score Point 2 • Demonstrates minimal use of basic conventions with regard to skills 1–7 as listed under Trait 3, Score Point 2 • Contains numerous significant errors in mechanics and conventions that impede comprehension; overall usage is at an unacceptable level for on-demand draft writing OR • Response is insufficient to show level of proficiency involving conventions and usage
Non-scorable	• Response consists only of text copied from the prompt or source text(s) • Response shows that test-taker has not read the prompt or is entirely off-topic • Response is incomprehensible • Response is not in English • No response has been attempted (has been left blank)

Sample Score 6 Essay

The inaugural addresses of Presidents Bush and Obama have one key difference that is immediately apparent: President Bush's address is focused on the past, while President Obama's speech is focused on the future.

Neither speaker gives an exact description of the historical context of his address, but even someone unfamiliar with the history of the past fifteen years can pick up a few clues. President Bush states: "A civil society demands from each of us good will and respect, fair dealing and forgiveness." Forgiveness is something offered for past wrongs. He also speaks of "civility" and "compassion." It seems clear that President Bush was assuming office at a time when people were angry and divided over an issue or issues, and that he feels the need to urge forgiveness.

President Obama, on the other hand, is a bit more explicit about his context, saying: "The state of our economy calls for action, bold and swift." Obviously, Obama is assuming office in the midst of an economic crisis. But in his speech, he frames that crisis as an opportunity to envision and create a better future. In the same paragraph in which he mentions the economy, Obama repeatedly refers to what "we will" do in the future: "we will act," "we will build," "we will restore," "we will harness," and "we will transform."

This is not to say that Obama does not mention the past at all. Both presidents pay homage to previous generations. However, Obama does so in more concrete and inclusive terms, mentioning experiences and events that resonate with a wide range of Americans—working in sweatshops, enduring slavery, and fighting in the Civil War, in World War II, and in Vietnam. In contrast, Bush speaks vaguely, though fondly, of our "democratic ideals."

Though, in essence, both speeches touch on many similar points—that America is a land of promise and that we should make sure all American enjoy the fruits of that promise, Obama's speech is more powerful because he seems to have a clear vision of how to move forward. Bush's speech seems like it was designed to soothe an angry electorate, not to lay out a clear agenda. His speech was fine, in that it was well organized and included the usual patriotic language. But in my opinion, any inaugural address should acknowledge the current state of the nation's affairs and lay out a plan for the future. Obama's speech does this, while Bush's does not.

About this essay:

This response is a six-point response because it is well organized, free of major grammatical or mechanical problems, and it uses details from both passages to make a coherent and even-handed argument that is based more on fact than on personal emotions.

Trait 1: Creation of Arguments and Use of Evidence

This response evaluates the arguments in the source texts, develops an effective position supported by the texts, and fulfills the criteria to earn 2 points for Trait 1.

This response establishes its stance in the first sentence (*President Bush's address is focused on the past, while President Obama's speech is focused on the future*) and develops it a step further in the conclusion (*But in my opinion, any inaugural address should acknowledge the current state of the nation's affairs and lay out a plan for the future. Obama's speech does this, while Bush's does not*).

The writer also provides a summary of support for that stance (*It seems clear that President Bush was assuming office at a time when people were angry and divided over an issue or issues, and that he feels the need to urge forgiveness. President Obama, on the other hand, is a bit more explicit about his context, saying: "The state of our economy calls for action, bold and swift."*)

Trait 2: Development of Ideas and Organizational Structure

This response is well developed and fulfills the criteria to earn 2 points for Trait 2. It is well organized, from the writer's clear point of view in the first paragraph, to the side-by-side comparison of the strengths of each speech.

The writer's vocabulary and sentence structures are sophisticated, and the tone shows an intensity of purpose.

Trait 3: Clarity and Command of Standard English Conventions

This response fulfills the criteria for draft writing and earns 2 points for Trait 3. Besides employing sophisticated sentence structure (*However, Obama does so in more concrete and inclusive terms, mentioning experiences and events that resonate with a wide range of Americans—working in sweatshops, enduring slavery, and fighting in the Civil War, in World War II, and in Vietnam.*), this response uses clear transitions in its compare and contrast construction (*In contrast, Bush speaks vaguely, though fondly, of our "democratic ideals."*)

Sample Score 4 Essay

People become president need to make sure they appeal to all Americans, not just a few. This is why President Bush's inaugural address was more effective than President Obama's. President Bush reminded listeners repeatedly of their common heritage. President Obama's speech seemed more self-centered because he talked about all the things he wanted to accomplish, but did not consider the concerns of average Americans.

President Bush talks about issues that all Americans are related to. For example he says "The grandest of these ideals is an unfolding American promise that everyone belongs, that everyone deserves a chance, that no insignificant person was ever born." He is talking about democracy here, and that is something all Americans agree with. But Obama seems to be picking a fight with political opponents when he says things like "What the cynics fail to understand is that the ground has shifted beneath them, that the stale political arguments that have consumed us for so long no longer apply." To me, Obama seems to be saying that people who don't agree with him are cynics with "stale" arguments. That could be denigrated to many people.

A president is president to all Americans, not just a few. That is why I think that the way President Bush talks about the need for all of us to practice "civility" is so important. Our country has many problems to solve, and we can't solve them without civility and being willing to forgive each other and operate with good will.

In conclusion, I believe President Bush did the best job in introducing himself and his plans as president to the country. He did so by appealing to everyone, not just to his supporters.

About this essay:

The essay is well structured, and the writer uses multiple quotes from the passages to back up key points. However, there are some minor grammatical/mechanical errors, and the writer uses opinion and emotion as much as supporting evidence from the passages.

Trait 1: Creation of Arguments and Use of Evidence

This response attempts to evaluate the arguments in the source texts, develops a position supported by the texts, and meets the criteria to earn 1 point for Trait 1. The writer establishes their perspective in the first sentence (*People become president need to make sure they appeal to all Americans, not just a few.*) and uses quotes to support their opinion (*Obama seems to be picking a fight with political opponents when he says things like "What the cynics fail to understand is that the ground has shifted beneath them, that the stale political arguments that have consumed us for so long no longer apply."*) though they also make leaps without textual evidence.

Trait 2: Development of Ideas and Organizational Structure

This response fulfills the criteria to earn 2 points for Trait 2. The writer begins by establishing their opinion, examines specific facets of each speech, and concludes by comparing the two speeches directly (*In conclusion, I believe President Bush did the best job in introducing himself and his plans as president to the country. He did so by appealing to everyone, not just to his supporters*).

Trait 3: Clarity and Command of Standard English Conventions

This response fulfills the criteria for draft writing and earns 1 point for Trait 3. There are some errors that make understanding the writer's meaning challenging (*That could be denigrated to many people.*)

Sample Score 3 Essay

If you look at President Bush's speech and compare and contrast it with President Obama's speech, you can see right away that Obama's is better.

Bush and Obama both talk about the path of America. But Obama makes Americans sound strong. He talks about the whip and the lash, and working your hands raw, and you can just feel how tough Americans are. But Bush just talks about how we are "flawed" and that sometimes we "halted." I don't think this is how people are aspired. It's not who we are.

Obama gets on a roll near the end of his speech with all the talk about "we will do this" and "we will do that," but all Bush does is say "be nice" and "be forgiving." Forgiving for what? Right away, you get your suspicious up.

That's why Obama's speech is better. He isn't afraid to call it like it is and he won't let anything stand in his way. All Bush seems to worry about is good manners.

About this essay:

This is a three-point response: although it does have a structure, it lacks a clear central argument and features scant support from the passages. It also has grammatical errors that interfere with meaning.

Trait 1: Creation of Arguments and Use of Evidence

This response attempts to evaluate the arguments in the source texts, though they struggle to develop a position supported by the texts, and so they earn 1 point for Trait 1.

Trait 2: Development of Ideas and Organizational Structure

This response has a structure but features little to no development of ideas, instead relying on a fairly straightforward recap of the texts. It meets the criteria to earn 1 point for Trait 2.

Trait 3: Clarity and Command of Standard English Conventions

This response attempts to fulfill the criteria for draft writing and earns 1 point for Trait 3. The spelling and syntactical errors reflect insufficient time revising or a lack of facility with written English (*aspired, "get your suspicious up"*).

Sample Score 0 Essay

President Bush knows what it means to be American. He talks about patriotism and civil society and about how immigrants can find opportunities to be American here. President Obama's speech is just scary. All that talk about the hard work people are supposed to like and the hard work we have to do. What about our government?

It's like Obama forgot that you have to talk like a president when you are giving a speech to the American people. This isn't a pep rally. You have to show you know yor stuff. That is what Bush does. He knows his American history. He quotes the facts.

Obama talks about what he wants to do and the work we are supposed to do. That's not facts. That's just wishes. Facts are what make speeches important.

About this essay:

This is a zero-point response because it is poorly structured, features multiple spelling and grammatical errors, and relies very little on evidence from the passages. Rather, it is based on the writer's unsupported emotions.

10 ▶ GED® RLA PRACTICE TEST 2

This practice test is modeled on the format, content, and timing of the official GED® Reasoning through Language Arts test.

Part I

Like the official exam, this section presents a series of questions that assess your ability to read, write, edit, and understand standard written English. You'll be asked to answer questions based on informational and literary reading passages. Refer to the passages as often as necessary when answering the questions.

Work carefully, but do not spend too much time on any one question. Be sure you answer every question.

Set a timer for 95 minutes (1 hour and 35 minutes), and try to take this test uninterrupted, under quiet conditions.

Part II

The official GED® Reasoning through Language Arts test also includes an Extended Response question—an essay question. Set a timer for 45 minutes and try to read the given passage and brainstorm, write, and proof-read your essay uninterrupted, under quiet conditions.

Complete answer explanations for every test question and sample essays at different scoring levels follow the exam. Good luck!

Part I

48 total questions
95 minutes to complete

Please use the following to answer questions 1–8.

This excerpt is from the Declaration of Independence.

1   When in the Course of human events, it becomes necessary for one people to dissolve the political bands which have connected them with another, and to assume among the powers of the earth, the separate and equal station to which the Laws of Nature and of Nature's God entitle them, a decent respect to the opinions of mankind requires that they should declare the causes which impel them to the separation.

2   We hold these truths to be self-evident, that all men are created equal, that they are endowed by their Creator with certain unalienable Rights, that among these are Life, Liberty and the pursuit of Happiness.—That to secure these rights, Governments are instituted among Men, deriving their just powers from the consent of the governed,—That whenever any Form of Government becomes destructive of these ends, it is the Right of the People to alter or to abolish it, and to institute new Government, laying its foundation on such principles and organizing its powers in such form, as to them shall seem most likely to effect their Safety and Happiness. Prudence, indeed, will dictate that Governments long established should not be changed for light and transient causes; and accordingly all experience hath shewn, that mankind are more disposed to suffer, while evils are sufferable, than to right themselves by abolishing the forms to which they are accustomed. But when a long train of abuses and usurpations, pursuing invariably the same Object evinces a design to reduce them under absolute Despotism, it is their right, it is their duty, to throw off such Government, and to provide new Guards for their future security.—Such has been the patient sufferance of these Colonies; and such is now the necessity which constrains them to alter their former Systems of Government. The history of the present King of Great Britain is a history of repeated injuries and usurpations, all having in direct object the establishment of an absolute Tyranny over these States. To prove this, let Facts be submitted to a candid world.

3   He has refused his Assent to Laws, the most wholesome and necessary for the public good. He has forbidden his Governors to pass Laws of immediate and pressing importance, unless suspended in their operation till his Assent should be obtained; and when so suspended, he has utterly neglected to attend to them. He has refused to pass other Laws for the accommodation of large districts of people, unless those people would relinquish the right of Representation in the Legislature, a right inestimable to them and formidable to tyrants only. He has called together legislative bodies at places unusual, uncomfortable, and distant from the depository of their public Records, for the sole purpose of fatiguing them into compliance with his measures. He has dissolved Representative Houses repeatedly, for opposing with manly firmness his invasions on the rights of the people.

1. Write your answers in the boxes below.

Based on the excerpt, "He has dissolved Representative Houses repeatedly" is an example of an injustice committed by the [   ] of [   ].

2. Paragraph 3 can be summed up as
   a. a list of laws for life in the colonies written by the King of Great Britain
   b. a list of laws created for the newly independent United States of America
   c. a list praising the many good acts carried out by the King of Great Britain
   d. a list of injustices committed by the King of Great Britain against the colonies

3. Which of the following quotations expresses the Declaration's main idea that the American colonies want independence from Great Britain?
   a. "We hold these truths to be self-evident, that all men are created equal"
   b. "it becomes necessary for one people to dissolve the political bands which have connected them with another"
   c. "He has refused to pass other Laws for the accommodation of large districts of people"
   d. "they are endowed by their Creator with certain unalienable Rights"

4. Which of the following quotations builds on the argument that governments should get their powers from the consent of the governed?
   a. "He has refused his Assent to Laws, the most wholesome and necessary for the public good"
   b. "whenever any Form of Government becomes destructive of these ends, it is the Right of the People to alter or to abolish it"
   c. "He has dissolved Representative Houses repeatedly"
   d. "He has called together legislative bodies at places unusual, uncomfortable, and distant from the depository of their public Records"

5. What evidence supports the claim that the King of Great Britain has wronged the colonists?
   a. a list of court rulings against the King in favor of the colonists
   b. a list of all his wrongdoings provided by other world leaders
   c. a list of the King's wrongdoings
   d. a list of names of colonists whom have been personally wronged

6. How would you evaluate the list of grievances given to support the claim that the King of England wronged the colonists?
   a. relevant and sufficient
   b. relevant and insufficient
   c. irrelevant and sufficient
   d. irrelevant and insufficient

7. Which of the following claims is supported by evidence?
   a. All men are equal.
   b. The King of Great Britain is a tyrannical leader.
   c. All men have certain unalienable rights.
   d. Governments should be controlled by the governed.

8. The quotation "to secure these rights, Governments are instituted among Men, deriving their just powers from the consent of the governed" is an example of which of the following?
   a. an explanation
   b. factual evidence
   c. valid reasoning
   d. false reasoning

Read the following excerpt and answer the next four questions.

What Was Her Life About?

(1) We were married and lived together for seventy years,
(2) Enjoying, working, raising twelve children,
(3) Eight of whom we lost
(4) Ere I had reached the age of sixty.
(5) I spun, wove, kept the house, nursed the sick,
(6) Made the garden, and for the holiday
(7) Rambled over the fields where sang many larks,
(8) And by the Spoon River gathering many a shell,
(9) And many a flower and medicinal weed—
(10) Shouting to the wooded hills, singing to the green valleys.
(11) At ninety-six I had lived enough, that is all,
(12) And passed a sweet repose.
    —Edgar Lee Masters, *Spoon River Anthology*

9. Based on the excerpt, what does the woman mean when she talks of passing "a sweet repose" (line 12)?
   a. her death
   b. her old age
   c. how well she slept at night
   d. needing to rest more as she grew older

10. Which of the following words best describes the overall mood of the poem?
   a. joy
   b. anger
   c. acceptance
   d. wonder

11. Which of the following is the most likely explanation of the line from the poem that reads, "Shouting to the wooded hills, singing to the green valleys" (line 10)?
   a. The speaker had a fine singing voice.
   b. The speaker loved the countryside.
   c. The speaker preferred sounds to silence.
   d. The speaker spent of a lot of time working in the fields.

12. Which can you infer about the couple's marriage?
   a. They were never meant to be together.
   b. They could not deal with the loss of their children.
   c. They had an extremely happy marriage.
   d. They had their sorrows and their joys.

Please use the following passage to answer questions 13 and 14.

This excerpt is from a speech by George W. Bush delivered on March 19, 2008.

1   Operation Iraqi Freedom was a remarkable display of military effectiveness. Forces from the UK, Australia, Poland, and other allies joined our troops in the initial operations. As they advanced, our troops fought their way through sandstorms so intense that they blackened the daytime sky. Our troops engaged in pitched battles with Fedayeen Saddam, death squads acting on the orders of Saddam Hussein that obeyed neither the conventions of war nor the dictates of conscience. These death squads hid in schools, and they hid in hospitals, hoping to draw fire against Iraqi civilians. They used women and children as human shields. They stopped at nothing in their efforts to prevent us from prevailing, but they couldn't stop the coalition advance.

2   Aided by the most effective and precise air campaign in history, coalition forces raced across 350 miles of enemy territory, destroying Republican Guard divisions, pushing through the Karbala Gap, capturing Saddam International Airport, and liberating Baghdad in less than one month. . . .

3   Because we acted, Saddam Hussein no longer fills fields with the remains of innocent men, women, and children. . . . Because we acted, Saddam's regime is no longer invading its neighbors or attacking them with chemical weapons and ballistic missiles.

13. Based on this speech excerpt about Operation Iraqi Freedom, take the following list of events and write them in the correct order of occurrence on the lines below.

   coalition forces cross 350 miles of enemy territory
   Operation Iraqi Freedom is launched
   Baghdad is liberated

1. _____

2. _____

3. _____

14. In the excerpt from Bush's speech, what does the Middle Eastern setting, comprising "sandstorms so intense that they blackened the daytime sky," add to the first paragraph, which mentions troops fighting death squads?
   a. a heightened sense of beauty
   b. a heightened sense of contentment
   c. a heightened sense of danger
   d. a decreased sense of danger

Please use the following to answer questions 15–20.

The 1976 Democratic National Convention Keynote Address, delivered by Barbara Jordan

1   Throughout—throughout our history, when people have looked for new ways to solve their problems and to uphold the principles of this nation, many times they have turned to political parties. They have often turned to the Democratic Party. What is it? What is it about the Democratic Party that makes it the instrument the people use when they search for ways to shape their future? Well, I believe the answer to that question lies in our concept of governing. Our concept of governing is derived from our view of people. It is a concept deeply rooted in a set of beliefs firmly etched in the national conscience of all of us.

2   Now, what are these beliefs? First, we believe in equality for all and privileges for none. This is a belief—this is a belief that each American, regardless of background, has equal standing in the public forum—all of us. Because—because we believe this idea so firmly, we are an inclusive rather than an exclusive party. Let everybody come.

3   I think it no accident that most of those immigrating to America in the 19th century identified with the Democratic Party. We are a heterogeneous party made up of Americans of diverse backgrounds. We believe that the people are the source of all governmental power, that the authority of the people is to be extended, not restricted.

4   This—this can be accomplished only by providing each citizen with every opportunity to participate in the management of the government. They must have that, we believe. We believe that the government which represents the authority of all the people, not just one interest group, but all the people, has an obligation to actively—actively—seek to remove those obstacles which would block individual achievement—obstacles emanating from race, sex, economic condition. The government must remove them, seek to remove them.

5   We are a party—we are a party of innovation. We do not reject our traditions, but we are willing to adapt to changing circumstances, when change we must. We are willing to suffer the discomfort of change in order to achieve a better future. We have a positive vision of the future founded on the belief that the gap between the promise and reality of America can one day be finally closed. We believe that.

6   This, my friends is the bedrock of our concept of governing. This is a part of the reason why Americans have turned to the Democratic Party. These are the foundations upon which a national community can be built. Let all understand that these guiding principles cannot be discarded for short-term political gains. They represent what this country is all about. They are indigenous to the American idea. And these are principles which are not negotiable.

15. What is the main idea of the second paragraph?
   a. Every citizen is welcomed by the Democratic Party.
   b. Immigrants have often chosen to support the Democratic Party.
   c. Barbara Jordan approves of the Democratic Party.
   d. The Democratic Party accepts only the best of the best.

16. Which of the following statements supports Barbara Jordan's belief that the government must represent all people?
   a. "Because we believe this idea so firmly, we are an inclusive rather than an exclusive party."
   b. "This can be accomplished only by providing each citizen with every opportunity to participate in the management of the government."
   c. "We do not reject our traditions, but we are willing to adapt to changing circumstances, when change we must."
   d. "These are the foundations upon which a national community can be built."

17. Based on the text, which of the following scenarios would Barbara Jordan most likely support?
   a. A Democratic Party presidential candidate holding a private dinner for a select group of people.
   b. Members of a political party focusing on recruiting only those who can donate large amounts of money.
   c. A Democratic candidate running for the state senate.
   d. A local Democratic Party group holding an open forum for members of the community.

18. Which of the following statements best summarizes the main idea of the address?
   a. Many people have chosen to support the Democratic Party over the years.
   b. The values of the Democratic Party represent American ideals.
   c. The Democratic Party has evolved when necessary.
   d. all of the above

19. In which of the following phrases does Barbara Jordan criticize the Democratic Party?
   a. When she calls it "the instrument the people use when they search for ways to shape their future."
   b. When she says that those in the party "believe in equality for all and privileges for none."
   c. When she says that it is a "party of innovation."
   d. none of the above

20. From which statement can you infer that Barbara Jordan believes the government should enact laws against race and gender discrimination?
   a. "What is it about the Democratic Party that makes it the instrument the people use when they search for ways to shape their future?"
   b. "We believe that the people are the source of all governmental power, that the authority of the people is to be extended, not restricted."
   c. "We have a positive vision of the future founded on the belief that the gap between the promise and reality of America can one day be finally closed."
   d. "We believe that the government which represents the authority of all the people . . . has an obligation to actively—actively—seek to remove those obstacles which would block individual achievement."

Please use the following to answer questions 21–25.

To: All Staff
From: Allison Lewis, Manager
Date: July 15, 2016
Subject: Piles of Books

It has come to our attention that there have been piles of books that (1) on the floor in the fiction, cooking, and teen sections of the bookstore by the end of every day. It has gotten so bad that some customers are complaining that they are in the way of a large portion of shelved books. (2), we are introducing a new policy that mandates employees check their assigned sections for piles every hour and that employees then shelf any books found out of place.

(3) make sure to follow this procedure regularly. Even piles of a few books can cause unnecessary obstacles for customers.

Thank you for (4) cooperation!

(5)

Allison Lewis

21. Choose the correct form of **accumulate** for (1).
   a. accumulate
   b. accumulates
   c. accumulated
   d. will accumulate

22. Which word fits correctly in (2)?
   a. Therefore
   b. However
   c. Meanwhile
   d. Instead

23. Which word fits correctly in (3)?
   a. please
   b. pleases
   c. Please
   d. Pleases

24. Which word fits correctly in (4)?
   a. my
   b. your
   c. their
   d. her

25. Which word fits correctly in (5)?
   a. Best.
   b. Best!
   c. Best'
   d. Best,

Please use the following to answer questions 26–29.

This excerpt is from *The Fall of the House of Usher*, by Edgar Allan Poe.

During the whole of a dull, dark, and soundless day in the autumn of the year, when the clouds hung oppressively low in the heavens, I had been passing alone, on horseback, through a singularly dreary tract of country; and at length found myself, as the shades of the evening drew on, within view of the melancholy House of Usher. I know not how it was; but, with the first glimpse of the building, a sense of insufferable gloom pervaded my spirit. I say insufferable; for the feeling was unrelieved by any of that half-pleasurable, because poetic, sentiment, with which the mind usually receives even the sternest natural images of the desolate or terrible. I looked upon the scene before me—upon the mere house, and the simple landscape features of the domain—upon the bleak walls—upon the vacant eye-like windows—upon a few rank sedges—and upon a few white trunks of decayed trees—with an utter depression of soul which I can compare to no earthly sensation more properly than to the after-dream of the reveler upon opium—the bitter lapse into everyday life—the hideous dropping off of the veil. There was an iciness, a sinking, a sickening of the heart—an unredeemed dreariness of thought which no goading of the imagination could torture into aught of the sublime. What was it—I paused to think—what was it that so unnerved me in the contemplation of the House of Usher? It was a mystery all insoluble; nor could I grapple with the shadowy fancies that crowded upon me as I pondered. I was forced to fall back upon the unsatisfactory conclusion that while, beyond doubt, there are combinations of very simple natural objects which have the power of thus affecting us, still the analysis of this power lies among considerations beyond our depth. It was possible, I reflected, that a mere different arrangement of the particulars of the scene, of the details of the picture, would be sufficient to modify, or perhaps to annihilate its capacity for sorrowful impression; and, acting upon this idea, I reined my horse to the precipitous brink of a black and lurid tarn that lay in unruffled luster by the dwelling, and gazed down—but with a shudder even more thrilling than before—upon the remodeled and inverted images of the gray sedge, and the ghastly tree stems, and the vacant and eye-like windows.

26. The words **sorrowful, sickening, melancholy,** and **dreary** serve to give the excerpt a
   a. joyous tone.
   b. foreboding tone.
   c. courageous tone.
   d. silly tone.

27. Based on this excerpt, take the following list of events and write them in the correct order of occurrence on the lines below.
   rides through the countryside
   feels a sense of gloom
   reins his horse near the house
   comes to the House of Usher
   1. _____
   2. _____
   3. _____
   4. _____

28. The phrase "vacant eye-like windows" is an example of
   a. alliteration.
   b. hyperbole.
   c. onomatopoeia.
   d. personification.

29. Replacing "insufferable gloom" with which of the following words changes the tone of the phrase "a sense of insufferable gloom pervaded my spirit"?
   a. melancholy
   b. joy
   c. sadness
   d. despair

Please use the following to answer questions 30–35.

From the personal memoirs of Ulysses S. Grant, LXX

1   Things began to quiet down, and as the certainty that there would be no more armed resistance became clearer, the troops in North Carolina and Virginia were ordered to march immediately to the capital, and go into camp there until mustered out. Suitable garrisons were left at the prominent places throughout the South to insure obedience to the laws that might be enacted for the government of the several States, and to insure security to the lives and property of all classes. I do not know how far this was necessary, but I deemed it necessary, at that time, that such a course should be pursued. I think now that these garrisons were continued after they ceased to be absolutely required; but it is not to be expected that such a rebellion as was fought between the sections from 1861 to 1865 could terminate without leaving many serious apprehensions in the mind of the people as to what should be done.

2   Sherman marched his troops from Goldsboro, up to Manchester, on the south side of the James River, opposite Richmond, and there put them in camp, while he went back to Savannah to see what the situation was there.

3   It was during this trip that the last outrage was committed upon him. Halleck had been sent to Richmond to command Virginia, and had issued orders prohibiting even Sherman's own troops from obeying his, Sherman's, orders. Sherman met the papers on his return, containing this order of Halleck, and very justly felt indignant at the outrage. On his arrival at Fortress Monroe returning from Savannah, Sherman received an invitation from Halleck to come to Richmond and be his guest. This he indignantly refused, and informed Halleck, furthermore, that he had seen his order. He also stated that he was coming up to take command of his troops, and as he marched through it would probably be as well for Halleck not to show himself, because he (Sherman) would not be responsible for what some rash person might do through indignation for the treatment he had received. Very soon after that, Sherman received orders from me to proceed to Washington City, and to go into camp on the south side of the city pending the mustering-out of the troops.

(continues)

4   The march of Sherman's army from Atlanta to the sea and north to Goldsboro, while it was not accompanied with the danger that was anticipated, yet was magnificent in its results, and equally magnificent in the way it was conducted. It had an important bearing, in various ways, upon the great object we had in view, that of closing the war. All the States east of the Mississippi River up to the State of Georgia, had felt the hardships of the war. Georgia, and South Carolina, and almost all of North Carolina, up to this time, had been exempt from invasion by the Northern armies, except upon their immediate sea coasts. Their newspapers had given such an account of Confederate success, that the people who remained at home had been convinced that the Yankees had been whipped from first to last, and driven from pillar to post, and that now they could hardly be holding out for any other purpose than to find a way out of the war with honor to themselves.

5   Even during this march of Sherman's the newspapers in his front were proclaiming daily that his army was nothing better than a mob of men who were frightened out of their wits and hastening, panic-stricken, to try to get under the cover of our navy for protection against the Southern people. As the army was seen marching on triumphantly, however, the minds of the people became disabused and they saw the true state of affairs. In turn they became disheartened, and would have been glad to submit without compromise.

30. Why were garrisons left in the South?
   a. Violence was still prevalent.
   b. The Civil War is brewing.
   c. Grant thought it was necessary at the time.
   d. Sherman made the order.

31. What historical event can you infer was drawing to a close at the time this was written?

   [   ]

32. How would the tone of the passage change if the word **outrage** was replaced with **injustice** in the sentence, "It was during this trip that the last outrage was committed upon him"?
   a. It would support Grant's disapproval of Sherman's March.
   b. It would strengthen Grant's support of Sherman's March as necessary.
   c. It would increase Grant's list of criticisms of Sherman.
   d. It would confirm Grant's claim that the Confederates believed they had succeeded.

33. Which of the following quotations reveals Grant's disagreement with the Confederate viewpoint after the Civil War?
   a. "[B]ut it is not to be expected that such a rebellion as was fought between the sections from 1861 to 1865 could terminate without leaving many serious apprehensions in the mind of the people as to what should be done."
   b. "It was during this trip that the last outrage was committed upon him."
   c. "Their newspapers had given such an account of Confederate success, that the people who remained at home had been convinced that the Yankees had been whipped from first to last, and driven from pillar to post. . . ."
   d. "In turn they became disheartened, and would have been glad to submit without compromise."

34. Put the events in chronological order.

    A—Sherman's men were ordered not to listen to him

    B—the Confederates "saw the true state of affairs"

    C—the Civil War

    D—Sherman's March

  a. C, A, D, B

  b. C, A, B, D

  c. A, C, D, B

  d. A, C, B, D

35. What does the word **triumphantly** mean in the following sentence: "As the army was seen marching on triumphantly, however, the minds of the people became disabused and they saw the true state of affairs"?

  a. sheepishly

  b. victoriously

  c. angrily

  d. defeatedly

Please use the following to answer questions 36–39.

"Watching Volcanoes," by Millie Ceron

1 Scientists who watch volcanoes bear a great responsibility. It is up to them to alert the public when they think that a volcano is about to erupt. But it is not always easy to tell when an eruption is imminent. I know, because my whole career as a scientist has been spent studying volcanoes. I've learned that predicting eruptions is a very inexact science. There often are certain warning signs, but they can be very difficult to interpret. What should you do when you see them? You certainly don't want to cause a panic or tell people to flee unless it is really necessary, yet you also don't want to underestimate the danger. Scientists like me usually try to steer a path between these two extremes. But we also try to err on the side of caution: It's always better to be safe than sorry!

2 What are the signs that an eruption may soon occur? The main ones are earthquakes beneath the mountain, bulges in the sides of the mountain, and the escape of volcanic gases.

3 **Watching for Earthquakes.** Earthquakes often occur for some time before an eruption of *magma* (molten rock) and volcanic gases force their way up through underground channels. Sometimes the force causes a continuous shaking called *tremor*. To record earthquakes, a device called a *seismometer* is used. Four to eight seismometers are typically installed close to or on the mountain. Only by being very close to the volcano can seismometers pick up the tiny earthquakes that may be the first sign that a volcano may erupt.

4 When an eruption is just about to take place, earthquakes often occur in "swarms." Scientists monitor these swarms around the clock. The reason is that variations in the type and strength of the quakes are often the best indication that an eruption is just about to happen.

(continues)

5 **Watching for Bulges in the Sides of the Mountain.** During the months or weeks prior to an eruption, magma rises inside a volcano. The pressure created by this magma often causes the sides of the mountain to "tilt." Sometimes it even causes visible bulges in the mountainside. To monitor these bulges, scientists use a sensitive instrument called a *tiltmeter*. Today they also use satellite-based technology to take precise measurements. By these methods scientists discovered that in the months before Mount Saint Helens erupted in 1982, one side of the mountain swelled by more than 100 meters.

6 **Watching for Volcanic Gases.** The gases dissolved in magma provide the main force in a volcanic eruption. Consequently, it is important to find out whether any gases are present and if so, what kinds of gases. However, collecting these gases is not easy. They are often found escaping from vents high up on the mountain or in the crater. Scientists may visit the vents themselves and collect the gases in bottles for analysis in the laboratory. But such visits are dangerous: the climb can be difficult, the gases themselves can be hazardous to breathe, and there is always the danger of an eruption. Scientists may also place automated gas monitors near the vents, but these devices are often destroyed by the acidic gases. Another way to collect the gases is by flying through the gas clouds above the volcano in specially equipped airplanes. But it is difficult to obtain good samples by this method, and bad weather can keep planes on the ground just when monitoring is most urgent. However, when scientists succeed in collecting volcanic gases, they can tell a lot about how a volcano works and what effects it may have on Earth's climate and environment.

"The 1992 Eruptions at Mt. Spurr, Alaska," by Ling Chen

1 Mt. Spurr is a small volcano located 80 miles west of Anchorage, Alaska. In August 1991, eight seismographs placed on the mountain began recording many very small earthquakes. Airborne gas sampling was used to check for the presence of volcanic gases.

2 In early June 1992, earthquake activity increased. Then on June 27 a "swarm" of earthquakes suggested magma moving at shallow depth. As the earthquakes grew stronger, scientists broadcast a warning that an eruption might be about to occur. Later that day, pilots reported ash plumes erupting from the mountain.

3 After the June 27 eruption, earthquake activity declined rapidly to its lowest level in months. Scientists concluded that the danger of further eruptions was low. During July, bad weather often grounded pilots, preventing airborne observation of the volcano and collection of volcanic gas samples. Weeks passed during which little occurred at the mountain.

(continues)

4   On August 18, however, a pilot suddenly reported a huge ash plume above the crater. Scientists immediately broadcast a warning that an eruption was occurring.

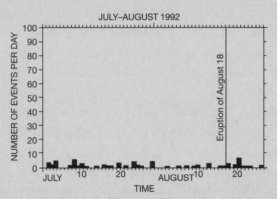

This graph shows earthquake activity recorded at Mt. Spurr before the eruption of August 18. The eruption ended after a few hours, and earthquake activity remained low, so the likelihood of further eruptions again seemed to be low.

5   That fall, however, earthquake activity increased once again beneath Mt. Spurr. "Swarms" of strong earthquakes were recorded in both early October and early November. Each time, scientists issued warnings that "a large eruption is likely within the next 24 to 48 hours." However, no eruption took place. When another "swarm" of earthquakes occurred in December, scientists decided not to issue an eruption warning.

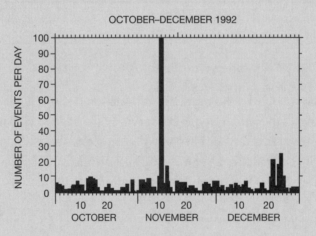

This graph shows earthquake activity recorded at Mt. Spurr from October through December 1992.

36. What is the main purpose of paragraph 3 in "Watching Volcanoes"?

  a. to describe how scientists monitor earthquakes to predict volcanic eruptions

  b. to define scientific terms, such as magma, tremor, and seismometer

  c. to explain how scientists use seismometers to record earthquakes

  d. to show how earthquakes cause volcanic gases to escape

37. Which of the following best summarizes "Watching Volcanoes"?

  a. Scientists monitor bulges in the sides of mountains with tiltmeters because bulges may indicate a volcanic eruption will soon occur.

  b. Scientists should not visit vents on mountaintops to collect and analyze gases because it is extremely dangerous.

  c. Scientists were concerned enough about a small volcano near Anchorage, Alaska, to issue a warning it might erupt in June 1992.

  d. Scientists who watch volcanoes monitor signs of eruption by various means to ensure the public is aware of possible dangers.

38. How are "Watching Volcanoes" and "The 1992 Eruptions at Mt. Spurr, Alaska" different?

  a. "Watching Volcanoes" focuses on a particular eruption, and "The 1992 Eruptions at Mt. Spurr, Alaska" is about volcanoes in general.

  b. "Watching Volcanoes" is a personal account, and "The 1992 Eruptions at Mt. Spurr, Alaska" is an objective report.

  c. "Watching Volcanoes" discusses seismometers or seismographs, and "The 1992 Eruptions at Mt. Spurr, Alaska" does not.

  d. "Watching Volcanoes" is a diary entry, and "The 1992 Eruptions at Mt. Spurr, Alaska" is a newspaper article.

39. Considering that there were never more than ten events in a single day from July to August 1992, why might the first graph allot space for as many as 100 events?

  a. to illustrate how Mt. Spurr was not capable of erupting

  b. to forecast a major rise of events in September

  c. to contrast the dramatic number of events in November on the second graph

  d. because this is the standard graph that all volcano-watching scientists use

Please use the following to answer questions 40–43.

This excerpt is from *Pride and Prejudice*, by Jane Austen.

1 It is a truth universally acknowledged that a single man in possession of a good fortune must be in want of a wife.

2 However little known the feelings or views of such a man may be on his first entering a neighbourhood, this truth is so well fixed in the minds of the surrounding families, that he is considered as the rightful property of someone or other of their daughters.

3 "My dear Mr. Bennet," said his lady to him one day, "have you heard that Netherfield Park is let at last?"

4 Mr. Bennet replied that he had not.

5 "But it is," returned she; "for Mrs. Long has just been here, and she told me all about it."

6 Mr. Bennet made no answer.

7 "Do not you want to know who has taken it?" cried his wife, impatiently.

8 "You want to tell me, and I have no objection to hearing it."

9 This was invitation enough.

10 "Why, my dear, you must know, Mrs. Long says that Netherfield is taken by a young man of large fortune from the north of England; that he came down on Monday in a chaise and four to see the place, and was so much delighted with it that he agreed with Mr. Morris immediately; that he is to take possession before Michaelmas, and some of his servants are to be in the house by the end of next week."

11 'What is his name?'

12 "Bingley."

13 "Is he married or single?"

14 "Oh, single, my dear, to be sure! A single man of large fortune; four or five thousand a year. What a fine thing for our girls!"

15 "How so? How can it affect them?"

16 "My dear Mr. Bennet," replied his wife, "how can you be so tiresome? You must know that I am thinking of his marrying one of them."

17 "Is that his design in settling here?"

18 "Design? Nonsense, how can you talk so! But it is very likely that he may fall in love with one of them, and therefore you must visit him as soon as he comes."

19 "I see no occasion for that. You and the girls may go, or you may send them by themselves, which perhaps will be still better, for, as you are as handsome as any of them, Mr. Bingley might like you the best of the party."

20 "My dear, you flatter me. I certainly *have* had my share of beauty, but I do not pretend to be anything extraordinary now. When a woman has five grown-up daughters, she ought to give over thinking of her own beauty."

21 "In such cases, a woman has not often much beauty to think of."

(continues)

22 "But, my dear, you must indeed go and see Mr. Bingley when he comes into the neighbour-hood."

23 "It is more than I engage for, I assure you."

24 "But consider your daughters. Only think what an establishment it would be for one of them. Sir William and Lady Lucas are determined to go, merely on that account; for in general, you know, they visit no newcomers. Indeed you must go, for it will be impossible for *us* to visit him, if you do not."

25 "You are over scrupulous, surely. I daresay Mr. Bingley will be very glad to see you; and I will send a few lines by you to assure him of my hearty consent to his marrying whichever he chooses of the girls; though I must throw in a good word for my little Lizzy."

26 "I desire you will do no such thing. Lizzy is not a bit better than the others: and I am sure she is not half so handsome as Jane, nor half so good-humoured as Lydia. But you are always giving *her* the preference."

27 "They have none of them much to recommend them," replied he: "they are all silly and ignorant like other girls; but Lizzy has something more of quickness than her sisters."

28 "Mr. Bennet, how can you abuse your own children in such a way? You take delight in vexing me. You have no compassion on my poor nerves."

29 "You mistake me, my dear. I have a high respect for your nerves. They are my old friends. I have heard you mention them with consideration these twenty years at least."

30 "Ah, you do not know what I suffer."

31 "But I hope you will get over it, and live to see many young men of four thousand a year come into the neighbourhood."

32 "It will be no use to us, if twenty such should come, since you will not visit them."

33 "Depend upon it, my dear, that when there are twenty, I will visit them all."

34 Mr. Bennet was so odd a mixture of quick parts, sarcastic humour, reserve, and caprice, that the experience of three-and-twenty years had been insufficient to make his wife understand his character. *Her* mind was less difficult to develop. She was a woman of mean understanding, little information, and uncertain temper. When she was discontented, she fancied herself nervous. The business of her life was to get her daughters married: its solace was visiting and news.

40. What is the number of the paragraph that supports the idea that a wealthy man is always looking for a wife?

Paragraph [   ]

41. What is the theme of the excerpt?

   a. travel

   b. divorce

   c. holidays

   d. marriage

42. In paragraph 14, what does "four or five thousand a year" refer to?

  a. the number of Mr. Bingley's annual trips to the Bennets' town

  b. Mr. Bingley's annual income

  c. Mr. Bennet's annual income

  d. Mrs. Long's annual income

43. What conclusion can you draw about Mrs. Bennet's wishes?

  a. She wants to marry Mr. Bingley for his money.

  b. She wants one of her daughters to marry Mr. Bingley.

  c. She doesn't want any of her daughters to marry Mr. Bingley.

  d. She wishes she had married someone with more money.

Please use the following to answer questions 44–48.

To: All Staff
From: Allison Lewis, Manager
Date: June 5, 2016
Subject: Bookstore Procedures

I am writing to clear up some issues dealing with our bookstores procedures. I have been getting a lot of questions about what procedures bookstore staff members are meant to follow on every shift. Recently, I have taken it upon myself to write a list of the procedures for reference.

1. at the beginning of a shift, all staff must sign in through our computer system.
2. Staff members assigned two the floor shift should check for misplaced books regularly and reshelf those books.
3. Staff members assigned to the stock shift should keep the warehouse clean and organized.
4. No staff member is allowed to give a discount to any customer without manager approval.
5. Staff members do not receive free and complimentary drinks at the in-store café.
6. Customers are not allowed to preorder books that are not yet on our preorder list.
7. Before leaving a shift, all staff members must perform one last check for cleanliness and organization of the store and must sign out though our computer system.
8. If a staff member forget to sign in or sign out, he or she must consult the manager before estimating his or her sign in and sign out times.

Thank you for your cooperation!

Best,
Allison Lewis

44. In the first sentence of the company memo, what should be added to make it correct?
a. an apostrophe at the end of *procedures*
b. an apostrophe at the end of *bookstores*
c. an apostrophe between *bookstore* and *s*
d. nothing

45. Reread the first list item:

1. at the beginning of a shift, all staff must sign in through our computer system.

Now, rewrite the sentence to correct any errors by writing it in the box below:

1. [   ]

46. In the second list item of the company memo, what should be changed to make it correct?
a. change *two* to *to*
b. change *for* to *four*
c. change *and* to *or*
d. no change

47. In the fifth list item, which of the following changes would improve the sentence?
a. delete *and complimentary*
b. delete *in-store café*
c. insert *on the house* before *free*
d. no change

48. In the eighth list item of the company memo, what should be changed in order to make it correct?
a. change *forget* to *forgets*
b. change *he or she* to *they*
c. change *consult* to *consults*
d. no change

Part II

1 question
45 minutes to complete

This practice allows you to compose your response to the given task and then compare it with examples of responses at the different score levels. You will also get a scoring guide that includes a detailed explanation of how official GED® test graders will score your response. You may use this scoring guide to score your own response.

Before you begin, it is important to note that on the official test this task must be completed in no more than 45 minutes. But don't rush to complete your response; take time to carefully read the passage(s) and the question prompt. Then think about how you would like to respond.

As you write your essay, be sure to:

- Decide which position presented in the passages is better supported by evidence.
- Explain why your chosen position has better support.
- Recognize that the position with better support may not be the position you agree with.
- Present multiple pieces of evidence from the passage to defend your assertions.
- Thoroughly construct your main points, organizing them logically, with strong supporting details.
- Connect your sentences, paragraphs, and ideas with transitional words and phrases.
- Express your ideas clearly and choose your words carefully.
- Use varied sentence structures to increase the clarity of your response.
- Reread and revise your response.

Good luck!

Please use the following passages to answer the essay question.

An Analysis of Stem Cell Research

1   Stem cell research is research using embryonic and "somatic" or "adult" stem cells for the purpose of advancing medicine. This research has been in existence since the beginning of the twentieth century, and over the years many breakthroughs have come from it. In 1998, scientists discovered methods to derive stem cells from human embryos. In 2006, researchers made another breakthrough, which involved reprogramming some adult cells in certain conditions to assume a stem-cell-like state. Stem cells themselves are useful in medical research because they are at the early state of reproduction, where the cell can either remain a stem cell or become a cell that would be involved in the formation of bones, brain cells, skin, the nervous system, organs, muscles, and every other part of the body.

Benefits of Stem Cell Research

2   Theoretically, research points to stem cell research being of great value in medical advancement. At this time, it is not yet clear how much can be done with stem cell research, and the possible benefits are incalculable. It could lead to cures for diabetes or heart disease. It is also seen as a potential resource to help cure cancer and Parkinson's disease, or even to regenerate a severed spinal cord and allow someone to walk who has been confined to a wheelchair. Although this sounds miraculous, it will not happen without extensive work and time.

3   Currently, adult stem cell therapies are used in the form of bone marrow transplants for treating leukemia. In 2006, researchers created artificial liver cells from umbilical cord blood stem cells. And in 2008, a study was published of the first successful cartilage regeneration in a human knee using adult stem cells. The variety of ways in which stem cell research could aid in curing many diseases has just begun to be explored.

4   While there are questions regarding human embryo stem cells for research, there are a variety of ways to acquire stem cells. As noted in a 2008 Stanford publication, regarding human embryo stem cell research specifically, a majority of the researchers are not actually touching newly derived stem cells, but are instead using the lineage and data of stem cells that have already been researched by other scientists. They have made these cell lines available for others to work with and learn from. Along with advances regarding adult stem cell research, this could be a fruitful direction for medical inquiry.

(continues)

Arguments against Stem Cell Research

5   Stem cell research is a risky endeavor that does not have clear-cut benefits, and a lot of moral questions are involved. While it seems clear that certain diseases are being treated by stem cell therapies, there are too many questions regarding further study and use.

6   With human embryo stem cells, a major concern is where they are coming from. One suggestion is for these stem cells to be taken from embryos that have been created for reproduction via in vitro fertilization. These embryos could be donated for scientific research after it is confirmed that they are not going to be used for reproduction. While this seems like a simple solution, there's also the question of the actual usefulness of those stem cells. With all stem cell therapies, *Consumer Reports* in 2010 noted the concern regarding transplanted cells forming tumors and becoming cancerous if the cell's division continued uncontrollably. There are also concerns of immune rejection by the patient being treated. While immunosuppressant drugs are used in organ transplant surgery, would this work on a body with new cells injected into it? There's also the additional question of whether the correct cell types can be induced in the stem cells, since the stem cells themselves are undifferentiated and can become many different kinds of cells.

7   While certain therapies have been successfully created, this research is still very untested. More conversations and clear education of the public are needed regarding this controversial form of medical therapy and the research behind it.

PROMPT:

While the first passage outlines the benefits of and identifies arguments for stem cell research, the second passage identifies arguments against stem cell research.

In your response, analyze both passages to determine which position is better supported. Use relevant and specific evidence from both sources to support your response.

Answers and Explanations

Part I

1. **The correct answer is the King of Great Britain.** The second to the last sentence in the second paragraph states, "The history of the present King of Great Britain is a history of repeated injuries and usurpations, all having in direct object the establishment of an absolute Tyranny over these States." The America colonists rebelled against the King of Great Britain's control of the colonies.

2. **Choice d is correct.** This paragraph incorporates a list of injustices that had been committed against the colonies by the King of Great Britain. The previous paragraphs describe suffering that the King caused the colonies, and paragraph 3 provides examples of those injuries.

   Choice **a** is incorrect. This paragraph incorporates a list of injustices that had been committed against the colonies by the King of Great Britain. It is not a list of laws written by the King, but a list of acts he committed.

   Choice **b** is incorrect. This paragraph incorporates a list of injustices that had been committed against the colonies by the King of Great Britain. It is not a list of laws for the newly independent United States of America because the colonies were not yet independent when the Declaration was written.

   Choice **c** is incorrect. This paragraph incorporates a list of injustices that had been committed against the colonies by the King of Great Britain. It is not a list of his good acts due to the fact that they are all negative things, and because the previous paragraphs mention that the King has committed repeated injuries against the colonies.

3. **Choice b is correct.** This quotation explicitly states that one group of people wishes to dissolve political ties with another group of people, meaning the colonies dissolving political ties with Great Britain.

   Choice **a** is incorrect. This quotation supports the idea of equality for all men, but does not express the desire to be free from Great Britain.

   Choice **c** is incorrect. This quotation expresses one of the grievances that the colonists have against the King of Great Britain. It is one of the reasons why the colonies want to split from Great Britain, but it does not express that desire itself.

   Choice **d** is incorrect. This quotation supports the idea of certain rights for all men, but does not express the desire to be free from Great Britain.

4. **Choice b is correct.** This quotation goes into more depth about what it means to have a government that gains its power from the consent of the governed and that is essentially controlled by the governed. This helps build the argument for popular sovereignty that this excerpt expresses.

   Choice **a** is incorrect. This quotation expresses a grievance that the colonists have against the King of Great Britain. It does not specifically help to build an argument for popular sovereignty.

   Choice **c** is incorrect. This quotation expresses a grievance that the colonists have against the King of Great Britain. It does not specifically help to build an argument for popular sovereignty.

   Choice **d** is incorrect. This quotation expresses a grievance that the colonists have against the King of Great Britain. It does not specifically help to build an argument for popular sovereignty.

5. **Choice c is correct.** The final paragraph of the excerpt is a list of the King's wrongdoings against the colonies.
Choice **a** is incorrect. The excerpt does not list court cases against the King.
Choice **b** is incorrect. The list of wrongdoings in the excerpt is by American colonists, not by other world leaders.
Choice **d** is incorrect. This excerpt does not name any specific individuals; it attempts to speak for the colonists as a whole.

6. **Choice a is correct.** The information given in the list of grievances is made up of examples of wrongdoings that the King has done against the colonists. This is definitely relevant to a claim that the King has carried out wrongs against the colonists. Furthermore, the list goes on for a long paragraph, making it more than sufficient to support the claim.
Choice **b** is incorrect. While the choice of relevancy is correct, the list goes on for a long paragraph, making it more than sufficient to support the claim. Therefore, the choice of insufficiency is incorrect.
Choice **c** is incorrect. While the choice of sufficiency is correct, the information given in the list of grievances is made up of examples of wrongdoings that are relevant to the claim. Therefore, the choice of irrelevancy is incorrect.
Choice **d** is incorrect. The information given in the list of grievances is made up of examples of wrongdoings that the King has done against the colonists. This is definitely relevant to a claim that the King has carried out wrongs against the colonists. Furthermore, the list goes on for a long paragraph, making it more than sufficient to support the claim.

7. **Choice b is correct.** The whole last paragraph of the excerpt is a list of tyrannical actions the King of Great Britain committed against the colonists.
Choice **a** is incorrect. The excerpt claims that "all men are created equal," but it does not provide evidence as to why this is true. No evidence is given to support this claim.
Choice **c** is incorrect. The excerpt claims that all men "are endowed by their Creator with certain unalienable Rights," but it does not provide evidence to support this claim.
Choice **d** is incorrect. The excerpt discusses the idea of popular sovereignty, but it provides no evidence to support this claim.

8. **Choice d is correct.** Factually, there is no validity to the claim that the only way to secure certain rights is through a government controlled by the governed. Logically, there is really no reason why this would be the only way to secure those rights. Therefore, this is an example of false reasoning.
Choice **a** is incorrect. This statement is not really an explanation of anything but rather an opinion that in order to secure certain rights, governments should derive their power from the governed.
Choice **b** is incorrect. This statement does not give any evidence based in actual fact. Instead, it expresses an opinion that in order to secure certain rights, governments should derive their power from the governed.
Choice **c** is incorrect. Factually, there is no validity to the claim that the only way to secure certain rights is through a government controlled by the governed. Logically, there is really no reason why this would be the only way to secure those rights. Therefore, this is an example of false reasoning, not valid reasoning.

9. a. Based on the excerpt, the reader can determine that the woman is talking about her death. The other choices do not fit in with the context of the poem.

10. c. This is the best answer. The speaker tells about her life in a matter-of-fact manner. She does not seem to be in a state of *wonder*. She certainly does not seem *angry* or particularly full of *joy*.

11. b. The line suggests that the speaker loved nature. It does not suggest that she worked in the fields or that she had a fine singing voice. No other choice is supported by the poem.

12. d. The poem recounts what occurred in their marriage, both good and bad, so this is the best answer. The other choices are not supported by the poem.

13. The correct order is:

1. **Operation Iraqi Freedom is launched**
2. **coalition forces cross 350 miles of enemy territory**
3. **Baghdad is liberated.**

This order is correct due to the implied order of events that Bush mentions in the excerpt. Operation Iraqi Freedom had to have been launched before coalition forces could cross 350 miles of enemy territory. The ultimate outcome of the operation was the liberation of Baghdad; therefore, that is the last event in the progression.

14. Choice c is correct. The setting is described as harsh and unforgiving. This technique is used to heighten the sense of danger to the troops fighting death squads, in order to persuade the audience of its truth.

Choice **a** is incorrect. The choice of describing an extreme climate with intense sandstorms in this paragraph is not meant to express beauty. This technique is used to heighten the sense of danger to the troops fighting death squads, in order to persuade the audience of its truth.

Choice **b** is incorrect. The choice of describing an extreme climate with intense sandstorms in this paragraph is not meant to express contentment. This technique is used to heighten the sense of danger to the troops fighting death squads, in order to persuade the audience of its truth.

Choice **d** is incorrect. The setting is described as having intense sandstorms and pitched battles. This technique is used to heighten the sense of danger to the troops fighting death squads, in order to persuade the audience of its truth.

15. Choice a is correct. In the paragraph, Jordan states that the party is "an inclusive rather than an exclusive party" and that "everybody" should come.

Choice **b** is incorrect. This is what the third paragraph is about, not the second paragraph.

Choice **c** is incorrect. Although it can be inferred that Jordan approves of the party, this is not the main point of the second paragraph.

Choice **d** is incorrect. This is the opposite of the meaning of the second paragraph.

16. Choice b is correct. Here, Jordan says that everyone should be able to participate in government. This is what the question is asking for.

Choice **a** is incorrect. In this sentence, Jordan is stating that the Democratic Party accepts all people. It slightly fits the question, but there is a better answer.

Choice **c** is incorrect. Jordan is speaking about how the party evolves, not about how the government represents all people.

Choice **d** is incorrect. This is a summary of all the values that Jordan brings up and is too broad to be just about the representation of everyone.

17. Choice d is correct. Jordan says the party is for all people and that everyone should be represented in government. An open forum is an inclusive event that allows people to speak their mind.

Choice **a** is incorrect. Jordan explicitly states that the Democratic Party is inclusive. This would be an exclusive event, contrary to what she states.

Choice **b** is incorrect. This is an example of exclusivity, which is not in line with the values she expresses.

Choice **c** is incorrect. Although this would be a logical choice, this is a broader answer, and there is a better choice. Jordan does not talk about senate races in the passage.

18. Choice b is correct. Throughout her address, Jordan compares American values to the party's values and claims that they are in line with each other. This is the best summary.

Choice **a** is incorrect. This is a detail Jordan includes, but it does not represent the main idea of her address.

Choice **c** is incorrect. This is another detail rather than a summary.

Choice **d** is incorrect. This cannot be correct because choices **a** and **c** are wrong.

19. Choice d is correct. Jordan praises the Democratic Party throughout her speech.

Choice **a** is incorrect. This phrase praises the party.

Choice **b** is incorrect. Jordan is commending the party.

Choice **c** is incorrect. Jordan is ascribing a positive quality, innovation, to her party's character.

20. Choice d is correct. Jordan does not come right out and say that the government should pass laws to combat racism and gender discrimination, which would block individual achievement, but she stresses the word "actively" in connection with the government's "obligation" to "remove those obstacles." Passing laws is "active" on the part of the government, and it is logical to infer that Jordan would support laws to curb discrimination.

Choice **a** is incorrect. Jordan is asking why people are drawn to her party, not calling on government to enact anti-discrimination laws.

Choice **b** is incorrect. Jordan is discussing political power in a democracy, not anti-discrimination law.

Choice **c** is incorrect. Jordan is talking about the beliefs of the Democratic Party, not about laws the U.S. government should enact.

21. Choice a is correct. In order to make the verb agree with the plural subject, *piles of books*, the verb needs to be in present tense and not end in *s*.

Choice **b** is incorrect. In order to make the verb agree with the plural subject, *piles of books*, the verb needs to be in present tense and not end in *s* (*accumulate*), not the present tense ending in *s* (*accumulates*).

Choice **c** is incorrect. In order to make the verb agree with the plural subject, *piles of books*, the verb needs to be in present tense (*accumulate*), not in the past tense (*accumulated*).

Choice **d** is incorrect. In order to make the verb agree with the plural subject, *piles of books*, the verb needs to be in present tense (*accumulate*), not in the future tense (*will accumulate*).

22. Choice a is correct. *Therefore* is the correct transition word to use when describing a cause-and-effect relationship. And as the first word in the sentence, the word is correctly capitalized.

Choice **b** is incorrect. *However* is a transition word used to show contrast. Since the accumulating piles of books cause the effect of instituting a new policy, *Therefore* is the correct transition word to use when describing a cause-and-effect relationship.

Choice **c** is incorrect. *Meanwhile* denotes time. Since the accumulating piles of books cause the effect of instituting a new policy, *Therefore* is the correct transition word to use when describing a cause-and-effect relationship.

Choice **d** is incorrect. *Instead* is a transition word used to show contrast. Since the accumulating piles of books cause the effect of instituting a new policy, *Therefore* is the correct transition word to use when describing a cause-and-effect relationship.

23. Choice c is correct. Because this word starts a sentence, the first letter needs to be capitalized. Choice **a** is incorrect. Because this word starts a sentence, the first letter needs to be capitalized. Choice **b** is incorrect. Because this word starts a sentence, the first letter needs to be capitalized. Also, *please* is being used as a command, and the addition of an *s* at the end does not make sense in this context.

Choice **d** is incorrect. *Please* is being used as a command, and the addition of an *s* at the end does not make sense in this context.

24. Choice b is correct. Of the possessive pronouns listed, *your* in the second person is correct to address the reader.

25. Choice d is correct. The closing of a letter or memo ends with a comma, followed on the next line by the letter writer's name.

Choice **a** is incorrect. The closing of a letter or memo ends with a comma, followed on the next line by the letter writer's name.

Choice **b** is incorrect. The closing of a letter or memo ends with a comma, followed on the next line by the letter writer's name.

Choice **c** is incorrect. The closing of a letter or memo ends with a comma, followed on the next line by the letter writer's name.

26. Choice b is correct. The author chose these words to create a dark and foreboding tone.

27. The correct order is:
    1. **rides through the countryside**
    2. **comes to the House of Usher**
    3. **feels a sense of gloom**
    4. **reins his horse near the house**

This is based on the order of events recounted by the narrator in the excerpt.

28. Choice d is correct. Personification is giving human characteristics to inanimate objects. The phrase "vacant eye-like windows" gives the human quality of vacant eyes to windows.
Choice **a** is incorrect. Alliteration is a repetition of consonant sounds at the beginning of several words in a row. An example would be "brightly beautiful butterflies."
Choice **b** is incorrect. Hyperbole is extreme exaggeration, for example: "He walks louder than an elephant."
Choice **c** is incorrect. Onomatopoeia refers to words that mimic the sounds they describe, for example: "The fire hissed, crackled, and popped."

29. Choice b is correct. The word *joy* changes the tone and meaning of the phrase from an expression of unhappiness and gloom to a positive and happy expression.
Choice **a** is incorrect. *Melancholy* preserves the unhappy and negative tone of the original phrase.
Choice **c** is incorrect. *Sadness* preserves the unhappy and negative tone of the original phrase.
Choice **d** is incorrect. *Despair* preserves the unhappy and negative tone of the original phrase.

30. Choice c is correct. Grant admits that he did "not know how far this was necessary," but "deemed it necessary, at that time." He feels later that his decision was justified.
Choice **a** is incorrect. The passage opens with the statement "things began to quiet down," the opposite of widespread violence.
Choice **b** is incorrect. The first words in the first sentence report that the war was winding down.
Choice **d** is incorrect. Grant deemed the garrisons necessary "at that time."

31. The correct answer is the Civil War. It can be inferred from the passage that the Civil War had just concluded. The passage clearly describes the "rebellion as was fought between the sections from 1861 to 1865." There are many other context clues. In addition, the excerpt is from Grant's memoir after 1865 and Sherman's March through the South.

32. Choice b is correct. Grant refers to Sherman's March as "magnificent" and as signifying "closing the war."
Choice **a** is incorrect. Grant obviously approves of the march.
Choice **c** is incorrect. Grant is sympathizing with Sherman, not criticizing him.
Choice **d** is incorrect. The word change is unrelated to Grant's feelings about how "[t]heir newspapers had given such an account of Confederate success."

33. Choice c is correct. Grant is describing how the Confederate view is false.
Choice **a** is incorrect. Grant is expressing sympathy with the general consensus of feeling after the war.
Choice **b** is incorrect. This sentence comments on Sherman's March, not Grant's disagreement with the Confederate viewpoint.
Choice **d** is incorrect. This sentence describes how Grant assumed the Confederates felt upon seeing Sherman, not Grant's disagreement with the Confederate viewpoint.

34. Choice a is correct. The correct order is C—the Civil War, A—Sherman's men were ordered not to listen to him, D—Sherman's March, then B—the Confederates "saw the true state of affairs."

35. Choice b is correct. Grant is describing how seeing the victorious soldiers' march reminded the South of what really happened.

Choice **a** is incorrect. The opposite is true for the victorious army. For example, Grant emphasizes how the march was a positive thing because it set the Confederates straight on who won.

Choice **c** is incorrect. There is no evidence in the excerpt to support this conclusion.

Choice **d** is incorrect. The opposite is true for the victorious army.

36. Choice a is correct. Paragraph 3 is mainly about how scientists monitor earthquakes to predict volcanic eruptions.

Choice **b** is incorrect. Although these terms are defined in this paragraph, they are supporting details.

Choice **c** is incorrect. The paragraph does not explain how seismometers work.

Choice **d** is incorrect. Although the paragraph mentions that volcanic gases force their way up through underground channels, this is a small detail and not the paragraph's main idea.

37. Choice d is correct. This best summarizes the main ideas of "Watching Volcanoes" by referencing the scientists who watch volcanoes, the ways they monitor volcanoes, and why their work is important.

Choice **a** is incorrect. This is a good summary of the section titled "Watching for Bulges in the Sides of the Mountain," but it does not summarize the entire passage.

Choice **b** is incorrect. The article mentions that vents are dangerous, not that scientists should not visit them for study. This is a small detail and not a summary of the complete article.

Choice **c** is incorrect. This answer refers to the second article, "The 1992 Eruptions at Mt. Spurr, Alaska," not "Watching Volcanoes."

38. Choice b is correct. "Watching Volcanoes" is a first-person account of watching volcanoes from the perspective of a volcano-watching scientist. "The 1992 Eruptions at Mt. Spurr, Alaska" is an objective report without any indication that the journalist is involved in volcano science.

Choice **a** is incorrect. The opposite is true. "Watching Volcanoes" discusses volcanoes in general, and "The 1992 Eruptions at Mt. Spurr, Alaska" focuses on the volcano at Mt. Spurr, Alaska.

Choice **c** is incorrect. Both passages discuss seismometers or seismographs, the instruments that scientists use to measure earthquake magnitude.

Choice **d** is incorrect. Although "Watching Volcanoes" is written from the first-person point of view like a diary, it does not describe what the writer did on a particular day as a diary does. Although it is possible that "The 1992 Eruptions at Mt. Spurr, Alaska" was published in a newspaper, there is no way of knowing this based on the passage.

39. Choice c is correct. Having vertical axes to 100 incidents on both graphs dramatizes the explosion of 90 more incidents than on any day in the first graph occurring in November 1992 in the second graph.

Choice **a** is incorrect. Based on the dramatic rise in events in November 1992 shown in the second graph, the volcano was close to erupting, and the threat was serious enough that scientists warned, "a large eruption is likely within the next 24 to 48 hours."

Choice **b** is incorrect. September is not charted on either graph.

Choice **d** is incorrect. There is no evidence to support this claim.

40. **The correct answer is paragraph 1.** Paragraph 1 explicitly states that "a single man in possession of a good fortune must be in want of a wife."

41. **Choice d is correct.** The topic of marriage is the focus of the introductory paragraphs as well as the majority of the dialogue.

Choice **a** is incorrect. Travel is not the main topic of the excerpt.

Choice **b** is incorrect. Divorce is not a topic in the excerpt.

Choice **c** is incorrect. The Michaelmas holiday is a minor topic in the excerpt, not the main topic.

42. **Choice b is correct.** Mrs. Bennet is discussing Bingley's fortune—in other words, his income.

Choice **a** is incorrect. Mrs. Bennet is discussing Bingley's fortune—in other words, his income.

Choice **c** is incorrect. Mrs. Bennet is talking to Mr. Bennet in this dialogue, and she would not need to be telling her husband about his own money in the third person. Furthermore, they are just beginning to discuss Mr. Bingley when this number amount is mentioned.

Choice **d** is incorrect. Mrs. Bennet is discussing Bingley's fortune—in other words, his income.

43. **Choice b is correct.** This whole excerpt is about the supposition that wealthy men need to find wives and the topic of marriage in general. Mrs. Bennet spends most of the dialogue discussing the merits of Mr. Bingley and how he would be a good match for one of her daughters.

Choice **a** is incorrect. Mrs. Bennet is a married woman, and every time she mentions marriage it is in reference to her daughters.

Choice **c** is incorrect. This whole excerpt is about the supposition that wealthy men need to find wives and the topic of marriage in general.

Choice **d** is incorrect. The only time that Mrs. Bennet mentions money is in reference to the wealth of Mr. Bingley and how that makes him a good match for one of her daughters. She never implies that she wishes she had married someone wealthier.

44. **Choice c is correct.** The noun possessing *procedures* is singular.

Choice **a** is incorrect. *Procedures* is not being used as a possessive noun in this context. Therefore, an apostrophe is not needed.

Choice **b** is incorrect. There is one bookstore, so the possessive noun is singular, not plural.

Choice **d** is incorrect. The singular noun *bookstore* possesses *procedures*, so an apostrophe should be inserted between *bookstore* and *s*.

45. **The correct answer is: At the beginning of a shift, all staff must sign in through our computer system.** The first word in a sentence must always be capitalized.

46. Choice a is correct. This is a common homonym error. *Two* is a number designation, and in this context, the preposition *to* is necessary instead. This is to reference what the staff members are assigned to, not a number designation.

Choice **b** is incorrect. This change would cause a homonym error. The preposition *for* is needed to denote an action that the staff members should take. The homonym *four* denoting number does not make sense in this context.

Choice **c** is incorrect. The procedure listed here has two parts. The staff members need to look for misplaced books *and* reshelf them. The procedure does not imply that staff members can choose to do one thing or the other.

Choice **d** is incorrect. *Two* is a number designation, and in this context, the preposition *to* is necessary instead. This is to reference what the staff members are assigned to, not a number designation.

47. Choice a is correct. *Free* and *complimentary* mean essentially the same thing. *And complimentary* adds an unnecessary wordiness to the sentence and should be deleted.

Choice **b** is incorrect. *In-store café* is the object of the preposition *at* and is needed in order to make the prepositional phrase complete.

Choice **c** is incorrect. *Free, complimentary,* and *on the house* all mean the same thing. Therefore, the use of all three together causes unnecessary wordiness.

Choice **d** is incorrect. *Free* and *complimentary* mean essentially the same thing. *And complimentary* adds an unnecessary wordiness to the sentence and should be deleted.

48. Choice a is correct. In order for the subject *staff member* to agree with the verb, *forget* must end in an *s*. This is a common subject–verb agreement rule.

Choice **b** is incorrect. Since *he or she* is referencing a *staff member*, all the subjects in the sentence need to be singular. The change to *they* would change this number agreement, making the pronoun plural that is referencing a singular noun, which is incorrect.

Choice **c** is incorrect. In order for the subject *he or she* to agree with the verb, *consult* should not end in an *s*. This is a common subject-verb agreement rule.

Choice **d** is incorrect. In order for the subject *staff member* to agree with the verb, *forget* must end in an *s*. This is a common subject-verb agreement rule.

Part II

Your extended response will be scored based on three traits, or elements:

- **Trait 1:** Creation of arguments and use of evidence
- **Trait 2:** Development of ideas and organizational structure
- **Trait 3:** Clarity and command of standard English conventions

Your essay will be scored on a 6-point scale—each trait is worth up to 2 points. The final score is counted twice, so the maximum number of points you can earn is 12.

Trait 1 tests your ability to write an essay that takes a stance based on the information in the reading passages. To earn the highest score possible, you must carefully read the information and express a clear opinion on what you have read. You will be scored on how well you use the information from the passages to support your argument.

Your response will also be scored on how well you analyze the author's arguments in the passages. To earn the highest score possible, you should discuss whether or not you think the author is making a good argument, and why or why not.

For your reference, here is a table that readers will use when scoring your essay with a 2, 1, or 0.

	TRAIT 1: CREATION OF ARGUMENTS AND USE OF EVIDENCE
2	• Makes text-based argument(s) and establishes an intent connected to the prompt • Presents specific and related evidence from source text(s) to support argument (may include a few unrelated pieces of evidence or unsupported claims) • Analyzes the topic and/or the strength of the argument within the source text(s) (e.g., distinguishes between supported and unsupported claims, makes valid inferences about underlying assumptions, identifies false reasoning, evaluates the credibility of sources)
1	• Makes an argument with some connection to the prompt • Presents some evidence from source text(s) to support argument (may include a mix of related and unrelated evidence that may or may not cite the text) • Partly analyzes the topic and/or the strength of the argument within the source text(s); may be limited, oversimplified, or inaccurate
0	• May attempt to make an argument OR lacks an intent or connection to the prompt OR attempts neither • Presents little or no evidence from source text(s) (sections of text may be copied from source directly) • Minimally analyzes the topic and/or the strength of the argument within the source text(s); may present no analysis, or little or no understanding of the given argument
Non-scorable	• Response consists only of text copied from the prompt or source text(s) • Response shows that test-taker has not read the prompt or is entirely off-topic • Response is incomprehensible • Response is not in English • No response has been attempted (has been left blank)

Trait 2 tests whether you respond to the writing prompt with a well-structured essay. Support of your thesis must come from evidence in the passages, as well as personal opinions and experiences that build on your central idea. Your ideas must be fully explained and include specific details. Your essay should use words and phrases that allow your details and ideas to flow naturally. Here is a table that outlines what is involved in earning a score of 2, 1, or 0.

TRAIT 2: DEVELOPMENT OF IDEAS AND ORGANIZATIONAL STRUCTURE	
2	• Contains ideas that are generally logical and well-developed; most ideas are expanded upon • Contains a logical sequence of ideas with clear connections between specific details and main ideas • Develops an organizational structure that conveys the message and goal of the response; appropriately uses transitional devices • Develops and maintains an appropriate style and tone that signal awareness of the audience and purpose of the task • Uses appropriate words to express ideas clearly
1	• Contains ideas that are partially developed and/or may demonstrate vague or simplistic logic; only some ideas are expanded upon • Contains some evidence of a sequence of ideas, but specific details may be unconnected to main ideas • Develops an organizational structure that may partially group ideas or is partially effective at conveying the message of the response; inconsistently uses transitional devices • May inconsistently maintain an appropriate style and tone to signal an awareness of the audience and purpose of the task • May contain misused words and/or words that do not express ideas clearly
0	• Contains ideas that are ineffectively or illogically developed, with little or no elaboration of main ideas • Contains an unclear or no sequence of ideas; specific details may be absent or unrelated to main ideas • Develops an ineffective or no organizational structure; inappropriately uses transitional devices, or does not use them at all • Uses an inappropriate style and tone that signal limited or no awareness of audience and purpose • May contain many misused words, overuse of slang, and/or express ideas in an unclear or repetitious manner
Non-scorable	• Response consists only of text copied from the prompt or source text(s) • Response shows that test-taker has not read the prompt or is entirely off-topic • Response is incomprehensible • Response is not in English • No response has been attempted (has been left blank)

Trait 3 tests how you create the sentences that make up your essay. To earn a high score, you will need to write sentences with variety—some short, some long, some simple, some complex. You will also need to prove that you have a good handle on standard English, including correct word choice, grammar, and sentence structure.

Here is a table that outlines what is involved in attaining a score of 2, 1, or 0.

TRAIT 3: CLARITY AND COMMAND OF STANDARD ENGLISH CONVENTIONS	
2	• Demonstrates generally correct sentence structure and an overall fluency that enhances clarity with regard to the following skills: 1) Diverse sentence structure within a paragraph or paragraphs 2) Correct use of subordination, coordination, and parallelism 3) Avoidance of awkward sentence structures and wordiness 4) Use of transitional words, conjunctive adverbs, and other words that enhance clarity and logic 5) Avoidance of run-on sentences, sentence fragments, and fused sentences • Demonstrates proficient use of conventions with regard to the following skills: 1) Subject–verb agreement 2) Placement of modifiers and correct word order 3) Pronoun usage, including pronoun antecedent agreement, unclear pronoun references, and pronoun case 4) Frequently confused words and homonyms, including contractions 5) Use of apostrophes with possessive nouns 6) Use of punctuation (e.g., commas in a series or in appositives and other non-essential elements, end marks, and punctuation for clause separation) 7) Capitalization (e.g., beginnings of sentences, proper nouns, and titles) • May contain some errors in mechanics and conventions that do not impede comprehension; overall usage is at a level suitable for on-demand draft writing
1	• Demonstrates inconsistent sentence structure; may contain some choppy, repetitive, awkward, or run-on sentences that may limit clarity; demonstrates inconsistent use of skills 1–5 as listed under Trait 3, Score Point 2 • Demonstrates inconsistent use of basic conventions with regard to skills 1–7 as listed under Trait 3, Score Point 2 • May contain many errors in mechanics and conventions that occasionally impede comprehension; overall usage is at the minimum level acceptable for on-demand draft writing
0	• Demonstrates improper sentence structure to the extent that meaning may be unclear; demonstrates minimal use of skills 1–5 as listed under Trait 3, Score Point 2 • Demonstrates minimal use of basic conventions with regard to skills 1–7 as listed under Trait 3, Score Point 2 • Contains numerous significant errors in mechanics and conventions that impede comprehension; overall usage is at an unacceptable level for on-demand draft writing OR • Response is insufficient to show level of proficiency involving conventions and usage
Non-scorable	• Response consists only of text copied from the prompt or source text(s) • Response shows that test-taker has not read the prompt or is entirely off-topic • Response is incomprehensible • Response is not in English • No response has been attempted (has been left blank)

Sample Score 6 Essay

Stem cell research is a complicated topic to evaluate. While it is noted as having a lot of potential with regard to medical advancements, there are several elements of it that can cause moral quandaries, such as the use of human embryos in the research. At the same time, it is providing valuable therapies for diseases such as leukemia and could treat diseases like diabetes and heart disease. With that in mind and on reviewing the two passages, I find that I must argue in favor of stem cell research.

Since the passage against stem cell research makes several valid points, especially questioning the source of the stem cells used in the research, this is sure to inspire many readers to question the morality of the supporting argument. This concern does not actually have any evidence behind it, saying that only human embryo stem cells are being used, so it is difficult to know where this concern came from. In addition, the particular evidence noting that stem cell research itself is potentially harmful has no scientific basis and was simply based on concerns from the populace, as noted by Consumer Reports, *rather than actual research. At the end of the third paragraph, this passage even questions whether scientists could differentiate the cells properly to make them become what is needed for that specific stem cell therapy. Would the stem cells become actual brain cells or would they just become a bunch of organ cells and cause a tumorous growth? This is stated without any evidence to back up the concern at all. While it is clear that the reason stem cell research is interesting in any form is that the cells themselves can be formed into any other cell needed, this worry about differentiation seems to be idle speculation rather than something that would legitimately make this research impossible.*

In contrast, the passage supporting stem cell research is full of dates and specific examples. While the against passage only notes an article from Consumer Reports, *this passage notes research done in the 1900s, all the way through 2008. It points out some of the current research and medical benefits of stem cell research being used right now, including bone marrow transfu-*

sions to treat leukemia and the generation of artificial liver cells just in 2006. It also notes that the major concern regarding the source of the stem cells should be less of a concern due to a report from Stanford, a major research institute, about how researchers acquire the data of human embryo stem cells. It appears that not every single researcher is getting a new set of embryo stem cells to work off of. Instead, the information about one set is shared among all of the researchers. Also, the passage pointed to a 2008 article about medical advancements using adult stem cells. If stem cell research should be argued against, there needs to be more thorough and specific evidence provided to support that argument.

It is clear that the arguments against stem cell research are antiquated and have been addressed by the medical community. Perhaps there is research regarding why stem cell research should not be pursued, but it is unspecified in these passages. Overall, while the supporting passage addresses many of the same concerns as the "against" passage, it is better organized and supported throughout with actual referenced research.

About this essay:

This essay has earned the maximum number of points in each trait for a total of 6 points.

Trait 1: Creation of Arguments and Use of Evidence

This response evaluates the arguments in the source text, develops an effective position supported by the text, and fulfills the criteria to earn 2 points for Trait 1.

This response establishes its stance at the conclusion of the first paragraph (*I find that I must argue in favor of stem cell research*) and provides a summary of support for that stance in the second and third paragraphs.

In the second paragraph, the writer also weighs the validity of the evidence in the "against" argument, for example: "*the particular evidence noting that stem cell research itself is potentially harmful has no scientific basis and was simply based on concerns from the populace, as noted by* Consumer Reports, *rather than actual research."*

Trait 2: Development of Ideas and Organizational Structure

This response is well developed and fulfills the criteria to earn 2 points for Trait 2. It is well organized, opens with a definitive stance, offers a discussion of the pros and cons of stem cell research and the evidence provided, and then provides a summary in support of the chosen stance. The writer provides multiple, specific examples and then elaborates on them, using an appropriately formal tone throughout.

Trait 3: Clarity and Command of Standard English Conventions

This response also fulfills the criteria for draft writing and earns 2 points for Trait 3. Besides employing sophisticated sentence structure (*Since the passage against stem cell research makes several valid points, especially questioning the source of the stem cells used in the research, this is sure to inspire many readers to question the morality of the supporting argument. This concern does not actually have any evidence behind it, saying that only human embryo stem cells are being used, so it is difficult to know where this concern came from*), this response uses clear transitions in its "compare and contrast" construction (*In contrast, the passage supporting stem cell research is full of dates and specific examples*).

In addition, the writer adheres to proper grammar and usage.

Sample Score 4 Essay

It seems clear that we must not allow stem cell research. It may have been around since the early 1900s, but that does not outweigh the moral questions it raises.

I am against stem cell research for mainly the same reasons stated in the passage. Since stem cell research has been around, there is no clear answer

regarding where the human embryo stem cells come from. This was not answered in the supporting passage.

What's more, I also think the possibility that the cells could form tumors and become cancerous, as noted in the against passage, is pretty worrying. At the very least, more education and research into the risks of stem cells are very necessary.

Finally, while it may be true that the arguments for stem cell research list many favorable benefits, and those aspects of stem cell research seem intriguing, the arguments against the research are better than the ones for it. At the very least there needs to be more education on the dangers.

About this essay:

This essay earned 1 point each for Trait 1 and Trait 2, and 2 points for Trait 3.

Trait 1: Creation of Arguments and Use of Evidence

This response makes a simple argument, supports it with some evidence from the source text, and offers a partial analysis of the opposing argument, earning it 1 point for Trait 1.

The writer generates an argument against stem cell research and makes a clear statement of her position in the first paragraph (*It seems clear that we must not allow stem cell research*), in the second paragraph (*I am against stem cell research for mainly the same reasons*), and final paragraph (*the arguments against the research are better than the ones for it*).

The writer does cite some evidence from the source text to support her position (*Since stem cell research has been around, there is no clear answer regarding where the human embryo stem cells come from*). The writer offers a partial analysis of the issue (*At the very least, more education and research into the risks of stem cells are very necessary* and *it may be true that the arguments for stem cell research list many favorable benefits*); however, this analysis is simplistic and limited.

In addition, in the second paragraph the writer offers a partial evaluation of the validity of the "for" arguments (*there is no clear answer regarding where the human embryo stem cells come from. This was not answered in the supporting passage*).

Trait 2: Development of Ideas and Organizational Structure

Although this response has a general organization and focus, the supporting ideas are developed unevenly; thus, it earns only 1 point in this trait.

This response establishes a discernible organizational structure by introducing stance and a comparison of the source text's two positions (*It seems clear that we must not allow stem cell research. It may have been around since the early 1900s, but that does not outweigh the moral questions it raises*).

The second and third paragraphs focus on the troubling aspects of stem cell research, and the writer offers a clear progression of ideas. Her main points are clear but not sufficiently elaborated upon. Her argument is based solely on what is offered in the passage (*I am against stem cell research for mainly the same reasons stated in the passage*).

The concluding paragraph offers a very basic comparison of the "for" and "against" arguments, but not much development is offered (*while [the good] aspects of stem cell research seem intriguing, the arguments against the research are better than the ones for it*).

Trait 3: Clarity and Command of Standard English Conventions

This response earns the full 2 points for Trait 3. It employs sophisticated sentence structure (*Finally, while it may be true that the arguments for stem cell research list many favorable benefits, and those aspects of stem cell research seem intriguing, the arguments against the research are better than the ones for it*) and clear transitions (*What's more . . . Finally . . .*).

In addition, the writer adheres to proper grammar and usage.

Sample Score 0 Essay

Stem cell research is way too confusing and disturbing for a lot of people. While these scientists think that listing all of the accomplishemtns will mean that stem cell research should continue it's not clear at all whether that's true. If perhaps you had loukemia, then it would be ok for it to continue.

Also we don't know where the human embryo stem cells come from also some of them could become cancerous and that isn't a good idea either I thought Loukemia was some kind of cancer, that makes it even more confusing. Also the differentiation of cells. If you can't get the right kind of cells for your therapy, then those cells are useless and are a waste.

I think it's a better idea to not have stem cell research until we know more about what it could do. There are too many factors that seem harmful or dangerous in some way.

About this essay:

This essay earned 0 points in Trait 1, Trait 2, and Trait 3.

Trait 1: Creation of Arguments and Use of Evidence

In general, this response provides a minimal summary of the source text and lacks insight and topic analysis, earning this response 0 points for Trait 1.

The writer fails to summarize source texts in a coherent and organized structure. Though this response addresses the source material, the writer fails to cite evidence to support any arguments and does not take a firm stance until the final paragraph (*I think it's a better idea to not have stem cell research until we know more about what it could do*). She also seems to flip-flop on her stance (*While these scientists think that listing all of the accomplishemtns will mean that stem cell research should continue it's not clear at all whether that's true. If perhaps you had loukemia, then it would be ok for it to continue*).

Trait 2: Development of Ideas and Organizational Structure

Overall, the response is poorly developed, disorganized, and lacks any clear progression of ideas, earning it 0 points for Trait 2.

The writer uses informal and colloquial language (*Stem cell research is way too confusing and disturbing for a lot of people*) and fails to demonstrate awareness of audience and purpose. The response lacks organizational structure and a clear progression of ideas.

Trait 3: Clarity and Command of Standard English Conventions

Many sentences lack sense and fluency and are incorrect and awkward. The writer misuses and confuses words, punctuation, and usage as well as the conventions of English in general, making the response almost incomprehensible and earning it 0 points for Trait 3.

This short response shows flawed sentence structure, including run-on sentences (*Also we don't know where the human embryo stem cells come from also some of them could become cancerous and that isn't a good idea either I thought Loukemia was some kind of cancer, that makes it even more confusing*) and fragments (*Also the differentiation of cells*).

Using the codes below, you'll be able to log in and access additional online practice materials!

Your free online practice access codes are:

FVEQ1L73T11V3LD0R770

FVEOT2TSC0JT2376K7S8

Follow these simple steps to redeem your codes:

- Go to **www.learningexpresshub.com/affiliate** and have your access codes handy.

If you're a new user:

- Click the **New user? Register here** button and complete the registration form to create your account and access your products.
- Be sure to enter your unique access code only once. If you have multiple access codes, you can enter them all—just use a comma to separate each code.
- The next time you visit, simply click the **Returning user? Sign in** button and enter your username and password.
- Do not re-enter a previously redeemed access code. Any products you previously accessed are saved in the **My Account** section on the site. Entering a previously redeemed access code will result in an error message.

If you're a returning user:

- Click the **Returning user? Sign in** button, enter your username and password, and click **Sign In**.
- You will automatically be brought to the **My Account** page to access your products.
- Do not re-enter a previously redeemed access code. Any products you previously accessed are saved in the **My Account** section on the site. Entering a previously redeemed access code will result in an error message.

If you're a returning user with a new access code:

- Click the **Returning user? Sign in** button, enter your username, password, and new access code, and click **Sign In**.
- If you have multiple access codes, you can enter them all—just use a comma to separate each code.
- Do not re-enter a previously redeemed access code. Any products you previously accessed are saved in the **My Account** section on the site. Entering a previously redeemed access code will result in an error message.

If you have any questions, please contact Customer Support at Support@ebsco.com. All inquiries will be responded to within a 24-hour period during our normal business hours: 9:00 A.M.–5:00 P.M. Eastern Time. Thank you!

NOTES